D0364169

Awight Now

Awight Now

SETTING THE
RECORD STRAIGHT

Michael Barrymore

SIMON & SCHUSTER

London • New York • Sydney • Toronto

First published in Great Britain by Simon & Schuster UK Ltd, 2006
A CBS COMPANY

1 3 5 7 9 10 8 6 4 2

Simon & Schuster UK Ltd
Africa House
64–78 Kingsway
London WC2B 6AH

www.simonsays.co.uk

Simon & Schuster Australia
Sydney

A CIP catalogue record for this book is
available from the British Library.

Hardback:
ISBN-13: 978–0–7432–9554–3
ISBN-10: 0–7432–9554–4

Trade paperback:
ISBN-13: 978–0–7432–9579–6
ISBN-10: 0–7432–9579–X

Set in 12/14.5 pt Monotype Imprint by
Rowland Phototypesetting Ltd, Bury St Edmunds, Suffolk

Printed and bound in Great Britain by
CPI Bath

This book is dedicated to the memory of
Margaret Reilly, my mum

Contents

Contents

We are all on a journey.
This is the story of mine so far.
Wasn't I the lucky kid who grew into
the man who had something to say?

Foreword

It's 6.20 Saturday morning and I have woken up in one of the nicest places I have ever been in my life. I have woken up in true contentment and happiness. Probably not the best way to describe the book I have written.

I have never been great at talking about myself, so when I was asked to write my autobiography I didn't jump at the idea. It had nothing to do with not wanting to write – most of the time I actually love writing; it's become a way of helping me deal with so many situations. If you've never tried it, I recommend it. Don't be put off by the thought you can't do it: just sit and write how you feel – spelling mistakes and bad grammar included. It's amazing the difference between thinking or saying something, and actually writing it down. One of the reasons I can say that I am so contented and happy today is because of writing this book. At times it's been difficult – even painful – to write, because of the reality of what I was putting down. I write everything with a cheap pen on an A4 pad. I then get my, sometimes illegible, pages typed up by someone who (a) can understand what I've said and (b) is trustworthy. The publishing bookie-type people want me to say more about the successes I have had – which I have, but not in as many words as they would like, and I ain't about to make it up.

In many autobiographies, the author writes, 'In this book I have tried etc, etc.' Well, in this book, I haven't tried anything; I've just let the pen go in its own direction. And I'm writing this foreword before finalising the rest of the book. It's part of my nature: I never work in a logical order. However I feel, that's what you'll get for the day. I've always been like that. If I don't feel like being funny, I won't make it up. I never lied or pretended, even as a child. 'Oh, let's pretend!' Sod pretending, I always thought – let's do the real thing. I know why some people prefer to pretend. Being real isn't easy – but it's great if you can do it.

A very close friend had a long chat with me last week and concluded that for every good part of my life, I've had to pay a price far higher than the average. But I'm not average, so that's okay. For every smile in my life, every laugh, every great feeling, every joy and all the excitement, I've had to cough up. You're not having all that fun without cost, Mr Barrymore! No way! You pay! Looking back, I realise that what I've paid is nothing compared to what some people pay; some folks just don't survive the sad and horrible bits in their lives. They don't hang on for another day, they just give up on life, or life gives up on them. In a shop window in New York I read this: 'Live every day of your life like it's the last.' If you wake up and you have the choice of doing the laundry or taking a walk in the park, take the walk in the park. Wouldn't it be awful if you got to the gates of Heaven and St Peter asked what was the last thing you did on earth? You said the laundry?

Speaking of laundry reminds me of the old saying: 'Don't wash your dirty linen in public.' Looking back on my history, it would seem that I've never taken any notice of that piece of advice. For the record, though, most of my dirty linen has been publicly washed by other people, and they certainly never bothered to read the instructions. Always leaving me hung out to dry, rather than doing a quick rinse . . .

What you will read is an account of my journey so far. I haven't had all of my life yet; that will be for someone else to write about, because I won't be here. Even if I was, I doubt if I would read it. I've never bothered reading about myself. A lot has been printed about who I am, what I am, what I've done, where I've been, what I've said and who I've said it to. It's all other people's opinions of me – what they like, what they don't, what they think – but none of them know me. This book is mine: my words, my opinions and my version of my life. I have no doubt that many others will say their bit. Go ahead! Why stop now? The name 'Barrymore' has a life of its own, for some reason. It's got its own legs, and it walks on to front pages in all sorts of ways. You very rarely see a newspaper article that starts 'Michael Barrymore . . .' It's always: 'Troubled comic Michael Barrymore', or, 'Troubled gay comedian Michael Barrymore', or 'tortured', or 'saddened', or else, as is often the case, they use my Arabic first name, 'Sham–ed!', whatever the description. Strange – for every single thing that's been written, no one ever asked me how I felt. Well, that's showbiz, good old screw-everyone-you-know-biz, and before I get quoted on that one, it's the opening line of a Helen Reddy song.

Maybe one day I'll sit down and read everything that's been said about me. But then again, maybe I won't. Why bother reading about it? After all, I should know what happened. I was there. Wasn't I?

1

Bermondsey Boy

Eight o'clock in the morning, 4 May 1952. The midwife slapped my arse into life, cut the cord, made a hasty knot – which to this day still sticks out too much – and handed me over to my mother. The mistake had arrived: Michael Ciaran Parker. (Later, the English spelling Kieron was used.) Mum reminded me several times throughout my early years that I was a mistake. I'm the youngest of three: my brother John and sister Anne are ten and eight years older than me.

The room the midwife delivered me in was in Mum and Dad's small, three-bedroom 1950s council flat in Bermondsey, south London (or 'saff', in the local accent). By the age of four I was aware of my surroundings; I have no memory before that time. The front room was small, with a folding, mahogany-look table and heavy, fake shiny, brown leather chairs; I remember the polish of the table reflecting the candles of my fourth birthday cake. 'Happy Birthday Kieron' – everyone used my second name. With so many kids in so many flats all crammed together, there were too many Michaels, and a least if they called out 'Kieron!' in the playground I was the only one that would turn round. It wasn't much of a playground: six swings, a concrete boat and a roundabout, but what more could any of us want? We had each other. All those families on the Dickens Estate were close: we laughed together. Mr Gooch, who lived in the flat above us, drove a black V8 Pilot, which stood bold and proud in front of our block of flats, Darnay House, and I would stand for ages staring at it. I never envied Mr Gooch; I was just proud and pleased that the car belonged to someone in our block.

My mother Margaret was Irish, a Reilly from the west of Ireland. My father was adopted, and, according to Mum, the cruelty of his adopted parents went as far as naming him Sergeant Grayston Parker. He wasn't too keen on this, and preferred to call himself George. Where he came from varied from Yorkshire to Lithuania. It was never established whether there was any truth to either extreme. When pushed, Mum only said he just turned up one day, and any previous history he had made up, including his accent which, when mixed with alcohol, was what's commonly known as slurish. For years, I've been the first to make him the bad man, the one to blame. He was a compulsive gambler, drunk and violent. He never brought any money home, or, if he did, then the wages he handed over to feed us for the week were missing the next day from Mum's purse.

Poor Dad. I only found out in later life that it wasn't entirely his fault that he couldn't hold his drink, that Mum hit him as much as he hit her. I'm sorry that I was the one who told Mum that enough was enough, he had to go. But he hurt Mum. He never had enough money left after the gambling to buy himself a drink – drinks were bought for him so that he could drown his sorrows and stagger home penniless. That's when Mum hit him, for putting her in the position of having to bring up three kids on no money, for having to go out and do three jobs a day. But it wasn't the money that bothered me; what bothered me were all the eyes watching my dad staggering home, the eyes of all my mates. He would disappear for days, sometimes weeks, which from an early age forced me to be creative about where he was. Long-distance lorry driver was my favourite, until I was quizzed on it. There was a transport company beside the flats where big ERF lorries and spotless, plum-red Leylands pulled in every night from their long-distance travel. I would look at the drivers climbing down from the high cabs and ask them where they had been and what loads they had carried so that I could answer any questions about why my dad wasn't around. Life would have been so much easier if he had been that Long-Distance Trucker. He was cruel, but the kids were crueller, waiting to catch me out and make fun of me, to bully me about my dad, the man who could never walk in a straight line. But you know what? I soon found out that they wouldn't bully me any more if I got in there first and made them laugh. That way I could take control of the situation. When people laugh they don't ask questions, they don't poke fun. Those kids didn't realise that by bullying eight-year-old Kieron Parker they gave Michael Barrymore his first break. Eight years old – a good time to start entertaining people. Other kids just think you're stupid and silly – fine, no problem with that – and adults think it's cute, even adorable. It's just a question of how you use your eyes.

At my junior school, St Joseph's, I learned to use my

eyes mainly to keep a look-out for the nuns, who would send us to Hell if we didn't obey them. These were the nuns who had failed the audition for *The Blues Brothers* – white, starched veils down to just above their eyes, spotless black covering the whole of their bodies, leaving one square of bare skin, the face. And that final child-frightener, a rosary so heavy they could tow trucks with it, or lasso a lapsed Catholic. I put my hand up for everything: church duty, altar boy. Make yourself popular, I told myself, and keep your eyes open for the ones who don't like your popularity. I started on a course that dictated my entire life. I didn't know any other way.

My years at St Joseph's passed with nothing worse than a smack across the back of my long, far-too-skinny legs. (I'm sure the nuns insisted on those short grey trousers so that their spotless white hands could make a deep red mark when slapped against a young boy's legs.) Other boys and girls at school talked about what their parents did, what was on TV last night, but I never joined in the conversation. My mum was at home, Dad was there sometimes, and the TV was on if there was enough money left to pay the weekly rental. I was embarrassed.

Mum did everything she could to keep us together as a family, dressing me in second-hand clothes, buying me a tricycle – and Dad did absolutely nothing to help. She held down three jobs, getting up at five o'clock in the morning to go out and clean offices, then coming home to get me up for school, going out again to heave heavy tin boxes off the back of trucks. Home again to give me lunch and prepare our meals, then out again in the evening to clean yet more offices. Three jobs, three children. She was my teacher too, finding time to teach me how to read, because I hated school and learned nothing there. Dad only came home to carry on drinking with his friends, or to have another fight with Mum. Usually this went from verbal abuse to punching, but I remember one occasion, when I was eight years old, when Dad picked up a heavy wooden chair and swung it straight at Mum's head. The blood spurted out all over the wall. He didn't see me, so I ran – screaming inside for him to stop, but no voice coming to the surface, just a tidal wave of tears.

I became immune to the fighting, but I could never stand the noise. My eyes could watch the punching; my ears couldn't stand the screaming. My escape was to the cold concrete stairwell, where I'd squeeze my hands tight over the sides of my head to block it out. Johnny Williams, a neighbour, would pull me up from the stairs by my arms and carry me to the safety and quiet of his flat at the end of the landing, where he lived with his wife Val. They had a son, Terry, who had to walk around with heavy plaster casts on both legs to straighten them. I remember thinking that, even though Terry had a problem with his legs, at least he had a real family. I would happily have swapped legs with Terry, just to live in a quiet house. Eight years old and already I wanted twisted legs rather than a twisted home.

One evening my father arrived at the flat, made it as far as the hallway, glared at us – we tensed ourselves for the explosion – and then bang, fell flat on the floor, out for the count with not a punch in anger. Mum, John, Anne and I rifled his pockets – not enough to feed a family for a week, but enough for a treat. We reckoned his comatose state would last for at least three hours, and so we took a bus ride to the Elephant and Castle, where the Norman Wisdom film *Trouble in Store* was on at the ABC cinema. It lasted two hours, and Norman Wisdom made the audience cry and laugh, laugh and cry. I was crying and laughing with the rest of them, but I also took the time to look around at the faces in that cinema. The film finished, we crossed the road and waited for the bus to take us back to Bermondsey . . . and I knew from the experience of being in that cinema what I wanted to do with my life. Not just because Norman Wisdom made us smile, but because he made us forget our troubles for that short time. I remember thinking that it would be great if you could just turn off your troubles whenever you wanted to. But the stars aren't always there when you need them; they're up there in the sky, so high that you can't reach them. If only we could pull down a star to make us laugh and forget . . . And that was what I decided I was going to do. Make people laugh and make them forget their troubles – a comical doctor – laugh at me and laugh at what I do, and for that short time you won't worry about your problems.

How I was going to achieve this I had no idea, but from that night on nothing else ever came into my mind. It seemed simple enough: make people laugh, get paid for it, so there was enough money for Mum to look after the family, and get rid of Dad. I had the answer to all our problems. Sorted. In fact, the answer to all our problems would sort me before I sorted it. Whatever I was going to do in life, I wasn't in any way going to end up like him. It never occurred to me that if I had inherited any good from my father then some, if not all, of the bad would be in the mix. I was witnessing first hand what effect booze had on the house, and it was worse than gambling. I was too young to see it as a disease. Mum was far too busy trying to cope, to survive, rather than dealing with how it might have affected us mentally. Thinking back, I suppose, subconsciously, I did copy the behaviour, and the addiction was probably inherited, though it didn't surface until very late in my life. At a young age, my addiction came out as ambition – I was hooked, addicted to the business of show.

6

From that first night at the cinema. Nobody, including me, noticed the overdosing of extrovert.

I told Mum I was going to become a comedy actor, so she borrowed a small book from the library for me called *Do You Really Want To Be On The Stage?* It gave every reason not to venture into such a hard business. At the end it said, 'If after reading this you still want to try your chances in show business, then good luck.' There wasn't one single thing in it that put me off. How could there be? We had nothing but each other, so the only way was up to the stars. I was at the start of a very long ladder. Some of the rungs were missing and, as you'll see throughout this story, sometimes there were so many rungs missing that I fell hard back down that ladder. I'm still on it. I don't know how many rungs are left, but I'm still climbing, and I can still see that star.

More and more after that night, Dad fell down and couldn't get up again. He went down and down. I can remember sitting on his lap at the age of eleven as he rubbed his unshaven face against mine; I could smell the beer on his breath, but that's what I was used to. It was one of the few times he'd held me, done a dad-type thing. He sat with dead eyes wondering who I was. How did I know? I just did. Kids know what an adult's eyes are saying, and his told me that he was trying to work out who this kid was. I moved away and went to my room. Mum was in the kitchen trying to make another substantial meal from belly of pork – the cheapest cut – and Dad slammed the front door. He never closed it, always slammed it. Mum and I were on our own that night; my sister was in hospital being treated for polio, and my brother was away. Later I got into Mum's bed to keep her company. The flat was quiet – a rarity. Then: slam! The quiet ceased. Mum's bedroom door was a quarter open, and there was Dad, silhouetted against the hall light, standing in the doorway with a double-barrelled shotgun raised to his shoulder, pointing it at Mum. I didn't breathe. Mum said nothing. He changed his aim from Mum to me: two barrels, two people. The silence returned to the flat, and we waited for the noise of the barrels releasing their loads. Dad lowered the gun, turned and walked away – and, for once, didn't slam the door. He never opened that door again.

My brother John said he sighted him a couple of times in the street. John had a totally different attitude towards him. They had fought many times as my brother, being ten years older than me, was up to this, size-wise. My sister Anne had only just come back from hospital, and she wasn't too pleased that Dad had gone. I listened to all the arguments for and against him staying. Secretly I was hoping he would just disappear.

There was a Salvation Army hostel nearby and I overheard he was staying there. I went cold. It meant he was just two streets away. The building was that heavy, red-bricked Victorian type that often features in adaptations of Dickens. I walked round to the building opposite, looking for ages at all the men going in and out. For days on end I watched from a distance. Every man that walked, or mostly staggered, in and out looked no better than the one before and I was just relieved that none of them was my dad. That addictive side kicked in, in the form of obsessively going to see who entered that place. What was I doing? I wanted this man gone, so what did it matter to me where? It was because I had the tools to deal with him staggering back home, but I had no answer to, 'Is your dad one of the old dossers who lives in the Sally Army?'

Mum started to go out dancing on Saturday nights. I always made out I was asleep when she came home, but I was awake watching every single car that pulled into the estate, looking for any new ones. There weren't that many

8

around, so it wasn't hard to pick out the guy dropping Mum home from the dance. Her new date, his new car, my new dad? One guy came back a few times. I never met him, but I knew because the same car returned. It was a Ford Zodiac convertible. 'Are you going to marry that man, Mum?' I asked as she was preparing the Sunday roast. She carried on without making eye contact with me. 'What man?' 'The one with the big green and white car.' She shook the colander to show she was busy. 'Oh no, he's just a friend.' I followed her with my eyes so we had to make eye contact. 'It would be great if we had a car like that in the family, eh Mum?' I repeated this till it hit the spot. With body language only the Irish can do when it comes to anything to do with relationships – a disjointed jig – Mum paused the cooking. 'Darling you have to love someone. You can't marry them because they have a nice car.'

I didn't answer her. I just thought, 'What's love got to do with it?'

During the next week I returned to standing and watching all the Sally Army inmates fall in and out, in their unshaven filthy clothes and cut and bruised from fighting, comparing them unfavourably to the man in the shiny Zodiac. Maybe Dad had just gone away to get a shiny new car. I was a kid, what did I know? I knew that was just a dream. The reality was that that man walking towards the Sally Army's door was my dad. For some reason I made myself visible. He wrestled drunkenly with a couple of men. They seemed to growl, the noise made when the throat is shot to ribbons from spirit. He looked happy where he was. He also looked terrible. The army-smart man gone, the only thing he matched now were the others around him. He looked towards me and stared. I don't know what he saw. He turned and staggered away. I turned and walked away. Nobody would recognise him.

9

I didn't cry. I didn't have to. It was sorted. That was the last I ever saw of him.

I was eleven years old. To this day, I am convinced Dad never really knew I existed. Poor me, or poor Dad. Mum never actually divorced him, or remarried. I had to grow up to find out that she really did love him, whatever he had done to her.

All my summer holidays were spent on Grandma Reilly's farm in Bunnahowen, County Mayo, the Blacksod Mountains to the rear, the Atlantic Ocean in front. At the age of twelve I travelled on my own, clutching a small suitcase, from Euston Station overnight to Holyhead, in a huge steam locomotive – all very Harry Potter but not quite as magical, arriving at six in the morning to catch the passenger ferry across the Irish Sea to Dun Laoghaire, the port outside Dublin. It's an angry sea, and punishing, despite the lyrics of 'If you ever go across the sea to Ireland'. The ships were known as cattle ships, crammed inside and on the decks, and everyone on board would look after a 12-year-old boy travelling alone. Unimaginable today.

From Dublin I would catch the train across the width of Ireland to Ballina, where Uncle Paddy picked me up and drove the dangerous winding coast road to Grandma Bridgie's farm. Everyone was terrified of Bridgie: she ruled with a rod, a thin wooden cane to whip you into the rules of the farm. It was the first time I learned that rules were made to be broken. I played Bridgie like the fish I caught in the stream that ran along the edge of the farm, easy to catch, easy to wind up. She was forever charging me to mend my ways, much to everyone else's delight, and for six weeks she'd chase me, calling me an English pig (nice coming from your own grandmother), then sob and bawl when I had to leave to go back to London. She couldn't put

10

up with me and my pranks, but she could never bear me to leave.

Every night she would make us kneel on the cold floor, our arms resting on the back of a chair, to pray five decades of the rosary; ten Hail Marys every decade, five Our Fathers ... One night I was so fast I was two decades in front. 'The Lord save us, will you slow down! Glory be to God, Hell is the only place for a heathen such as yourself!' Whack! I'm sure to this day that one ear is larger than the other from having been hit with that heavy metal crucifix. If you look closely in a certain light you can see the face of Our Lord on my left earlobe.

I had one of my first sexual encounters on holiday in Ireland. Until then, I'd done nothing more than any of my peers in the stairwells of our council flats – putting my hand up a girl's dress, touching her knickers, if I was lucky. The girls picked a number between one and ten and, if it matched the number you had chosen, you could get in between their second and third floors! I always said three, knowing that Sally would have chosen the same. Not the brightest girl on the estate, but the one with the biggest knicker over-hang. It wasn't really sex; it was just children daring each other. I'm not sure if the next encounter in Ireland was anything more than that. A lad about two years older than me walked me back to my nan's farm late one night. In that part of Ireland the darkness is so heavy you can't see your hand in front of your face. Halfway up the dirt road, he stopped and told me to 'hold this'. What I was supposed to do with the stiff thing he put in my hand I wasn't sure.

'Just rub it up and down quick.'

I did as I was told. He zipped himself up and we walked back to the farm.

'But don't say a word to anyone, will you?'

I thought, 'What have I got to say? I don't know what happened?'

Naivety has always been one of my worst traits.

My first thought on moving across to my secondary school, St Michael's, was relief at getting away from the leg-slapping nuns. I was very tall for my age, and so thin that with my heavy Doc Martens boots I looked like the letter L. I hated being taller than the rest, so I developed a strange stooping walk to reduce my height; I still have that walk today. Knowing what I wanted to do when I was older meant that school was just a matter of doing whatever it took until I could get on with the real business of being a comedy actor. Reading was the only thing I had any interest in, and I'd put up my hand to read aloud at any opportunity. Drama classes were just then being introduced into schools – perfect for me, but not at all popular with the tough Docklands kids who thought that anything to do with the stage was sissy. The sixth form were putting on *Romeo and Juliet*, and the lad who was to play Friar Laurence became so terrified of learning all his lines that he dropped out two weeks before the show was due to go on. I was only in the third form, but I offered to take his part. The teacher said I was too young, but I convinced him I could play older – and, besides, what choice did he have?

One of the English teachers, Miss Jackson, did not like me at all. We were always clashing in class; I think she just hated teaching me. But after the production of *Romeo and Juliet*, she put her arms round me and said, 'I'm so proud of you. I never thought you were capable of doing such a thing.' I had won her round. I had made someone who didn't like me change her mind; it put me in control, made me powerful. There was no doubt in my mind: amateur dramatics had to be the next move.

I joined the local dramatic society, the Felton Players, who used a small theatre owned by St Michael's church in Bermondsey. I performed in two comedy dramas: *Sailor Beware!* and *Brush with a Body,* in which I played an Irish chimney sweep called Dermot Ignatius Eamon McMorag Flaherty. Like all amateur shows, the three nights were sold out to relatives and friends of friends. The buzz was electric. The hum of the audience filing in sounded so right as it distorted through the cheap dressing-room speaker. I remember being shown how to put on stage make-up for the first time and the smell of it. Best of all were those bright lights – endless rows of bulbs. Hearing for the first time the stage manager bellow, "Thirty minutes everybody. Half an hour, this is your half-hour call'. The nerves, the heavy breathing, the panic coming from every corner. Other actors and actresses struggling with costumes that fitted fine a week ago. 'Fifteen minutes. This is your fifteen-minute call.' The hum from the audience fighting to drown out the high pitch of all in the dressing room. The director shouting, 'Good luck everybody'. One last look at the words you already know backwards, loads of 'Oh my God', and unknown amounts of touching God-knows-what for good luck. No one needs any mind altering substance or liquid with this sort of high. As the show started I got myself into position to enter centre stage through the painted garden. On cue I opened the doors to enter the set and, in my best Irish accent, I delivered my opening lines. The laughter from the darkness of the auditorium only hooked me more. The audiences loved what I did, and I loved what they did, cheering and clapping; I was fast becoming addicted to it. It got to the point where the day just wasn't right for me unless I'd done some kind of performance. I knew I had to be in show business, and I didn't care how I went about it, but how was I going to achieve it? None of my family knew anything about show business, and my teachers just told me that the chances of my making a success in it were zero. Well, from zero you can only add on. One of my school reports said, 'If only he concentrated on his maths as much as he does on school plays, he would make a fine academic.'

All during this time at school, after my dad had left home, I was, I suppose, looking for a father figure – and I found one among the priests who taught us. I can't remember his name. He seemed always to be looking out for me in the classroom, making eye contact, and I would wait around after lessons to get closer to him. I told him that I wanted to become an altar boy and eventually a priest, and I started volunteering for every religious duty possible. It was just another stage for me, putting on a costume, being on the high altar in front of the crowd – and when I found out you got paid for doing weddings, that was even better. The priest listened to me, encouraged me and told me that if I was serious about the priesthood, he would give me some private tuition after school.

The priest's house smelt so holy – over-waxed, I suppose, thinking back on it. He took me to a small room on the ground floor, sat me down at a table and began to talk about what it meant to be a priest. I listened intently, but he kept breaking off to stare at me. I had no cause to wonder why; in this house of God he was my surrogate father, and I had no reason to feel uneasy when he told me to come and sit on his knee.

'You are a very special boy,' he said. That was fine; that was what dads did with their boys. He put an arm round my shoulder, which felt very reassuring. My real dad never held me like this. He spoke very softly.

'Do you like cars?'

My face said it all. 'Yeah, I think they're great!' I could

---

see myself reflected in his glasses: not just one happy boy, but two.

'Would you like to go for a ride in the country this week-end? We can have some afternoon tea and, if you're really good, you can steer my car.'

I couldn't wait. After all the shit with my real dad, God was giving me something nice. I didn't tell Mum where I was going. I got to the priest's house early, I was so anxious to ride in the car and get out into the country. I don't remember where we went, but all the trees and fields and grass seemed massive to an inner-London kid. As we drove through this new-found heaven, he would look across and smile and every now and again pat me on the head. This was how it should be. This was perfect.

The trees grew thicker and taller until I could no longer see the top of them. We were headed into deep forest. This was nothing like the vast open fields of Nan's farm in Ireland.

'Do you want to steer the car?'

For the first time he said something without looking at me, just stared straight ahead. I sensed a change in his tone which I didn't like, just as I didn't like the way the forest was closing in around me. It looked like one of those scary drawings in a children's book; the sort of forest that has a wicked witch living in it. My small hands gripped the big, oversized bakelite steering wheel. There wasn't another soul about; I couldn't even hear birds. I started to feel uneasy. He put his hands over mine, steering hard right, then hard left into a space between the trees. I tried to slide my hands away, but he held me tight. He braked hard and we came to a standstill. My fun was turning into fear.

He spoke in a low whisper. 'Do you know what people do when they love each other?'

I was trapped, caught by my own desire to have a father.

15

I stammered out, 'No . . .' His face came closer, a breath away from mine.

'They kiss each other.' Two very frightened little boys were reflected in his glasses.

The whole forest seemed to lean towards me. I pulled away as hard as I could, and started to cry. My happy day was turning out to be very unhappy. I just had to get out of the car.

'It's going to be all right. Come here.'

Here was not where I wanted to be. I knew that this wasn't right, this wasn't how happy families worked. I pulled hard on the door handle, released myself from the car and ran into the forest. He ran after me. The forest thickened. I glanced back and his whole body seemed twice the size seen from that steep angle. The bushes and leaves were getting taller than me, and they entwined around my skinny frame. As I fell to the ground I gave in to the horror of whatever was the conclusion to this now twisted day. His spotless white priest's hand reached to the side of my neck, and tightened, grasping at my shoulder. He spun me round.

'Come back with me, don't be silly.'

I nodded my head in agreement, but said nothing. We climbed back through the forest, no words, just heavy breath from him. He held on tight to me, keeping me moving forward and into the car.

'Let's go for another ride,' he said.

He must have picked the spot well; no one was in sight at all. I took the steering wheel again and we pulled away, driving along the edge of a cliff. I was so tempted to swerve the car right over the edge. All this time the priest said nothing. Eventually I told him that I didn't want to drive any more, and he took over. The silence in the car was eerie. We drove back through the forest to a house where the priest's two older sisters lived. They made me tea and cakes

16

and generally made a fuss of their brother's new protégé. They all smiled and chatted as if nothing had happened. One of them said, 'You're a very quiet boy,' and looked at her brother. 'Is he always this good?' He just nodded and smiled. I wanted to say 'Help me', but I couldn't get the words out.

Later on, he told me to go and wait in the car while he said goodbye to his sisters. I sat and watched them talk in the doorway; they must have known what was going on. It was so bizarre.

The journey home didn't take long at all. He pulled up a short distance from my mum's flat and, as I opened the door, he never turned to look at me, just stared straight ahead.

'You won't tell anyone about today, will you? It will just be our secret.'

I had nothing to tell. What was there to say? It was just a horrible day. My first real one.

In 1965 I was thirteen years old, a Beatles fan, trying to discover what my part was in this world. A few spots to deal with in the bathroom mirror, which I was well tall enough to stare into. I was already earning my own money: I had a paper round, a car-cleaning business, and I sold sweets to all the other kids. Plus my brother John and I sold toiletries in the doorway of a closed shop in Deptford High Street; we did well, but we needed transport. John somehow got hold of a wheelbarrow, which was pushed to and from the cash-and-carry eight miles away on the other side of Tower Bridge. No problem: a barrow full of Dettol, squeaky right wheel, one skinny little kid and his 21-year-old rocker brother – a rocker without a motorbike. Dad was long gone; after a few sightings, he disappeared for good, and I didn't think about him.

I was thinking about girls.

I had discovered how to get a crowd of people to like me: just perform for them. Part of my repertoire was to sing 'Michael, Row the Boat Ashore' to an assembled audience of girls and boys sitting on the concrete steps of the council flats, faces cupped in their hands, as I performed on the lower floor. 'Michael, row the boat ashore, hallelujah, Michael, row the boat ashore, hallelujah,' over and over – it was the only song I knew at least half the words to.

The next addition to my repertoire came when I dis- covered that, with my late-breaking voice, I could scream at least as high as any of the girls. One good scream and all the worried parents would come bursting out of the flats to see which child was being murdered – which made my friends laugh, and made me popular. Just what I wanted. I took requests, and for some strange reason the screaming was always more popular than 'Michael, Row the Boat Ashore'.

The Rolling Stones were becoming popular at this time, so although I kept my hair Beatled, I added a Mick Jagger impersonation to my rapidly expanding repertoire.

This became a highlight of the show I now gave every Saturday evening. Mum went up to the West End to go dancing most Saturdays, trying to put some kind of life together for herself, so I opened up the front room for all my friends. I sang along to records that I took from my brother's Elvis collection. I did the Everly Brothers using an old tennis racket as a guitar, I did silly walks, I stretched my face as far as it would contort and for as long as it took to get the audience laughing. During the interval I made sandwiches, laid them neatly out on plates and offered them around, always asking for 'Sixpence, please'. And if anyone asked why I was charging, I'd say, 'I haven't got a dad. Sixpence, please.' Most of them paid; to those who didn't I gave the option, 'Pay up or I won't perform.'

They paid. I performed.

At school I discovered that we were all growing up rapidly – I was getting taller and taller, but no wider, and I was nicknamed 'Twig'. I wasn't a great fighter, but Mickey Jarman was, so he took care of that side of things for me. I also amused Johnny Alan, the second-best fighter in the school, so he didn't pick on me either.

There were hundreds of us, all living on top of each other in the flats and, as our puberty progressed, we started to get on top of each other in other ways as well.

By fourteen, the school playground was a place to meet and talk about music. The first record I bought was Millie's 'My Boy Lollipop'. I loved the bits where you put your finger in your mouth and made it pop. I also loved Pauline Hart, the school's best-looking bird, but she was Johnny Alan's girlfriend.

I looked the dog's bollocks by now: skinhead haircut, mohair suit, trousers just exactly short enough above my Doc Martens boots. Something was stirring in me as a teenager as well. I wanted to join in what all the other lads were doing, or so the rumour went . . . going round to each other's flats when the family was out and doing things together. From playground talk, if you did this sort of thing you were queer. That was a word I'd never heard at home, and not even at school until this point.

Was I doing what qualified as this word? No way! Then why was I more interested in going round to my friends' flats to mess around with them than I was in finding a girlfriend? There was no way I was going to survive in the Docklands if I was queer. Queer boys had no chance. After all these years of getting everyone to like me – boys, girls, mums, dads, nans, grandads – I wasn't going to blow it. I was the funny one, not the queer one.

'Wanna come back to my flat?'

'Yeah.'

Bob was one of my best mates; I really got on with him. I don't know why; I had loads of mates, but I just always felt good around him. His mum and dad were always out working and, rare in those times, he was an only child. The first time I went back to his flat I noticed an odour. At first I thought it was the flat itself, which was on the top floor of one of the other blocks on the Dickens Estate, but then I realised it was him. Not an unpleasant smell, just the natural smell of a young man's body. When I was with him I felt physical changes. We sat on the long couch in the front room; there was no reason for him to sit as close as he did, as we were the only two there, but I didn't tell him to move away. I could see he was aroused, and I knew from my own experience what was stirring inside him. I had the same feeling myself.

He said nothing. I said nothing. My mouth went dry and I suppressed gulps. My body buzzed like it never had before. His hand lowered to hold himself, I copied in silence. My head was rushing like mad.

But neither of us could stop or wanted to. I can only remember the overwhelming feeling of that first step into sexuality – a word that would not have been in our vocabulary at the time. Nor would 'gay'. Only queer. But you couldn't be queer, and no one could know, so Bob and I met every occasion we could and never once in all that time of early discovery did we speak.

I hope Bob is well today. I don't know if our early experiences together were just that for him – an experience – or whether he is a happy straight man today, or if he's gay and happy too. I know you, Bob, and you know me. My name's Michael. And yours ain't Bob . . .

Around this time I began to indulge my love of cars. Having a good income from my various scams funded many things for me, including my first motor, an ex-GPO (General Post Office) Morris van which cost me £80. I loved that van. Being fourteen did have its problems: for one thing, I could only drive it around the block of flats, but I did at least teach myself to drive. In the process I reversed too fast into the bike sheds, demolished four of them, then ran around the block and screamed, 'Who the hell moved the van?' I got away with that one, but I didn't get away with my first venture on to the main road. I took a chance and drove up to Tower Bridge, and on my return I was pulled over by a motorbike copper who was surprised to see the skinny young kid at the wheel – surprised because I was driving so well. He nicked me for having no insurance and driving without a licence. I attended Tower Bridge Magistrates' Court and was fined £40. This was my first ever experience of being in a courtroom, and it terrified me.

I changed the Morris van for a three-wheeler Bubble Car, because at the time you could drive one with just a motorbike licence – not that I had one of those either, you understand. The car seated two people, or one and a pile of boxes full of toiletries to flog down Deptford High Street. Top speed 30 mph, or so they told me. Cost me a fiver, paid for itself in two days. But they lied about the speed: on my first return trip from the cash-and-carry I hit the accelerator and it flew along at 75 mph, screaming its bubbly head off, swerved right, then left, of its own free will and hit a bollard at top speed. I wasn't injured – only my pride. Bubble Cars only had one door, at the front, and that was smashed in, so I ripped my way through the cloth sun-roof, climbed out and left it there. I've driven past that spot since, and that bollard's still in exactly the same position. Next time I pass I might sign it. The council obviously think it's a piece of art.

Another new discovery were the many pubs that filled

Bermondsey: the Lilliput, the Dun Cow, the Red Lion. My mates and I were all tall enough to pass for the right age, and we started going out to the pubs all the time. I loved them – though not for the booze, because I didn't drink, as I just didn't like the taste. What I loved about them was that they gave me another platform on which to perform. Every time we went out I would get up and do my party piece, just fooling around, no jokes, no comments. I don't know how to describe what I did, because I didn't know then and I don't know now. But my friends found it funny and that was what counted.

I left school at fifteen with no qualifications. That didn't matter: I was free! Now I could start on my chosen career – but how? When I told a careers officer what I wanted to do, he replied, 'No, seriously, a proper job.' Like everyone else, he thought a show-business career was not for the likes of me. I had to do something. I'd read an article in the paper about a hairdresser called Vidal Sassoon, 'the king of hairdressing', so I decided to become an apprentice at Sassoon's for the very simple reason that all the big stars were having their hair done there, and I reckoned that I would get close to them, be discovered and get paid. The last thing in the world I wanted to be was a crimper, but I took a chance and took the job.

My first job, my first pay: £3.50 a week plus tips, which was a bit of a drop in wages, as I was managing to pull in £36 a week from various scams around Bermondsey. But what the hell, I was heading for the West End of London, the glamour, the glitz, the reality of life about to unfold. Sassoon had three salons at the time: Sloane Street, Bond Street and Grosvenor House, Park Lane. I didn't get on too well in Sloane Street; one of the juniors found out that most of the famous heads were teased out at Grosvenor House, where Vidal himself would occasionally put in an appearance if there was a big American star staying at the hotel. Ricci Burns was one of the top stylists at Grosvenor House: very popular with the clients, less so with the juniors, because of his temperament. They were all delighted when I volunteered to work for him. I couldn't give a toss how hard he was to work for, he had what I wanted – the star list: Lulu, Candice Bergen, Dusty Springfield, Dudley Moore, Shirley Bassey . . . Maybe, just maybe, one of them would discover me. I used to hold the door open for them, smiling so hard they just had to notice me. They probably just wondered, 'Who's this six-foot stick-insect with the skinhead haircut and the inane grin?'

Ricci was always immaculately turned out: no ordinary blazer for Ricci, his had to have gold buttons. For some reason he took to me, and instead of just getting me to do the usual junior duties, like holding hair to one side or handing him the rollers, he got me to do impressions to amuse the clients. I did them to order – mostly Shirley Bassey, unless, of course, she was the client. Through Ricci I met a client called Dora Ravis, dress designer to the rich and famous, who had a stunning apartment in Argyll Street. This was the first time I learned that if you're rich, it's called an apartment; if you're poor, it's a flat. Dora invited a friend of hers round to meet this young and, in her opinion, talented junior – a man called Bertie Green, who owned a nightclub called The Astor. I didn't realise it, but this was my first audition. I nervously did a few impressions, and his only comment, after a long silence, was, 'He looks like a young Frank Sinatra.' What a start! What a waste of time. Wake up, Michael: you're fifteen, you've got no experience, and you've just learned that knowing people in power does not make a career.

Well, if that wasn't going to work for me, something else

would. Hughie Green hosted the biggest star-making show of the day, *Opportunity Knocks* – that had to be the answer to all my prayers. I attended an audition. Hughie Green sat there with his team and watched me do what I always did to make my friends laugh. It felt strange this time; the roof of my mouth went dry, and my legs were so shaky I was having trouble standing up. This had never happened before, with my mates; what was so different? Why weren't they laughing? After the audition, Hughie Green said something, but it didn't contain the words, 'We would love to see you again.' Well, what did he know? He only had the biggest-rating, most successful show of its kind ever on British television.

I left Sassoon's because some of my mates at home had found out I was working in a hair salon in the West End, and the word 'poof' was starting to be thrown around. Well, I couldn't have that; I wanted to be liked, and having a gang of lads shout out, 'Oi! Poof!' in the middle of Bermondsey didn't go down too well. And if they'd known that I was actually wondering myself whether I was a poof or not, they would have been even less happy about it. Well, I consoled myself with the fact that I was still only fifteen, and I'd heard someone in the West End saying that if you got past twenty-one and you still had leanings towards your own sex then that was the time to worry; before that it was probably just a phase. Thank God for that: six years to go! Maybe I could do some research. But how? I lived in the Docks. We were geezers! Poofs came from another planet, not Bermondsey. Not us lads – us Jack-the-lads who supported Millwall, whose older brothers were Dockers, painters, barrow boys, all of us dressed real tasty as mods, real tasty for the birds.

I loved my mates, and my Millwall mod well-hard mates loved me. My mum was the only parent who allowed a crowd of loud teenagers to crash at their flat and this only added to my popularity. By now my brother had married and moved out, so I had a room to myself, and when I had my first taste of booze in the pubs it gave me the confidence to get closer to my mates.

'You know what, mate, you're my best mate.'

'Yeah, you're my best mate too.' Then both having another drink and passing out.

'Stay here if you want.'

Sleep together for the night, fiddle around a bit . . . wake up the next morning, and just grumble to each other.

Uneasy two seconds, and a strange look from Mum as we leave the bedroom together. 'See you later, Mum . . .'

Walk down the stairs of the flats, no conversation, just looking straight ahead, hoping to God he wouldn't say anything. Open the doors of the Lilliput pub on the corner, meet back up with the gang from the night before, start the Sunday lunchtime drinking and all was forgotten. Nothing had happened. Just got pissed, the cold lager drowning any memories.

It seemed to me that that was the way it worked: say nothing. Anyway, most of us had birds, so . . . well . . . know what I mean? They knew, and I knew, but how could you ever find any answers when nobody was even asking the questions? Is he gay? Or, as it was more often said, is he a bit funny?

Me, I was bloody hysterical.

Sixteen years of age and various jobs down the line, I still hadn't started my career as far as I was concerned. Hairdressing hadn't worked, and opportunity hadn't knocked, but I'd learned one thing: being sixteen and cute wasn't going to be enough to get me noticed, I needed to get some experience. Mum gave up most of her savings so I could buy a set of keyboards and join a band that were looking for a keyboard player; they took me on because I don't think anyone else could afford the instrument. I had a few lessons from an organ teacher in Sidcup, about whom I remember very little apart from the fact that he used to sit far too close when he was showing me which chords to bang, munching Madeira cake, which sprayed all over the keys.

Joining the band was a big step for me. We started off as a soul outfit, covering all the standards of the day: '(Your Love Keeps Lifting Me) Higher and Higher', 'Down at the Club', later graduating to Traffic and Jethro Tull. We weren't bad, but we weren't good enough to make a career of it. Still, I learned some important lessons through being in the band: mainly I discovered that I liked people, I could communicate with ease, and I spent all my time observing their mannerisms, how they talked and walked. I threw myself into the business of pleasing people, and it worked.

As well as getting on with my career, I decided it was time to become a man and have sex with a girl. Time to stop all this mucking around with my mates – time to get a girl. Yeah, that would sort me out.

One thing I'd learned from my mother was good manners. Which knife and fork to pick up, how to light a lady's cigarette by holding the flame away, then offering it up, how to walk on the outside of a lady down the street, open doors for her, walk behind her if you're going upstairs, in front if you're going down. I was well-mannered, and the girls noticed that I knew how to treat a lady. One night I was at a party with a couple of my mates from Bermondsey at a flat in Fulham, and my good manners led to what I regarded, at the time, as my first sexual experience.

There were six of us at the party, three lads and three girls, and the others had all paired off, leaving me with the tall thin one with short hair. We must have looked like the last two matches in the box. She took me to the bedroom, closed the door and leaned back, letting her arms fall down by her side. Her eyes were flickering rapidly: it must have been all the strong tobacco we'd been smoking. I placed both hands on her tits; I had big hands, and she had small tits. I rubbed my palms in a circular motion, which made her rock from side to side, her head lolling, the door rattling in unison. I lowered my left arm down through the elasticated waistband of her trousers. She said, 'Urrr ...', I said 'Woooh!' and began rotating my hand, in the opposite direction. I thrust my middle section against her, and now the door started to bang rather than rattle. Somehow she managed to get her hands down my jeans, while making a strange sort of snoring noise. She grabbed my dick and turned it like a starting handle, while I pulled down her knitted slacks. She finally got one whole word out – 'Yes!'

Having absolutely no experience at all, I didn't really know much about how a woman was put together. I pulled her hand away, pushed forward ... and missed. Oh Jesus, why did my first time have to be standing up with my jeans round my ankles? I was all over the place bending to the left, to the right, up, down. But I wasn't giving in, I had to become a man. Oh God, finally, thank you, thank you. It felt strange. She pulled herself up higher and higher against the door. I followed. Almost as soon as it had begun, it was all over. I pulled up my jeans and left the house. That was it, then: my first heterosexual experience. It was like being in one place in body, another in mind.

Next time I saw my mates, nothing was said, typical Bermondsey style. If it's anything to do with sex, say nothing. Maybe it put an end to the whispers. Me, a homosexual? My God! No way! I shag birds! I was as straight as any of them. Which, at the age of sixteen, playing keyboards in a band and touring around Europe, I was about to prove.

2

A Foot on the Ladder

The only reason I joined the band was to get on to a stage. My music skills alone weren't going to get me very far, though I could punch out a few chords, thanks to the strange organ teacher in Sidcup. It didn't take much to work out which organ he wanted me to practise on, needless to say that was a short course, but I knew instinctively how to perform.

I think it must have come from Mum, having seen her always get up at family gatherings acting the eejit, as she called it. I suppose Mum always making others laugh was her way of dealing with adversity. It was noticeable she did this whenever there was a crowd. I was too young to know if that was for acceptance or attention, but Mum always encouraged me to follow suit. Whereas my brother and sister always shied away from any kind of exhibitionism, I took any opportunity to get up and perform to my aunts and uncles. At six or seven it had to be some sort of in-born trait to know that it would work better if I was on a stool rather than just on the floor. This was just a young guy with a dream – no ideas, just a dream. Nobody mentioned Dad much any more. He wasn't about to get praise for having anything to do with a young wannabe, though much later I would find out that Dad had other talents besides losing money and getting drunk. (Thinking about this has made me wonder what Mum and Dad were like when they first got together. It's made me smile, which is just one of the upsides of writing. Lovely.) So with a mix of their talents and a few chords under my belt I considered myself fit for musical service.

Whenever there was a song that I couldn't play, I let the rest of the band get on with it, while I went mad, throwing myself around or standing on my head on top of the keyboards. Standing on my head was my only forte at PE in school. I was far too skinny to do anything else. I found moving my legs around and talking kept the blood flowing whilst upside down. I could stay up for twenty minutes without going dizzy. Why has the word nerd just entered my head?

One of our mates managed to borrow some money off his dad so that we could be a proper professional band – and in the 60s, you weren't a proper band unless you had a six-wheeled Ford Transit van with aeroplane seats fitted in two rows and the rest of it empty for your equipment. So now we were ready to take the music business by storm: we'd practised hard, we had the van and we looked the part. I had crushed velvet trousers, a long trench coat and a fluffy sort of cotton-wool beard. I looked an absolute prat. We even had a name: Fine China. I don't know who thought that one up, as there was nothing particularly fine about us, but I presume it must have been during one of our acid trips.

Sex and drugs and rock 'n' roll – that's what you join a band for, isn't it? Well, the rock 'n' roll wasn't up to much, but we certainly had our fair share of the first two-thirds of the equation. I had my first taste of acid in the form of a little pink pill in one of the band's houses in Camberwell. His mum and dad were away, which is always a good time to indulge in a bit of growing up, and I took a taste of another world. I sat in the corner of the front room, crossed my legs, put my hands on top of my head and sat like that for two days. The others tried to get me up, but I wouldn't let them touch me because I was a strawberry and wasn't ripe yet. I had to be left till I was ripe, red and ready for plucking . . . The true meaning of a fruitcake, and a waste of two days of my life, but so what? At sixteen we have the rest of our lives. That was my one and only acid trip. Being a strawberry for two days didn't do much for me, but one little experiment with drugs wasn't going to hurt . . . was it?

So with three musical chords and a head-standing trick to my name, I took myself and five other band members and a roadie off to Germany for our first gig, a month's residency in a little southern town called Schweinegen. Which translated means Pigshire. Who said that Germans don't have a sense of humour? It was a long drive, but we all wanted to have a go at the wheel of the Transit, even though not one of us had a licence. It didn't matter: we could do what we wanted – all for one and one for all in a foreign land. Why we think that the moment we get out of Great Britain other countries' laws don't apply to us I've never really worked out.

We made our way across Belgium and Germany with absolutely no money. No problem! If we needed petrol, we just refilled the Transit and then drove off without paying.

Hungry? We just went into a food store, picked up what we needed and ran. Some new equipment for the band? Same story.

When we arrived in Pigshizer, everything seemed fine. The club owner was friendly and put us up in a small, family-run hotel; our board and lodging was part of the deal. The gigs were going okay, but we had made a much more important discovery: the groupie. They're a breed of their own, just made for any up-and-coming band – up and coming being the groupie's motto. My first encounter with a groupie took place in Pigshipenze, not in a bed, because they were all full, but in the next obvious place – the back of the Transit. Not being experienced, I went for the standard, 'you lie on the floor and I'll do all the hard work' approach. Well, I may not have been experienced, but I wasn't stupid: the steel floor of the van was freezing, so her arse took the chill. She had blonde hair and glasses and seemed to have been in this position before. She handed me a large white tablet, about the size of a two-pence piece, which she told me to place inside her. 'Das ist very gut. Now, ven it stops the, how you say, fizzing, you may enter yourself.' Oh, the excitement!

So this was sex: fizzing and warm, then screaming in agony as my balls hit the cold floor of the van. I shot my arse heavenwards, she pulled me back down, the van doors flew open and there were my long legs flailing around for all the world to see. I don't know if anything like sex happened, but the fizz tablet won the day. Thinking back, I suppose it must have been some early form of contraceptive – unless it was just a personal quirk of hers. What would I know?

It was during this time that I signed my first autograph. One of the girls had come back to the hotel with us, and wanted all our autographs, only she didn't have an autograph book, so naturally we decided to sign her breasts. Felt tips for felt tits. For once in my life I saw an advantage to having a long name – Michael Kieron Parker – as it increased the time that I could spend signing her. To this day, I still sign my name with two dots underneath. I really enjoyed the experience. Me, gay? No! Proper geezer this one.

The owners of the hotel never complained, despite what we were doing to their rooms and, moreover, to the young girls of their town. But the club owner wasn't so pleased with us, and decided that we weren't up to standard and thus weren't going to get paid. So we did what any ordinary group of people would do: we kidnapped his wife. We drove up to his house. He wasn't there, but she was, so we loaded her into the van and drove off. We parked up and got her to ring him with an ultimatum: pay us our money or lose your wife. He told us in no uncertain terms to keep her. Shit. Bad idea. No money, no food, no roof, and a terrified German woman that nobody wanted. Eventually we took her back home and apologised for what we'd done, and for the fact that her husband didn't want her.

She became strangely calm and asked us if we would like some tea. This, as anyone who has studied women will know, is a danger sign. We sat there politely drinking tea and eating cakes, when in walks Mr Club Owner. He mumbled something to his wife. She didn't reply, just went into the kitchen and left us to beg, threaten and plead for our money. Then suddenly the club owner slumped forward, face down on the carpet, and there was his wife standing behind him holding a large copper frying pan. She quietly walked over, pulled out his wallet and directed us to the nearest bank. I don't know if he ever got up, but having seen the look on her face I personally would have stayed in a coma.

*

Goodbye small-town Pigshittenhousen, hello swinging Frankfurt! (German for hot dog farting.) Big town, big time, big trouble. The K52 Club on Kaiser Strasse was an important gig, and we had more to do: five, one-hour spots a night. Accommodation came with the gig: no nice hotel this time, but self-catering in an old town house on a busy road. We were shown to our room: 'This is yours, this is yours, this is yours' and so on; one room for all seven of us, four bunk beds, a coffee table and a lamp. I don't remember any one of us making a complaint, just arguing over who was going to have the top bunk. Everyone wanted to *sleep* in the top bunk, but when it came to a bunk-up they all wanted the lower one, because the only way you could get any privacy was to hang blankets around the side while you were shagging. The rest of the band stayed in the room while you and the groupie were grunting away, so it was privacy of a strictly limited kind.

Al, the bass player, always had an opinion on other people's sexual performance, particularly if he wasn't getting any. One night it was my turn to get behind the blankets with my groupie and, as I was fumbling away, I heard the words, 'You're not doing it right.' I hadn't seen her lips move; just my luck, I'm shagging a ventriloquist. But no: it was Al peering through the blankets and giving his expert advice. 'Okay,' I said, 'you know so much: show me how it's done.' So we changed places and I watched. I learned a few new tricks that certainly seemed to be giving Al pleasure, although the poor girl lay motionless. Just as his 'Ah! Ah! Ah!' was starting to get louder, I said, 'Thank you, I think I've got the idea now.'

I did everything I could to get a reaction, the bunk bed was rocking, the bolts and screws that held it together were shaking themselves loose ... Then I heard Jon, the drummer, say, 'I'm going down the train station. Anyone want anything?' The bunk bed ground to a halt, I pulled back the blanket, stuck my head out and said, 'Get us a bar of chocolate, will you?' At the time I didn't understand why they all burst out laughing. Maybe I see it now.

The crowds at the K52 Club seemed to like us, particularly in the small hours when the drug dealers arrived. One of the dealers liked us so much that he gave us huge lumps of cannabis and various pills as a reward. In fact, we had so much cannabis that we used to spend our spare time rolling it into packets of twenty joints. Being the youngest and the most stupid, I was nominated the pill-tester. They would lay me on the top bunk, insert a pill and wait for a reaction. One pill made me laugh for eight hours solid. Another made me feel very horny. On that particular evening all the groupies were taken, apart from one huge girl sitting at the coffee table smoking a huge joint with a huge grin on her face. Everything about her was huge. Normally I would have given her a huge berth, but the pill was telling me that she was pretty. Pretty what, was never confirmed. All the lower bunks were busy going backwards and forwards, but the bathroom was empty – it always was, it was freezing and damp.

So I led Huge Smile into the privacy of our unused bathroom and indicated to her that she lower herself down between the bath and the wall. It was a tight fit, and as she squeezed in she started to fold in on herself. I pushed her down to get her arse somewhere near the floor, and by this time she was well and truly stuck, her legs forced together by the bath and the wall. Then, with one giant thump, the eagle had landed. There was no way that I was going to get anywhere like this, so I suggested that we go back to her place. I tried, believe me I tried, to pull her up. I called for help, and it took four of us to pop her out. The rest of the band were looking at me in disbelief: 'Why do you think she was left alone at the coffee table?'

I offered to drive her home, but by the time we had got to her place she was looking good again and I started kissing her in the van. This was one weird pill. I kicked the passenger seat down, she found a comfortable position between the front and rear seats, I jumped out and slid open the passenger door, intending to leap on top of her. But her huge legs came dropping out of the van and hammered me straight into the ground. The snow and ice broke my fall, and my legs slid under the van like a mechanic's. Huge Smile was stuck yet again. I stood up; the fall had sobered me up a bit, and I felt sorry for her, this poor, broad-smiling girl with not a single place in the world to park her arse. With no back-up this time, I pulled her free from the van one leg at a time.

'You give me the bumpsie-bumpsie?' German for a shag, I am led to believe, but by now the pill was wearing off and I realised that perhaps she wasn't the girl for me. I told her that she could do better than me, that the likes of me were not for her. I walked back to the driver's side and started the engine.

'You know what you need, love?'

'Nein ...'

'You need someone strong.'

I hit the accelerator hard. I hope she did find someone. And if she did, I certainly wouldn't like to upset him.

On our return home the band drifted apart; we'd given it a go and it hadn't worked out. The actual split came after an audition for a manager who wanted to put together a new pop band and at the end said he only wanted Al the bass player and me, which even I agreed was a joke, as my musical abilities were the worst – not that that's ever stopped anyone in the business. But this didn't go down too well with the other lads, and so we called it a day. We'd had a lot of fun playing around in Europe, mostly with girls, and I had gained experience of being on stage. It was, and still is the only place I always feel at home. The stage, to me, is my front room, and the audience, whatever size, my friends.

The rest of the lads went on to take up different careers; for me, the band was just the beginning, now it was time to get on to the next stage – any stage. But what? The answer came in an advert in the *Evening Standard*: 'Wanted, young men and women to become Redcoats at Butlins, minimum age 18.' And the money wasn't bad – £7 a week, with everything thrown in, uniform, accommodation, food. Fantastic! A chance to do exactly what I wanted and get paid for it as well. And I'd read about stars who had got into the big time by being Redcoats. Perfect – apart from the fact that I was only seventeen.

I walked down Oxford Street to the Butlins Head Office just opposite Selfridges, smiling so hard – I wanted this job so much. Just as long as they didn't ask my age. I'd do anything to be a Red. The nice Butlins man smiled almost as much as I did.

'Hello, Michael.'

'Hello!' I gushed, much too loud, never losing my smile.

'So you want to be a Redcoat?'

'Oh yes, I do!' Smile, smile.

'Do you have any stage experience?'

'Oh yes, lots!'

'Great,' he said. 'Do you know Clacton-on-Sea?'

My smile froze. 'Yes, I've heard of it.'

'Well, Michael, I know you will be perfect for us.'

The interview was over. As easy as that.

All I had to do was smile at everything and everyone

(rather like my German girl, Huge Smile), and do the Redcoat show six days a week. Give me seven! I wanted it all! Mum was pleased for me, and I promised to come home every Sunday to tell her how my climb to stardom was going. Bags packed, a few more quid borrowed from Mum – who else? – and down to Liverpool Street Station, single to Clacton, please. The engine steamed out of the station, I beamed out of the window. I couldn't tell you what the scenery was like because, in my imagination, I was up there on the big Butlins stage. The applause, the adoration ... I would be the best Redcoat ever. A star was on his way. I'll make them laugh, I'll tear them apart, I didn't know how. Just act stupid – it worked with my mates, why not for Butlins?

Like everyone else, I was called down a week before the paying crowds arrived for my training. I can still see myself walking along Clacton Station, carrying my suitcase, practising my smile. I looked right, smiled – nothing. Looked left, smiled – nobody. I crossed the road, looked left and right, but there was no need because there wasn't a single car in the town, and even if one had hit me, I would have carried right on smiling. On the other side of the road there was a high fence with rolls and rolls of barbed wire stretching for hundreds of yards. I remember thinking that they must have held German POWs here during the war, and I was surprised that they hadn't got round to knocking it down yet and making better use of all that prime land right by the sea. But that wasn't my problem: I had to find Butlins.

I walked further and further along the fence and eventually I came to a security hut with two uniformed guards in it. Poor sods, I thought, having to guard an old prison camp with no prisoners in it. I smiled at them, they stared at me. I thought it best to break the silence.

———

'I'm looking for Butlins.' Smile.

One of them stood up. 'Name?'

With confidence I replied, 'Butlins.'

The other one stayed sitting down, and smirked. 'He must be a bloody Redcoat.' He jerked a thumb in the direction of the prison camp.

I walked on, and after ten yards they hit a switch and the barbed wire gates swung open in front of me. I stepped inside and the gates closed behind me. I walked on, singing, 'Smile, though your heart is aching . . .'

Before I go on I must make it clear that Butlins has changed dramatically over the years, and I even believe that Clacton has cars going through it these days. But this was my experience, and I was always taught to speak as you find. My first discovery was that, as a fully fledged 17-year-old Redcoat, I only got to do one show every two weeks. The rest of the time was yours to work your bollocks off. Redcoats' duties were to be there from the first sitting for breakfast till the last dance with anyone who asked in the evening. The only reason I stuck the whole season was because I told myself that if you can't stand this, you will never last in show business. And I was there to learn as much as I could.

The resident comedian was a man called Mike Onions, who was small and skinny with long hippy hair, and sat on stage telling jokes while knitting a scarf in a variety of colours. He had a different act for every night of the week, and then he compered the fortnightly Redcoat show. Over the twenty-week season he really made his mark on me – and he made a scarf long enough to cover a thousand necks.

Competition amongst the Redcoats was stiff, and I had to battle hard to get a place on every show. That wasn't the only thing that was stiff amongst the male Reds. My chalet-mate Barry, like most of the other Redcoats, had no interest in show business whatsoever. Sod doing the shows: let's just do the customers. New ones every week: young mothers away with the kids while Daddy's off fishing with his mates. The set-up was perfect: the children were looked after all day, and all night if you wanted, so Mummy could have a good time and not worry. In the theatre there was a big electric sign that would flash up, 'Baby crying in Chalet 14'. And, depending on where Barry was at certain times, 'Mother screaming her tits off in Chalet 15'.

A Redcoat's duties were endless. Snooker tournament, darts tournament, table-tennis tournament, swimming tournament, football tournament, dancing tournament, glamorous granny tournament, knobbly knees tournament, talent contest. Oh Christ, there's a change, a contest crept in. Donkey derby, disco, old-time music hall, bingo. Now I like bingo – playing it, that is. But believe me, calling the numbers is an art, and not one that I ever mastered.

'Two and one, twenty-one, four and eight, forty-eight, seven and three, seventy-three . . .'

Voice from the back of the room: 'Slow down!'

'On its own, number three, seven and eight, seventy-eight, four and—'

Voice from the left-hand side of the room: 'Speed up!'

Remember, no one's called House yet, and it's only two quid for a top line. Take a breath, smile, have a bright idea: I'll say all the fancy sayings that precede a number at high speed, but I'll say the number itself slowly.

'Downing Street – number ten! Kelly's Eye – number one! Two fat ladies – eighty-eight! Top of the shop, blind—'

Before I could finish, some old girl in the middle of the room shouts 'Eeer-yah!'

I continue, 'Hold all your cards, please. Top line called

on number two.' Huge ooooh from the crowd. Then the old girl raises her voice, 'Wot yer min, too?'

I reply, 'The last number I was about to call was top of the shop, blind—'

The crowd interrupts as one voice: 'Blind ninety!'

'No, no, top of the shop, Blind Pew, number two.'

Some old gent on their behalf: 'It's top of the shop blind ninety, not Blind Pew number two! How long have you been doing this?'

Remember, at this point, I am very tired, it's mid-season, I've danced with every granny, bounced every child. I've ridden donkeys front ways, sideways, back ways, astride two who parted in mid-ride, smiled so much I can now lick my own ears with the edge of my tongue, goose-stepped outside my chalet to the rhythm of Barry's shagging until they finished at two in the morning and I could at least get a few hours sleep before being woken up by some happy campers who thought it would be a great idea to dunk me in the boating lake, from which I caught some filthy disease not even registered in any medical journal, but which causes me to vomit continuously – and this old fart is upset because I thought a little change like, 'Top of the shop, Blind Pew number two' might bring a bit of variety into their lives.

So I answer him, 'All the fours, forty-four, why don't you piss off through that door?' Not, I must admit, one of my best ad libs, and I was sacked for it. But Mike Onions spoke up for me, and I don't think the manager had a lot of choice but to keep me, as I was the only Redcoat who regularly did the show. I got sacked four times that season and was taken back every time. I learned one useful thing from Butlins: never say to anyone 'You'll never work in this business again.' There is no such word as never.

*

At the end of the season I returned to reality. I took any job that was available, but the one that paid best was cleaning cars for Sainsbury's. They had a fleet of cars for their managers, going right up to Rolls-Royces and Bentleys for the family itself and, as I loved cars, it wasn't a bad job. I did long hours and worked my way up to being relief chauffeur. At the age of eighteen, driving Rolls-Royces was my idea of heaven.

Barry, my mate from Butlins, encouraged me to work on my impressions. At this stage I was doing Alan Whicker, David Frost, Larry Grayson and a few others, but I never really put my heart and soul into it as I was earning such good money at Sainsbury's. For a while, I lost my enthusiasm for the business. One of the clerks at the garage said, 'You always go on about wanting to be on the stage, but you can't, can you? You're not a member of Equity.' Not knowing what he was talking about, I bluffed. 'I am a member. I'm just resting in between jobs.' He was involved in amateur dramatics and always bought the weekly showbiz paper *The Stage*, and there were always loads of auditions advertised in the back.

When I started going for auditions I would try anything, even if I wasn't suitable for it. Trapeze artist? Yeah, I'd go, just in case I discovered a talent I didn't know I had. Mind you, walking a straight line has always been difficult for me, so doing it on a rope sixty feet off the ground was never going to be easy. I auditioned at the Haymarket Theatre, London, went on, stood on my head, sang some cockney song and walked off to the sound of nothing! Several years later I met a producer who said, 'Actually, we have sort of met before'. I was surprised. He said, 'Do you remember doing an audition at the Haymarket?' 'Oh Christ,' I said, 'I died on my arse!' He smiled and said, 'Well, I was one of the producers. We couldn't work out why you stood on your head. Did you have any idea what you were auditioning for?' I couldn't lie. I had no choice but to say, 'No, not really, my agent at the time just told me to go along. Why?' He replied, 'The auditions were for *Hans Christian Anderson*'. I just stared at him and said, 'Well, he couldn't have done much better than me, he's never been heard of since!' He gave me that look we all know, the one where their eyes blink in slow motion that translates to 'You fucking dip-stick!'

Most of the auditions were in the daytime, and the only way I could attend them was to leave Sainsbury's and find a job with more flexible hours. So I bought an ice-blue Austin Cambridge and became a minicab driver for a firm in Bromley called Speedy Cars. I used to work one solid shift from Friday night through to Monday morning with no sleep break, just making as much money as I could so that I could attend auditions during the week. After a few weeks like this, I could see it wasn't going to work, because I had to sleep all day Tuesday and Wednesday, which only left Thursday free to look for work. I mentioned to one of the drivers that seventy-two hours' solid driving was doing me in, so he suggested I take some pills. He said they'd be fine, no problem, they'd just keep me awake. One of my biggest problems in life, as I tell myself until I'm blue in the face but still never learn, is naivety. I trust everyone and take everything at face value. So all they do is keep me awake? Great! That's just what I need!

So I started taking the pills. I don't know what they were, but I was certainly living up to the firm's name of Speedy Cars. My call sign was 69 Wilco, and the controller would be calling me for hours at a time trying to find me. 'Wilco, where are you? Come in, sixty-nine!' On one occasion I'd ground to a halt at three in the morning: the whizzing around had stopped and I sat staring in the parked car, the engine off, frozen. Eventually I answered, 'Sixty-nine here . . .' He snapped, 'Come back to base immediately!'

'I can't.'

'Where are you?'

'Trevillion Road.'

'Sixty-nine, you are one street away from base. Come back.'

'It's snowing, the road is covered in ice, it's steep and I'll never make it.'

'Sixty-nine, it is not snowing, Trevillion Road is not steep and if you want any more convincing, it's sixty degrees Fahrenheit and it's the middle of August. Now come back.'

It was time to find a different job.

One of the advertisements in *The Stage* was from a holiday camp in Dartmouth, Devon, looking for a compere for the summer season: apply to agents Trevor and Billie George, Torquay. So I jumped in my car and drove down to Devon – a journey that took for ever in those days before the motorway. I had never seen such a beautiful place. Tired as I was, I felt at home right away. The audition took place in a club called the Dorado. It was early in the week, out of season and very quiet – there were only about twenty people in the audience. I did my so-called act to a very muted reaction, then went backstage to meet Trevor and Billie. I knew I hadn't been good enough, and prepared to make my excuses, but Billie got there first and asked me how much money I wanted. I just answered instinctively, 'As long as I have a roof over my head, food to eat and something to send home to Mum, that's enough.' I got the job, and it was only at the end of the season that Billie told me why. It wasn't my act or my experience – it was, she said, because I'd said I needed the money to send home to

Mum. Strange how you get some of your breaks in this business.

As Entertainments Manager of the Dartmouth Holiday Camp, I organised everything with a staff of one – me. My wages were £36 per week – probably another reason why I got the job – plus a percentage of the bingo takings. I used to count every sixpence carefully, as anything over a certain amount was mine.

One of my duties was to entertain the children for an hour every evening from six o'clock. Seven days a week for twenty-six weeks was not going to be an easy task, as the only song I knew was 'She'll Be Coming Round the Mountain'. Even the youngsters couldn't stand a whole hour of 'Singing aye aye yippee yippee aye'. I've always got on great with kids, but what do you do with sixty to a hundred of them for an hour every night? My answer was cowboys and Indians. Behind the function hall was a small wooded area which my room overlooked, so every night after fifteen renditions of 'She'll Be Coming Round the Mountain' I'd say, 'Okay, who wants to play cowboys and Indians?' A huge 'Yeah!' from all the kids. 'Right, for those who haven't played before, you stay here while Uncle Eric plays the piano. Then, as soon as he stops playing you have to run out and find the cowboy – that's me. I could be anywhere, so look all over the camp!'

Eric would begin the music while I made a head start before the kids were let loose. Then they went mad around the camp making wild Indian noises while I sat at my window on the second floor drinking tea until two minutes before the end, when I climbed down the drainpipe, up the nearest tree and waited until I was captured by a tribe of a hundred little 'uns, who then beat me up. Every bruise was worth it for this magic solution of how to entertain one hundred kids. Recipe: ten minutes 'Aye aye yippee yippee aye', ten minutes Uncle Eric on the piano, thirty-five minutes Indian chanting for the kids, same thirty-five minutes me with my feet up, then five minutes Big Cowboy Michael getting seven bells bashed out of him. Perfect. Same routine every night.

It was at Dartmouth Holiday Camp that I got a taste for liquor. All through my teenage years I disliked the taste of booze; it never appealed to me, nor did smoking cigarettes. One night, before I introduced the cabaret, one of the holidaymakers offered me a drink. I said no at first, but they convinced me that lager wouldn't taste so bad if I put a drop of lemonade in it. Over the course of the evening I had to go on stage and make various announcements, and I can only assume that while I was gone the barman was putting something extra in my glass. When it came to 12 o'clock, time to say goodnight, I fell back like a stiff plank of wood, hit the stage with my microphone still in hand and carried on saying my goodnights from a horizontal position. The next day several of the campers said I should keep that falling backwards bit in my act, it really worked. I had a terrible hangover and felt dreadful, and vowed never again to touch a drop of drink when I was working. If only I had just vowed never to take another drop.

A taste for alcohol wasn't the only thing I came away from Dartmouth with; I also found a new name. Billie George got me to join Equity, and seeing as there was already a member called Michael Parker I had to change either my first or my second name. All sorts of suggestions were made, and then, in the middle of cooking dinner in the kitchen, Billie shouted out 'Barrymore'. I thought it was a bit of a mouthful, that it sounded more like an actor than a comedian, but it stuck, and from that moment on I was Michael Barrymore.

3

Finding My Way

At the end of the Dartmouth 1974 season, I stayed on in Torquay with Trevor and Billie George, the agents who had hired me. They were getting me shows around the local clubs for £12 a night, and I was going out with their daughter Anne, who also performed as a magician. Even her brother helped run the family business: it was like a showbiz version of *The Waltons*. It was the perfect set-up: I had transport, a girlfriend who could do tricks, and free accommodation at her mum and dad's. I was very fond of Trevor and Billie, and I liked Anne a lot – I think they would have been happy if we'd settled down together, but I wasn't really in love with her. As time went by, it became more and more of a brother-and-sister thing between us.

Eventually I moved out of Trevor and Billie's and took a

room in a converted barn near Dartmouth. It was my first taste of independence – and a place where I could spend some time with a guy I'd met. He was an actor, and we'd been in *Aladdin* together for two and a half weeks. I played the villain. He was very different from my mates: he was from a middle-class background, a bit older than me, very interested in theatre, and always travelling up and down to London where he had a boyfriend. He came over in rehearsals one day and started chatting to me, and I was immediately attracted to him; it wasn't so much a question of what he looked like, we just clicked. I wasn't thinking about blokes at that time; I'd had a lot of girlfriends, and I was concentrating on my work more than anything else. Work seemed to provide a kind of ease from worrying about my sexuality and it suited me to get my straight side going.

I was starting to get quite popular around the Devon and Cornwall area, and I made friends with one of the comedians on the circuit, Jack Lillie. We did a lot of shows together as an outfit: me as the compere and driver, Jack the star comedian, Anne the magician. I'd soak up all Jack's stories: he was about sixty by this time, larger than life, and larger than most guys, with the greatest smile, like an ageing Dennis the Menace. He'd talk for hours, puffing on his pipe, about all the acts he'd known, what things had been like in the old music hall days. But most of all he went on about his wife, who didn't understand him and thought that for all the years he'd worked he was just a fool, and now he was an old fool.

One day, Jack told me that there were auditions the following week at a working men's club outside Bristol for *New Faces*, the TV talent show that gave breaks to such future names as Jim Davidson, Lenny Henry, Elaine Paige and Marti Caine. Jack was planning to have a go at it, and he asked me to give him a lift. No problem – I was used to running Jack around, but I wasn't sure that this was such a good idea. The panel of judges on *New Faces* was notoriously cruel, and for all the stars they made there were many more careers that they ruined. When I told Jack this, he just took a heavy draw on his pipe, filled the car with smoke and said, 'To tell you the truth, Mike, I don't really care. I'm only doing it to wind up her indoors. If I get through, she'll be mortified that I'm on the telly, she'll deny she knows me!' But it mattered to me; I really loved old Jack, as did everyone I knew.

When we pulled up to the audition there were people everywhere: bands, comedians, singers, magic acts, clowns, dancers, pretend managers, kids, mums, dads, nanas, grandads, hundreds and hundreds of wannabes, plus Jack and me. I was pleased that I had just agreed to take Jack and not participate myself. No, this was not for me. I was happy earning £80 to £100 a week in the working men's clubs and holiday camps of Devon and Cornwall. Going on television and getting slagged off was not for me. I wanted to be on stage, not on trial. Jack and I found a space down one side of the hall and watched in pain as act after act fell flat in front of the production team. Now and again a talent would stand out and the crowd would cheer. The local club members were allowed in to watch the auditions, to help the producers make their choice, but they gave no reaction either way, so it was impossible to tell who would be picked to be on the show. There was so much heavy make-up on so many people in the room that the air smelled like coconuts.

Jack was given a number and a form to fill in, and was told to step up on the stage when his number was called and do no more than two minutes. I was anxious; I didn't want to see Jack die, he was my mate. Then someone thrust a form into my hand; I tried to give it back to the boy who had given it to me but it was too late, he was gone. "'Ere, Mike, why don't you fill that in and give it a go?' said Jack. I shook my head; it was hard enough just watching this circus. 'Go on, Mike! No one knows you're here and no one knows who you are.' So I filled in the form with Jack's phone number, the address of a friend I hadn't seen for years and the name of another comedian I had worked with once. If I was going to go through this farce, at least they'd never be able to find me afterwards.

Jack went up and did his two minutes, and they seemed to like him, which was a relief. Then it was my turn. I walked to the middle of the stage.

'My name is . . .' My mind went blank. I couldn't remember the name I'd put on the form. '. . . Michael, and I'm a comedian.' Shit. I wished I'd stuck to my guns. Why did I put myself in this situation? The whole room seemed to go deathly quiet as everyone stared at me. If this was the audition, how the hell would I cope with the actual show? No problem – I wasn't going to get it anyway.

My two minutes had started and I'd yet to break the silence. Then I went into my routine.

'Good evening, ladies and gentlemen. Let's go over to Sydney, Australia. Hello? Are you there, Australia?' I threw my hands to the floor, balanced on my head and turned myself upside down. Everyone in the room remained silent. Standing on my head and using my legs to talk instead of my arms, I said, 'G'day, my name is Bruce, how's it going?'

Everyone in the room remained silent.

'I wish that Sheila in the front row would cross her legs!'

The room remained silent.

'Would you please welcome Mr Alan Whicker!' Still

standing on my head and using my legs to indicate what I was saying, I said, in my best Alan Whicker voice, 'So it's up [legs thrust up], up [legs up again] and away [legs thrust apart] for another *Whicker's World*!'

The room remained silent.

'This week on *Whicker's World* my guests are Lester Piggott [legs folded down to the size of a jockey], Larry Grayson [legs shot upright, one foot hanging limp] and Joan Collins [legs wide apart].' I paused for a reaction then brought my feet back down and returned myself to standing position, deliberately stumbling as if I were really giddy, and again waited for a reaction.

The room remained silent.

I gave a lightning bow and walked off. The producers called for the next act and the audience clapped them on.

All I said to Jack on the way back was, 'Please don't ever put me through that again.' I didn't blame him, but I was very glad I'd put down the wrong name on the form. At least they'd never find me.

The weekend passed, and I went back to my digs. As I put my key in the lock my landlady Trish (a part-time belly dancer) called out from her kitchen that, 'A lady called Susie rang and asked if you could call her. Said it was urgent.' I didn't know anyone called Susie.

'Did she say what it was about?'

'No, dear. It's a Birmingham number, you can use the phone.'

I dialled. 'Hello, is Susie there? I got a message to call you. I'm in Torquay.'

She paused, not knowing who I was, and then, 'Oh yes! Tony!'

'No,' I said, 'Michael.'

'Oh, so that *is* your name! You've been really hard to track down.'

I had to ask. 'Excuse me, but who are you?'

'I'm one of the team from the *New Faces* auditions last week.'

I stopped her before she had a chance to go on. 'Look, I'm sorry it was so disastrous . . .'

'No, no, we liked you, we thought you were different. Could you do the show in a week's time?'

I didn't have time to think about my reply. 'No,' I said. 'No, I really don't want to do it.'

Susie was not, I am sure, used to this kind of rejection. 'Why not?'

'I just don't. I don't want to face that panel.'

'Look, Tony . . .'

'Michael.'

'Sorry, Michael. How old are you?'

'Twenty-two.'

She suddenly came over all schoolmarm-like. 'Whatever happens, Michael, you have the rest of your life ahead of you.'

'Do you think I should do it?' Looking back, that was a really stupid question. She talked me round and, after much deliberation, I arrived at the ATV Studios in Birmingham, all on my own with my best loud yellow-and-purple-check suit – my only suit – and a wooden box with a hole cut out of it to make it look like a television.

The format of *New Faces* was simple: six acts a week, with three minutes each in which to show why they should become stars. At the end, a panel of judges would say what they thought, and they'd vote for a winner. Over the following week, viewers voted for the act they liked the best. The cameras rolled, the acts rolled and then I was introduced. The panel that week included Jack Parnell, Arthur Askey and Mickey Most; I was lucky, no Tony Hatch. Every talent show panel has its Mr Bad Guy, and in the case of *New Faces* it was Tony Hatch, who could reduce acts to tears if he didn't like them.

My act began with, 'And now the news ...' – the box with the hole stuck over my head. 'An elephant has done a ton on the M1. Police are asking motorists to treat it as a roundabout.' Box off head and straight into the standing-on-my-head routine. The audience laughed, the panel said nice things and my total score was 115 out of a possible 120 – one of the highest ever recorded in the history of the show. I won the viewers' vote as well!

New Faces gave me exactly the kind of break I needed, although I can't say that it rocketed me to stardom over-night. But it established me as the new kid on the block, if you like, someone who could compete with the established comics, but who had something new and original to offer.

The first significant job was a six-month winter residency at the Showboat Club on The Strand in London. You would think that this was definitely the start of the big time. In this business, it's deemed that until you are top of the bill, they are doing you a favour by allowing you to appear in a prestigious venue which is reflected in your pay. I got paid £50 a week for a twelve-minute slot. Nevertheless I felt I'd really arrived. It was one of many arrivals; you have to arrive several times before you've really arrived. But I was delighted with the money, delighted with the attention that I was getting from one of the singers in the show, a beautiful 25-year-old divorcée called Cheryl, who had been a big hit as one of the dancers in the Young Generation on TV during the late 60s, early 70s. When we first met at rehearsals I thought she was Italian (she wasn't); then it was her well-spoken accent that impressed me. At this time I still had a thick south London accent that I was working hard to get rid of at evening classes in speech training. She asked me if I wanted a cup of tea; she could see I was the new boy, and she was looking after me. That's what Cheryl was good at: giving all her attention to one person, making them feel really special.

Her mother sat in the background puffing away on a cigarette, watching her daughter make a play for me. I had an idea that that's what she was doing from the outset – I was a bit less naive by this time. I had the usual amount of girlfriends for the usual amount of time, usually about a week. But Cheryl was different. She was a class act: she looked fantastic, had a great figure, and a great smile. She had a family, she had money, she'd been very successful in the business and knew a lot of important people. Great cook, great dresser, great ambition, great ideas, great sex. What was a skinny Bermondsey boy to do? I was twenty-three, she was twenty-five. I was on the road to the big time, she'd had enough of it. I needed someone, she wanted someone. I liked her, she loved me.

In time, my liking turned to love. In those early days, I always struggled with the concept of what love was. To be honest, it's taken me years to get to an understanding of it. I never experienced it around me growing up. I don't ever recall looking at anyone and saying to myself that's love. I didn't know how important it is to remind those around you, especially children, that they are loved. Without hearing it, strong hand shakes, ruffling the hair and pinching the nose don't tell a child you love them. It is so hard to have a feeling about another person and not be able to describe what it is or worse, not be able to say it.

Cheryl loved me from the word go. First of all, she loved my act, and started coming round to my dressing room to chat and encourage me, telling me I was the best thing she'd ever seen. Cheryl was a great singer, but she soon decided that she didn't want to be up there doing it any more. 'I'll be your manager instead,' she said. I just went along with it – it was an environment that was all new to me.

She sent me to a tailor called Robbie Stanford in Conduit Street, who used to make stage suits for Englebert Humperdinck and Tom Jones. He charged £800 for a stage suit, which was a lot of money in those days. Cheryl wanted me to wear a black tuxedo. It certainly changed the way I looked and it definitely changed the way I worked. Cheryl introduced me to a brand new world. Before I met Cheryl I was quite happy plodding along doing what I always did. I didn't feel the need to be top of the bill.

Then she asked me back to her mum and dad's place in Harlow. It was a lovely house, and I got on straight away with her father, Eddie. The classic cockney man, he was of average height, had a full head of shiny grey hair and owned a chain of shops. The first time I met him he was wearing a long, navy blue Crombie and smoking a Henri Wintermans half corona cigar with the same intensity that anyone else would puff away on a Silk Cut. Eddie and I hit it off immediately; there is no doubt he was the dad I was looking for. He was tough and feared no one and he greeted me with a smile and asked me how I was. He always had a tan from all the cruises he went on with his wife, Cheryl's mum, my future mother-in-law. There will be no mother-in-law jokes about Kit; she wasn't that funny.

I was soon well established as Cheryl's boyfriend and more or less part of the family. One night I'd been round there for another fantastic evening meal, Cheryl and I were cuddled up on the green velour sofa, Mum and Dad were upstairs in bed ... To this day, I don't know where the words came from.

'D'yer want to get married?'

'Do you mean it?'

'Of course I do, I wouldn't have said it otherwise.' More words that escaped me without permission.

54

There was no delay. Cheryl ran upstairs to tell her mum and dad. I heard nothing, no jumping for joy, no 'Aaaah! Well done, darling!' Nothing. She came back down; I asked her how they reacted.

'They'll be all right, don't worry.' But her body language told me something was wrong.

I stayed there the night; the spare bed had been made up for me. Cheryl came to me in the early hours, took me back to her room and we made love. Then I went back to the spare room to wake up as if nothing had happened.

The next morning, Eddie was very upset and said nothing. Kit asked me if I had any financial security, and whether I had given marriage a lot of thought. Her looks spoke clearly enough: 'You don't look the right sort of man to be marrying my daughter.' The more she scowled, the more determined I was to marry Cheryl.

At a much later date, Cheryl told me that when her mother first met me she assumed I was gay. Ha ha. I joined in with the laughter, but to myself I whispered, 'Bloody hell . . .'

We lived with Cheryl's parents until we could get a place of our own, saving up money by taking any jobs we could get. When the gig at the Showboat finished, Cheryl supplemented her income by working at one of Eddie's shops; I took a day job in the toy department at Selfridge's. Then a flat became free in Bishopsfield, Harlow. It was modern, it was cheap – £18 a week – and it was ours. Shit, but our own. We painted it green to match my brain, and the curtains were brown dress material. With a few cushions and a second-hand bed we were happy. We were independent.

No sooner had I asked Cheryl to marry me than it was all organised. I remember a mate of mine saying, 'Are you sure about getting married? Because it's not too late to change your mind.' But I was determined to go through with it; I'd said I was going to marry her, hadn't I? I couldn't have backed out then – not after her parents had arranged everything.

We got married on 10 June 1976 at Epping Register Office, with the reception at Harlow Mill. It was great fun: my mother was there with my brother and sister, and the whole thing had been organised beautifully. But I was a nervous wreck. Grooms are supposed to be nervous at weddings, aren't they, so nobody really thought too much about why I was in such a state – and neither did I. But halfway through the marriage ceremony I developed a nervous shake in my hand – I couldn't control it, and I couldn't take my eyes off it, which made me start laughing. That developed into a full-scale attack of the giggles, and I had to keep walking out of the register office. Every time we got to, 'Do you take this woman . . .' I started giggling and rushed out, got myself under control, came back in and it started all over again. People thought it was funny at the time, but I should have realised something was wrong. You don't though, do you?

At the reception, I gave a speech that went down well, along the lines of: 'As long as I can remember I always wanted something . . . and when I got it I'd know what it was . . . my great desire for the one thing in my life . . .' all of it leading up to '. . . and now I've found my beautiful bride' – or so you were meant to think. But in fact the punch line was '. . . and I never did get that bike.' I just had to make a joke out of it – and everybody laughed.

At first I really got into the idea of being married. After all those worries about my sexuality, Cheryl had made a man of me. Being gay was just a phase. I could see a bright future, married to a great-looking girl who had enough ambition for both of us. She quickly established herself as not only my wife but my manager, and focused her considerable gifts on my career. She took care of everything: how I looked, what I wore, how I behaved, who I mixed with. All I had to do was get up on stage and perform, then go home to bed and perform. No complaints from me: I loved working, and I wanted children, loads of them, so that I could be the father I never had. And that meant lots of baby-making business, no contraception. I even had the names ready: Ben if it was a boy, Rosie if it was a girl.

We tried and tried, but the children just didn't come. Cheryl had blocked Fallopian tubes, and after a couple of miscarriages we decided to adopt. If you've ever tried to adopt, you'll know how difficult it is: Are you suitable? Are you religious? Have you got money? A steady job? We went to one meeting and I drove away feeling really despondent about the whole thing, as we didn't seem to meet any of their criteria. It seemed total crap to me: I just wanted to have children and give them love. Cheryl had other ideas.

'Do you really want kids? She asked.

'Yes, I really do.'

'Because, if you're doing it for my sake, I'm not really bothered.'

This took the wind out of my sails; surely it couldn't be right to go to all the trouble of adopting a child if the wife wasn't really bothered.

'It's not that important to me,' she said. 'You are enough for me. And if I am enough for you, let's just stay like that. Besides, I don't need a child. I already have one: You.'

I carried on driving and said, 'I suppose so . . .' Inside I felt so sad: it takes two to want a child, and Cheryl didn't want one. Cheryl already had her baby, her lover, her husband, her career, all wrapped up in one person. Wasn't I lucky to have so much from one person? Why did I give in so easily? What was I scared of? Why didn't I call the marriage off? Was my self-preservation so important? Was I so selfish? It certainly sounds like it.

We'd been married less than a year, and already Cheryl was in complete control. I was always in the driving seat, but she was doing the steering. I began to feel that the only way I would ever achieve anything was if Cheryl sorted it out, that she was the only one who could make me into a new, faithful, complete human being, Well, I certainly never looked at another woman – but some of the guys were starting to look interesting.

As time wore on, Cheryl's father Eddie and I became great friends. From the very start he was the father I wanted. He taught me how to run a business and he would always say at any given opportunity, 'If you were my son I would have made sure you had a proper education.' I never told him that I wished I had been his son. He treated Cheryl and me as equals. If there was an argument over anything he treated us 50/50. It was never my daughter or my son-in-law. The in-law bit wasn't in his vocabulary. In the early days he subsidised everything he could. We had no money and he tried the approach of 'you have to fend for yourself' but somehow things seemed to get paid or he would come up with the idea of us having his old car until we could afford one. He would spend ages telling me how he survived being caught at the start of the Second World War and imprisoned in a POW camp by the Germans. How he overcame the odds. He was so smart, he never came downstairs without a shirt and tie on in his own home. I loved him and I know he loved me, even if his way of showing it was by how much he increased the grip on my hand. Sometimes almost crushing! As time went on we grew closer and closer.

Cheryl and I didn't have a honeymoon; we just carried

on working. I had a summer season booking at the Festival
Theatre in Paignton, Devon, as part of *The Black and White
Minstrel Show*. Roy Hudd was top of the bill, I was bottom.
The shows went well: audiences were turning up to see the
Black and White Minstrels and left talking about the new
young comedian Michael Barrymore. Larry Grayson was
appearing at the Pavilion Theatre in the same resort – so
here I was, the skinny new boy playing alongside the big
boys. I got on great with Roy Hudd, and Larry Grayson
wanted to get on great with me, despite the fact that I had
my new wife in tow. He'd invite us to these parties at the
house he'd rented in Torquay, and Cheryl didn't seem to
mind when Larry would lean all over me and tell me, for
the tenth time in an evening, that he loved me. After all, it
was just an act, wasn't it? Larry was the King of Camp, the
top of the bill, it wasn't hard to humour him. He liked me
and made me laugh. I just about managed to keep him away
from my lips; I could see his sister, Fran, quietly watching
us from the corner. His voice boomed in my ear, drawling a
little from the drink.

'Michael . . .'

'Yes, Larry?'

'You know that I love you very much.' He looked
over towards Cheryl; she smiled back, not threatened. He
made sure that she could hear his loud whisper. 'Who's
she?'

'That's Cheryl, Larry. My wife.'

He grimaced. 'Oh, really?'

'Yes, really.'

He moved his face closer to mine. 'Tell her to fuck off.'

I couldn't believe what he'd just said, and my face must
have shown it. Cheryl called over: 'You all right, Michael?'

'Course he is!' boomed Larry. 'I'm going to make him a
star!' Then he turned to me again and whispered in my ear.

'Michael, I'll give you one bit of advice. In this business, keep yer mouth shut and yer ears open.'

Then he walked over to the record player and put on the soundtrack of *A Star is Born*. As Judy Garland's voice belted out, I went and sat with Cheryl. I could hear Larry whispering to one of the other guests, pointing at me, 'Oh, he's anyone's for a doughnut.'

We came back from Paignton in good spirits. The money had been crap, just enough to survive on, but I'd done well and there were offers of work coming in from other quarters. I'd had my second TV slot on the BBC's *Seaside Special* after the producer had come to see me in Paignton. And we'd been sensible: we'd taken out a bank loan and invested in a shop unit in Ilderton Road, Bermondsey, as something to fall back on if show business turned out to be all show and not a lot of business. I put my brother John in charge of the shop, a combined newsagent and stationers, and from the outset it seemed to be a gold mine. The money flowed in, the family was happy and we were building up a nice little nest egg for the future.

When I got back home I phoned the shop to make sure that all was well. It wasn't. John had last been seen heading for the Irish ferry in a V8 Rover – and he hadn't come back. I went straight over to the shop and there was Mum, looking very tired surrounded by a lot of empty shelves. John's idea of running the business had been to order the goods, sell them at a profit and keep the profit, of which there was plenty, as none of the suppliers had been paid. In 1977, Cheryl and I moved into Mum's and worked from five in the morning till eight at night trying to sort things out. Eddie came over to check the accounts, which was a quick job as there weren't any. The creditors were pressing hard, and I promised to pay them all back if they'd only give me time. They didn't.

The phone rang one day: 'Mr Parker, I am one of the official receivers.'

It meant nothing to me. I thought the Official Receivers were a rock band who wanted me to do my act with them. But it was no act when, a few months later, I was made officially bankrupt for debts of £47,000. Cheryl and I had nothing, and they took that anyway. Cheryl blamed my whole family for what had happened; it wasn't enough just to blame John, she blamed anyone remotely associated with him as they must have all played their part in the plot. Being weak, I went along with her and cut off any association with my family. This was a mistake. It's true that John was wrong, stupid and greedy; Mum could have come and told us that she was worried, so could my sister Anne. And they didn't. But I knew in my heart that they never meant to hurt me. Cheryl could not believe this; as far as she was concerned, this was family war, and all communications ceased forthwith.

I didn't talk to my mother for many years. I haven't really spoken to my brother since, though I'm sure this would have changed if he hadn't later made things worse when he found a good income from talking to the newspapers. I suppose he took the stance that if I was not talking to the family that gave him the green light. When I did get back with Mum and my sister Anne again, John was not included, though I know that whatever I was giving to Mum she was using to help the others. I never had a problem with that. You cannot give a gift and tell the person what they can do with it. A short while before Mum passed away she said to me, 'I haven't left you anything in my will, is that okay?' I said, 'Yeah, that's fine, I understand,' and I did. I saw John at Mum's funeral and we just mumbled a few incoherent words to each other. It wasn't the time to make up, or at least it didn't feel like it. That's if there ever is a right time. I am sure there is. I hope so.

This marked the start of the degeneration in my relationship with Cheryl. I didn't have the strength or the guts to challenge her, and when her mother started in on me as well, I just caved in. Arguments would start, and Kit would end up shouting at Cheryl. Then I'd butt in with, 'Don't shout at my wife!' She'd come back with, 'She's my daughter, I'll do what I like,' and so on and so forth, the usual family discussion. Kit's attitude at this time was that I wasn't good enough for her daughter; I was a bottom-of-the-bill comic, a bankrupt, a bad lot. She kept bringing up Cheryl's first husband, the film producer Greg Smith. 'You should never have divorced him! What were you thinking of?' I don't think Kit ever forgave Cheryl for that; she loved being able to say to the neighbours, 'Oh yes, Cheryl's living in the West End with Greg – you know, Greg Smith, the film producer.' Being shacked up in a council flat in Harlow with a bankrupt unknown comic didn't have quite the same ring about it.

Eddie was a different matter. I truly believe that if it hadn't been for him, my relationship with Cheryl wouldn't have lasted for as long as it did. It was Eddie I couldn't give up, although, knowing Eddie, he would have kept in contact with me even if I'd finished with Cheryl – if he'd been allowed to. But whenever there was trouble, Eddie sided with Kit. Anything for a quiet life. And to be fair, he loved her more than life itself; even I had to get in line behind Kit.

Bankruptcy clears you out, and the only way to restart our lives was to take any job going. And the first job going was a stag night at the Room at the Top club in Ilford. Up to this point in my life I had never been to a stag night, never performed at one, and didn't really have a clue what was expected, so this was going to be a challenge. I wondered, as I walked into the function room, just where my career was leading me. Winner of a TV talent show, star of various theatre shows, nightclubs, holiday camps, with a clean-cut act and a clean-shaven image – what was I going to do in a room with 300 men and two strippers?

I asked for a dressing room; I wasn't expecting much, because when you're on the bottom of the bill you get whatever's given to you. A cupboard would do. This one looked more like the ladies' toilet – in fact it was the ladies' toilet. The two strippers were getting ready in there, sitting on the loo, chewing gum and pulling on their stockings, one of them sticking shiny paper stars around her crotch for extra effect.

'You new, darling?'

I found it hard not to stare between her legs.

The compere was a comedian called Ronnie Twist, who took pity on the new boy and put me on first. I climbed into my suit and waited at the toilet door while he introduced me. Well, I had nothing to lose. No money, bankrupt – nobody could take anything away from me. I went on to face that audience thinking, 'Do your fucking worst.'

It went well; not great, but well. As I came off, Paper Crotch congratulated me when we crossed in the corridor, 'Nice show darling'. Ronnie Twist was encouraging and took my number, saying he had to turn down loads of work which he'd pass my way.

'I like you,' he said. 'You're different.'

I hung on to that as I drove home – but not as tight as I hung on to the £25 in my hand. You're different – you're £25 better off.

Then £50, £100 better off, as my stature on the stag circuit grew and grew. Within a year I was working solid, three shows a night at venues all over the south east, driving from one to another; you'd bomb at one, you'd go well at another. It was one of the best schools to learn in because, unlike most schools, not only did you get paid, but you also got to see just how versatile some of the strippers were. Just how did she make *that* disappear?

The main booking agent was a guy named Bill Gordon, who would call me up in the morning to give me my bookings for the day.

'Hello, Michael, it's Bill 'ere. Now, tonight you've got two jobs, one's in Surrey, the other's in Lewisham. You have to get to the Lewisham one half an hour earlier than normal for security reasons.'

'Why's that, Bill?'

'It's the post office.'

'So?'

'So they'll be closing the gates at the sorting office half an hour before the show starts.'

'Why, Bill?'

'Because the strippers tonight are the Two Sarahs.'

'What do they do, then?'

'Er . . . they shag.'

'Shag what?'

'Er . . . the audience. On the stage. That's why it's better that you should go on first, then get out of there as quick as you can, because if the police raid the place, they'll arrest everyone.'

'Is the pay higher for the risk involved?'

'No, but you don't have to do as long.'

'Have you asked anyone else to do this?'

'Yes.'

'And . . .?'

'No. They can't.'

'You mean they won't.'

'Er . . . yes.'

'So, why should I do it?'

'It's £25.'

'Right. Where is it, then?'

So of course I did my spot, and then ran the risk of being arrested by staying on to see exactly what it was that the Two Sarahs did.

They came on to some music, the audience cheered and they got straight down to business.

Obviously I'll spare you the details of that evening, but, needless to say, I was full of admiration for the men of our postal service who could deliver so much so quickly, and I thanked God for revealing to me just what show business really had to offer.

4

Awight?

I needed a push. I'd had a bit of success, enough to get me regular work, but if I was ever going to get beyond the stag circuit I needed somebody with connections. Trevor and Billie George had got me the booking in Paignton, but they didn't get on with Cheryl, who made it very clear that from now on she was in charge, and her ambitions, in her eyes, were way beyond anything that they could get for me. So at the end of the summer season of 1978, I signed up with Norman Murray and Anne Chudleigh – big-time agents, who at the time were handling Les Dawson, Little and Large, Hinge and Bracket. They had the kind of clout that I needed, and they gave me the new-boy slot on all their big shows: summer seasons, pantomimes, tours and so on. In between times I earned money on the stag circuit.

Norman Murray is worth a book of his own: the classic, archetypal agent, Jewish in religion, mafia in looks and style, with grey hair and a magnificent tan. Anne had started off as his secretary, but soon she was as good as the boss and became his business partner. She was getting quite a reputation for getting great deals for her clients – something she did her own way. With her looking after me, under Norman's supervision, we really started going places.

The first time I met Norman was at his offices in Regent Street. He sat at his desk chewing endless sweets and talking on the phone; I sat opposite him in the only suit I owned, waiting for him to tell me that he was going to make me into a big star. He looked at me and said, 'Nice suit.'

'Thank you.'

'Well, that's a good start. I'll be in touch. Bye-bye.'

The next time I went to see him, I wore the same suit so that he would recognise me.

'Hello Norman.'

'Hello, Dolly.' He called everyone Dolly, male or female.

I wanted to know if he had any work for me, and I hovered around the doorway.

Norman looked up. 'Yes?'

'I was just passing . . .'

'So why didn't you?'

I stood there blinking. 'What?'

'Why didn't you just pass? Bye-bye.'

Later on he rang Cheryl. 'Look, Dolly, tell Michael not to surprise me like that. I need to know who's coming in and when. Otherwise he could pop in to tell me he's going a storm at the Palladium and I'd have to agree, whether I had booked him or not.'

I threw absolutely all my energies into my work. I had no distractions: no hobbies, no children. I may have gone on at the bottom of the bill, but I never intended to stay there. All the stars I worked with started off liking me, but as time went on it became clear that I was becoming ruthlessly ambitious. I'd do anything to get the most applause from the audience at the end of the show – a ritual known as 'Who's Best?' That was what I lived for. I discovered that my friends were not around as much. I wondered if it was down to being married or whether it was because I was changing as a person. There was no doubt that Cheryl was instilling a take-no-prisoners approach to my work. The one sentence she said at the time that stood out was, 'There is no point getting to the final of the FA Cup to come second.' As far as she was concerned you might as well have lost in the first round. Can you imagine Cheryl being the England coach? Actually I could!

By this time I even had what all comedians strive for – my own catchphrase. When I started doing stand-up and I was a bit insecure and green, I used to hide behind other people's catchphrases – so I'd come on and say, 'Hello, good evening and welcome'. Then someone pointed out that I shouldn't really be nicking David Frost's catchphrase, that I needed to get my own. On one of my return journeys home, just before I met Cheryl, I'd been sitting with my mates in the pub and I noticed something about the south London drawl that I'd never paid attention to before. It's all to do with using as few words and syllables as possible, to say what you mean.

''E'o mate, yawight?' (Hello friend are you all right?)

'Yeh, I'm awight.' (Yes, I am all right.)

''Ow's yer bird?' (How is your girlfriend?)

'She's awight.' (She is all right, thank you.)

'That's awight then.' (That's good news to hear.)

That could go on for about an hour, the lips barely moving, in a complete monotone. The south London accent is incredibly lazy compared for instance, to east London. So

---

I picked up on that and started saying 'Awight' to the audience when I came on stage. Then, because I'd been taught to encompass everyone, I'd say, 'Awight at the back?' That's what really caught on first.

A performer can't make a catchphrase; only audiences can do that. Before long, I was getting known for saying 'Awight', which struck me as really absurd at the time; I'd worked all these years to get stage experience, and suddenly everyone wanted me for this one word. I still get people shouting it at me in the street today, even though I hardly ever say it any more. What I tend to say now, if someone shouts it at me, is, 'Yes, I'm fine thank you'. People bring their children up to me and say, 'Oh, go on, she really loves you, please say "Awight" to her.' And if I say, 'Er, maybe not the right place,' they go, 'What's the matter with you? You say it on the telly!' Friends of mine are constantly amazed at how much I get this. People will come up to me in the street, nudge me in the ribs and mutter 'Awight', then scoot off. Do I hate it? No, of course I love it. Let's be honest, you can't spend twenty years of your life saying you want to be recognised and then turn round and not like it when you are.

As I got more and better work, the stage became the only place where I really felt in control. I never wanted to come off stage – and, increasingly, audiences didn't want me to leave either. The audience and I were slowly falling in love with each other. The more they cheered and laughed, the higher I climbed up the bill. I took no prisoners. If I did well, I got a better billing, and so spent more time on stage each evening – and that was all I really cared about. I had no fear on stage, only the fear of leaving it. Friends-wise, it was becoming increasingly obvious that they had to be approved by Cheryl. But I'm not so sure that it was a trait unique to her, rather that this is what often happens with couples. I didn't know, as I was too busy trying to get Michael Barrymore right. Michael Parker was definitely taking second place.

Most of the stars I worked with would sit and chat in their dressing rooms while they waited to go on; not me. I stood in the wings, watching and learning from everyone. I knew all their acts. I saw them getting applause just by walking on to a stage – the same applause that I had to work so hard just to walk off to. I asked Norman why this was.

'Because they're stars, Dolly.'

'What makes a star a star?'

He pointed up to the sky. 'See that star up there? Can you touch it?'

'No. It's untouchable.'

'Exactly, Dolly, That's what a real star is. You can see them, but you can't touch them. You're one of these stars. All you have to do, is persuade the powers that be in television to recognise that.'

Easier said than done. My live work was getting me a lot of recognition, but without TV, I would never reach real star status. Norman managed to get a few producers down to see me, but they could never understand what all the fuss was about. So far, my only TV experience had been *New Faces* and *Seaside Special* – and audiences' memories are short. I'd also done a couple of gigs as an extra – if anyone can find the tapes, I'm in two *Monty Python* sketches, 'The Piston Engine' and 'Louis XIII Glasgow Bovver Boys'.

Eventually, the producers stopped coming to see me, but Norman wasn't going to be put off that easily. He was going to get me into a TV studio if it killed him, or me. And so, using his contacts at the BBC, he got me a job as a warm-up man. 'You ain't going to get recognised unless you're in the corridors of power, Dolly.' Which is how I came to do warm-up for Les Dawson, Little and Large, all the stars

70

who had shows on the BBC at that time. I was always getting into trouble for running over. A more seasoned warm-up man gave me a piece of advice.

'You'd better toe the line. You're getting more laughs than the stars you're warming-up for. Tone it down or they'll throw you out.'

I wasn't toeing the line for anyone. I didn't want to be just a warm-up man for the rest of my life. But he was right. I did Mike Yarwood's show; I wasn't asked back. I managed to perform myself off *Are You Being Served?*, *The Generation Game* and even *Little and Large*, who were Norman and Anne's clients. The only one who wasn't bothered was Les Dawson. As long as he had his drink and a few nice women to talk to, he didn't care; he just wanted to do the job and get paid. He'd sit in the bar before the show, drinking with members of the audience; he didn't have any of that star mystique thing. I used to watch him downing gins, wondering how on earth he could go on and do a show in that state. Truth was, he wasn't in a state. Strange thing to admire!

A single telephone call changed the TV situation. It was Norman.

'BBC Television want you to do a series!'

'Fantastic! What's it called?'

'*Sebastian the Dog*.'

That sounded unusual. 'What is it? Half-hour or an hour?'

'Five minutes, Dolly. Children's TV.'

My excitement was beginning to diminish, but I'd learned by now to say yes to any TV that was offered.

Sebastian the Dog and I lasted for one series. David, Sebastian's creator, crouched behind a screen while I did dialogue with the posh pooch, who said things like, 'Oh really, dear boy?' while I attacked him and twisted his head.

I used to get a bit carried away sometimes, and David/ Sebastian would give very convincing yelps. After record- ing each episode, David would always ask me to go easy on Sebastian, as it wasn't really a dog, just his arm.

The BBC Children's Department liked me, and gave me another five-minute series, *Mic and Mac*, which I co-wrote with Geoff Atkinson. I played Mic, a bachelor who worked from his flat drawing a cartoon character called Mac, a strange-looking creature with a Scottish accent. The show had masses of visual gags, which was great for me, and it got me even more noticed around Television Centre. At the time they were casting for a new male presenter on *Crackerjack!* – which was the gig that everyone in kids' TV wanted. I wanted it so much: it would have been my biggest break to date. I'd have been following people like Eamonn Andrews, Michael Aspel and Leslie Crowther, who I'd watched as a kid. But the job went to Stu Francis; I was disappointed, and I didn't even get a *Crackerjack!* pencil. But I did present *Jackanory*; it was a great honour to read Noel Langley's *The Land of Green Ginger*.

That concluded my adventures in BBC Children's Television. I'm very proud of the work I did. For my fiftieth birthday, my partner Shaun got together all the tapes of those shows, and I watched them over and over. That's the magic of television: you can relive the past, with all the bad bits left out.

Another summer season came around, more TV producers came to see me and left saying, 'Not for us, thank you', until one day David Bell and John Kaye Cooper turned up. David was the head of entertainment at London Weekend Television, and when Anne rang him up to see if he wanted to use me, he said, 'I haven't got a clue what he did, darling, but he's got something. Not quite sure what it is, but I'll use him.' John Kaye Cooper was putting together a new series for Russ Abbot, and put me in the team that they were building around him.

So I joined *Russ Abbot's Madhouse* in 1982. The cast was Russ, Dustin Gee, Bella Emberg, Jeffrey Holland, Sherrie Hewson, Les Dennis and me. The show became a huge hit, Russ shot to mega-fame and the rest of us picked up the fall-out from that adulation. Russ did two-thirds of the show, the rest was divided up between the team. I remembered what Larry Grayson had told me – mouth shut, ears open – and I never complained about not being given enough sketches. As a result, John gave me as many cameo spots as possible.

Dustin Gee became a great friend. He was a wonderful impressionist, who worked hard on set and played hard off it. Dustin was openly gay, but he never confirmed his sexuality to the media; if anyone ever asked him directly, he toed the line. I really admired Dustin's attitude to life; he didn't take anything seriously. He had a boyfriend who came down to London now and again; I had a wife who packed me off from our Harlow council flat. When Dustin arrived at rehearsals, I would always stick near him to hear what he'd been up to the night before, where he went clubbing up West and where he ended up staying the night. I wanted to go out with him, do the showbiz bit, behave badly, be naughty – everything that Cheryl feared for me.

'You have to concentrate on your career,' she said. 'Turn up for rehearsals on time, looking smart, knowing your lines. The likes of Dustin won't have a career for long, carrying on the way he does.' I knew she was right, but couldn't I be wrong for just one night?

No. Not for Cheryl. I had to be Mr Clean, Mr Correct, Mr Perfect, twenty-four hours a day, seven days a week. So

I did what she wanted, and I started to resent it. Inside the Good Boy there was a very angry Bad Boy who was desperate to break out.

Dustin spent most of his earnings on his fast-lane lifestyle, which came to an abrupt end two years later. He was forty-four; he had lived life to the full, to the absolute full stop of a heart attack. Rest in peace, Dustin; thank you for your kindness and care and for the conversation we had at your house in Covent Garden when you told me you knew I was gay. I didn't answer you. I didn't have to. You were right, I knew it, but I just couldn't be it. Not like you. I wish I could have been as confident in myself, and I wish you were still here.

Given the success *Russ Abbot's Madhouse* was having, I was surprised when Norman wanted me to do another warm-up. I thought I was finished with all that, and my pride said no, but good sense said yes, it's for Thames Television. I hadn't done one there, besides which, the Beeb hadn't rung recently, so I didn't have too many options. So much for all the successful warm-ups I had done for them: they had led to absolutely nothing!

'What's the show, then?'

'*Give Us a Clue* with Michael Aspel.'

Another popular game show of the time, another chance to do my live act in front of a new lot of producers – but on the wrong side of the camera. David Clark produced *Give Us a Clue*, and I went down to Studio Two at Teddington Lock to meet him and the team captains, Una Stubbs and Lionel Blair. Una was lovely; Lionel was lovelier.

I went on and did my usual warm-up routine, got the audience going, and went back in the recording breaks to get even more laughs – not just from the audience, but from the whole team. At the end, David thanked me for doing a great job and said he would use me again. I don't know why, but I heard myself say, 'Thanks a lot, David, but I ain't doing any more warm-ups.'

He smiled. 'No, you're not. I want you to come back next week and be part of Lionel's team – on the right side of the camera. I'm not wasting anyone who gets laughs like you do on warm-ups!'

David was true to his word, and in a week's time I was back in the studio as a participant. *Give Us a Clue* was, basically, charades. I stood up to read what I had to mime. 'Nineteenth Nervous Breakdown' by the Rolling Stones – perfect for my style of visual comedy. Thames wasted no time in using me again, and after my second appearance I was given my own show. Just like that: a deal. Three series of six half-hour comedy shows over two years, simply called *The Michael Barrymore Show*.

You'd think that after all the hard work and plotting and planning we would have been out celebrating like mad when we got the commission for *The Michael Barrymore Show*. But I can't ever remember feeling, 'This is it!' In fact, if anything, it just represented a lot more pressure. It's funny: when you're the new boy you toddle along at the bottom of the bill, stealing a show here, a show there, and everyone pats you on the back. It's the bloke at the top of the bill who has to worry about things. When you're put in that position, you're up on a pedestal, and you feel very vulnerable and exposed. Someone comes along and gives you the chance you've always dreamed of, and suddenly you think, 'Oh God, where am I going to get six half-hours of material from?' You don't have much experience, but expectations are very high, everyone's running around you, wanting more, more, more. Success, to me, meant losing a little bit of control of myself – suddenly there were other people making decisions for and about me.

If anything, it was Cheryl who was having to deal with

more at this point, because suddenly there were all these other people who were telling me what to do and how they saw things. She felt she was being sidelined, as was made evident by one of the producers who, when Cheryl asked, 'What day next week are we rehearsing?' replied, pointing to me and himself, 'We are starting on Tuesday, so that's Wednesday for you'. There are only two things Cheryl ever rolled up her sleeves for. One was to work and you did not want to be on the end of the other. Right from this moment it became very clear that you did not just get me when you hired Barrymore.

I preferred it when it was just me dealing directly with a situation – right back from the time when I was entertaining the kids in the flats. If I made them laugh, I was in control; end of story. Now, however, it was a lot more complicated. It wasn't just a question of making my friends laugh; people were paying a lot of money to see me, and that's a whole different ball game. It turns into business. I really feel for those kids who win *Pop Stars* or *Pop Idol* – after all those years waiting for the phone to ring, suddenly it never stops, and you feel like screaming. You get a lot of praise, but you become a sitting target for criticism as well. When you're young, that's hard to handle. It was more pressure for my mum. Here was her son becoming well known and her neighbours asking all sorts of questions, none of which she could answer. Because I wasn't talking. This was not how it was supposed to be. I had promised her so much as a young lad. What happened to all the, 'One day, Mum', 'I'll look after you', 'I'll make you so proud'? Anytime I hinted at mending the situation with Mum, Cheryl made me feel that I was not thinking right. Somehow, the justification was a combination of my career and Cheryl's hold on me, which I allowed. And for what? Show business? My marriage? Or because I thought I would lose one or the other or both.

Whichever way you cut it, I was a piece of shit. Maybe my ambition had changed to ruthlessness!

The Michael Barrymore Show was all sketches, no gags, and a lot of guests. One sketch featured me as Parker from *Thunderbirds*, with thick wires attached to my limbs, and my legs going all over the place – very physical stuff. Britt Ekland appeared in a sketch as Desdemona, with me as Othello trying to smother her with a pillow. One of my regular guests was a young actor who I'd seen playing one of the sons in the BBC sitcom *Butterflies*, and who managed to be even skinnier than me: Nicholas Lyndhurst. Each week we did a sketch about two mods, Mick and Nick. During the recording, he told me that he'd got a job on a new comedy called *Only Fools and Horses*. I wished him well and told him that if it didn't work out, his spot on my show would always be there for him. Funnily enough, Nick never did take me up on my offer . . .

Just as well, really, because there was no second series of *The Michael Barrymore Show*. I walked out on my Thames contract. It wasn't my idea, or Thames's, but Anne and Norman's. They came to see me when I was back in summer season at Torquay, this time second on the bill to Little and Large at the Pavilion Theatre.

Norman said, 'Listen, Dolly. What I am going to say to you may seem like madness, but Anne and I don't think that you're being given the right support from Thames. Your first series was okay, but if you go back and make the second one in the same way, you won't have a career. My suggestion is that unless they give you Studio One, you walk.' At that time it was considered that anything other than Studio One was second division. He also added that I should demand top writers and a big star support artist.

I couldn't believe what I was hearing, but I couldn't

think of any good argument against it. The first series was okay, and that was the problem: it was just okay.

'Do I have any offers from elsewhere?'

'No, Dolly.'

'And you still think I should walk?'

'Yes, Dolly.'

Cheryl and I glanced at each other. 'Then if that is your advice, I'll walk.'

The rest of the contract was worth £20,000 – and I kissed it goodbye. One thing was certain: I'd never work for Thames Television again. I asked Norman how I was going to break the news to them. He looked over the top of his glasses. 'Just you leave them to me, and get out on the stage tonight and show Thames what they've lost.'

'But Norman, they might not lose me if they agree to your demands.'

'Believe me, Dolly, they won't give in. You ain't big enough. But you will be one day.'

Did I do the right thing? There's no way of knowing. Were Thames upset when they were told? Definitely. Was I back where I started? No, just free to wait for the next break. I didn't know where it would come from, but at least Norman hadn't left me with nothing to look forward to. As he left, he said, 'Oh, by the way, Dolly, you need to get a really good six-minute spot together for a TV show in November. I've got you on *The Royal Variety Performance*.'

The Royal Variety Performance had a reputation for making or breaking new stars. It was known as the comedian's graveyard. I was given the new-boy slot, fifth on at the Drury Lane Theatre in the presence of Her Majesty the Queen and Prince Philip. It was 1983.

I practised like mad. How was I going to steal the show? What should I do? LWT were recording it, and once again the producer was David Bell, who'd given me a break on *Russ Abbot's Madhouse*. His cultured Scottish accent boomed out from the darkness of the theatre.

'So, Mr Barrymore, what are you going to do for us?'

I beckoned across the footlights. 'Er ... David ... I want to go into the audience and get a woman up on the stage and dance *Swan Lake* with her.'

'Whatever, darling. Where will she be sitting?'

'No, David. Not a plant. I mean any woman who happens to be there. Don't worry. I won't go for the Queen.'

He didn't laugh. 'So you're going to come on, get a woman ...'

'No, I'm going to stand on my head first.'

'Stand on your head? Hmm ...' David was getting bemused.

'And before that I'll say, "Awight? You awight? Awight at the back?"'

'Aaah ...'

'Then I get the woman up. When she's here, I tell her that she's going to perform *Swan Lake* with me. The orchestra belts out the music, I throw my jacket off, run round like a ballet dancer, pick her up by the waist, try to lift her, then get her hands stuck between my legs and shout, "Not like that, love! New balls please!" Then put her down on one side, run over to the other side, put on a swan ...'

'A swan.'

'Of course. Then I dance behind her and lift the back part of her dress and shove the duck's head through her legs and shout out, "I'm soaked down 'ere, love!" Thank her, give her a bunch of flowers, put her back in the audience. Take a bow, one to her, one to Her Majesty, then off. What d'ya think?'

'I think you should keep quiet about it, Michael, because

if the Variety Show Committee hear about it, they won't let you go on. For my part, if that's what you want to do, fine. Just make sure that in rehearsals, you do something – anything – different. When the Queen's in, go for it. Good luck. Very good luck indeed.'

When the overture played that night, I was nervous as hell. We all were: Les Dawson, Billy Dainty, Kelly Monteith and three other music-hall acts, all stuck together in one big dressing room with our nerves cranked up to breaking point. Les was moaning about the fact that there was no booze. We heard 'God Save the Queen' playing in the background. I ran across the road and bought two bottles of wine, which I gave to Les; he calmed down immediately. There was a knock at the dressing-room door and I made my way to the wings, escorted by a stage assistant.

'Ladies and gentlemen, Mr Michael Barrymore!'

Polite applause. I shut out the last thing I saw: Kelly Monteith banging his head against the wall. He'd just been on, and he'd royally died.

I could just see the outline of the Queen's crown; I assumed she was beneath it.

I went on and did exactly what I said I'd do. I got a lady called Beryl out of the audience to dance *Swan Lake* with me. She was a friend of a friend and agreed to be plucked. That was the only time then and since that I've known who I was going for. Either way, Beryl did a brilliant job and it worked. We finished with a large woolly-necked swan stuck on my head, which I thrust between her legs and screamed, 'God, it's wet down here!' I know what you're thinking: pure class. Whatever it was, it was mine. The audience was looking up to the royal box to see if Her Majesty approved; seeing her laughing, they laughed too. A bow to Beryl, a bow to the Queen and I was off.

Did I do well? As always, even if the audience is clapping

and cheering, I never assume it's for me. I don't know why I'm like that at the end of a performance; I become almost apologetic, shy, not staying too long for the appreciation. The next day the press talked about the great new boy and how he made a dream come true for a fishmonger's wife from Harlow to dance before the Queen. So thanks, Beryl, for being such a good sport. In fact, thanks to all the people who have joined my shows over the years.

I waited for the phone to ring with an offer of a series, but nothing came. Jesus, what do you have to do? I had stolen *The Royal Variety Performance*; wasn't that enough?

'They ain't knocking the doors down yet, Dolly. Just be patient.'

I got several spots on other people's shows, and I started to get a bigger following. More people came to see my live shows; I started to do sell-out business. But every time I did anything on TV, no matter how successful, nothing came from it, except another guest spot.

Then one day Norman asked me to watch a tape of an American quiz show that a British TV company had bought the rights to. I watched it; it was naff. But I thought that if I could do my own version, it might work.

The producer, Maurice Leonard, came to see me perform at Lewisham Town Hall – top of the bill, sold out. He came to the dressing room before I went on; I was very quiet, as I often am before a show. Afterwards, as he later told me, he said to his associate producer, Johnny Graham, 'I think we've made a mistake. The man is totally devoid of personality.'

He changed his mind when Mr No Personality went on stage and moved like a hurricane for two hours and received a standing ovation.

I made a pilot of this naff American quiz show, then a series. It became an instant hit. The show was called *Strike it Lucky*. And the TV company? Thames, of course. Never say never.

I didn't really want to be a game-show host, but I had no other choices. I had to use *Strike it Lucky* as a vehicle for my comedy; the actual quiz part I battled through. I didn't meet the contestants beforehand, which gave the show a certain edge, and if I didn't like someone, I didn't hide it. It worked; it kept me on my toes. For the most part, I genuinely liked the other people and they liked me; we had some great characters as contestants, and it didn't matter that they didn't have a clue what the answers were. It was real television made with real people, and if the contestants got a laugh at my expense that was even better. I talked to the contestants as individuals, not as a group of bodies who should be grateful to be on television.

Maurice Leonard was the first producer to let me have my head and grow as a performer. He let me muck about with the format: giving prizes away if I felt like it, slagging them off if I thought they were rubbish. If I fell over or made a prat of myself, it wasn't edited out. At its height, *Strike it Lucky* attracted audiences of 17 million in the UK alone. It was shown all over the world, and the 150 episodes have been repeated several times. People still come up to me and make the 'woo-woo' noise that you got when you struck the screen. The secret of the show's success was Maurice's canny awareness that the show had to work not only as a quiz, but also as a vehicle for my comedy. You could enjoy it on both levels. And he was brilliant at picking the contestants – the unusual, the different, the nice, the kind, the young, the old, the newlyweds, the Jack-the-lads, the mad, the blind, the deaf, butchers, bakers, grandmas, grandads. Every single one of them has played a part in my career, and I thank them all. The ones that walked with sticks, the ones that did naff tricks, the ones too brainy for us, the ones who drove buses, the navy, the army, the air force too, the Catholic, the Buddhist, the Muslim, the Jew, the kids who halfway through needed a poo, the people from London, the man from Sri Lanka, the gay ones, the straight ones, the obvious wanker, the silly, the stupid, the total crackpot . . . I have met them all for the sake of a jackpot. To those I've forgotten, you're all in mind – I'll get to you someday. You're one of a kind.

So many people appeared on *Strike it Lucky*. It had a life of its own; each show wrote itself. In the very first episode, one of the contestants was called Mrs Clutterbuck. I know! But it's real. She was pure Lancashire.

'Okay, Mrs Clutterbuck, the next category is sport.'

'Oh no, luv, not for me, give me summat else.'

The audience loved her front, and so did I.

'You can't have "summat else", love. Sport *is* the next category.'

'Well, if I have to, I'll take two, although I don't know a bloody thing about sport. Actually, thinking about it, I'll have one.'

'You can't have one! You have to have a minimum of two!'

She looked me straight in the face and said, 'Who says?'

'What do you mean, "Who says?" The rules says!'

'Well, you want to change the rules.'

There were so many people like her, who wrote the unwritten script every week. Like the couple from Thailand . . .

'Hello, what's your names?'

With broad smiles, the answer came, 'Mr and Mrs Pong.'

I did nothing, just attempting not to say the obvious. The audience didn't even try; they laughed. I gave them a

---

look of disdain: how dare you laugh at someone's name? Then I carried on the interview with great dignity.

'Do you have any children?'

'Yes.'

'How many?'

'One.'

'Boy? Girl?'

'Girl.'

'And what's her name?'

'Ping.'

'Ping?'

'Yes, Ping.'

'So she's Ping Pong?'

The audience laughed even louder, and I glared at them with even more disdain. That only made them laugh more.

The still smiling couple corrected me. 'Actually, her name is Mai Ping.'

I told them that she may or she may not, but she's still Ping Pong.

Once everyone recovered, we got on with the game, but Mr and Mrs Pong had a few problems – like not understanding a single one of the questions and not answering anything correctly. They did, however, manage to smile right to the end.

They were the first of many couples who failed to get a single answer right, and the first of many I gave prizes away to. I felt it only right that they should get something just for being there.

A typical question would be, 'Can you fill in the missing word: The Princess and the ...' To those who know, it's an easy question. (The Princess and the Pea.) To those who don't, there's a choice of six answers on the screen, so a little elimination should give you the answer. The first person I asked said, 'The Princess and the Porker'. The next one looked at the remaining five options, decided against the right one and came back with, 'The Princess and the Yorkshire Pudding'.

We became known as the show that would take anyone on board. We had one young guy who came on with an extremely elderly lady in a wheelchair, well over ninety years old. She told me in the interview that the young man lived with her. I looked at him and his eyes shifted. She went on to tell me that he pushed her everywhere. I gave him another look; he shifted even more guiltily. I told her not to worry, she was in good hands now, and I'd look after her for the rest of the show. Then I did my usual introduction and pushed her to the start position. I left her there and walked away. The audience let out a gasp: she had started to roll backwards. I'd forgotten to put the brake on her wheelchair. I managed to get back to her just before she rolled off the back of the set, catching her wheelchair in mid-free fall. There was something so black about the whole thing that I just lost the plot and tried to apologise through an uncontrollable fit of laughter.

One of our contestants generated a little more interest than most. The show went out – and so did a warrant for his arrest. He'd been evading the police for some time and was wanted for questioning about three murders. Now they tell me! I can only believe what the contestants tell me; who knows what they've really been up to?

Another woman, despite having bottle-thick glasses, complained that she couldn't see the list of answers. So we gave her her own small screen, and, as she had bad legs as well, we sat her on a stool. The combination made her slump so far forward that she looked as if she was dead. I never saw her face for the rest of the show, only heard her voice shouting out answers every now and again.

One young man appeared with his new girlfriend, and

walked slowly on to the set. He told me that he'd been mugged, and that they'd hit him not once but three times. He was so happy just to be on the show, and so grateful that despite everything that had happened to him he was still alive and one of the gang – it made me cry. He never managed to get any of the answers right, but I gave a holiday to him and his girlfriend for no other reason than that he made me feel humble. He made me realise that it doesn't take much to be happy in this life, and made me wonder why, if that's the case, happiness eludes all of us at times. As I write this, I can see his face; I hope he's well and still happy.

Strike it Lucky started to get quite an off-stage reputation as well, for high jinks in Thames dressing room number one, or Room 101 as it was known. Some nights the drinking in Room 101 went on into the small hours. The shows were doing so well that we thought it was okay to celebrate every single evening. We were starting to become like one big family, and we got our fun by throwing sandwiches at each other or jumping out of cupboards at unsuspecting people who came in. Every night the games got louder and more adventurous. Sandwiches went flying, followed by teacups and coffee cups, teapots and coffee pots, trays, chairs and finally, the sofa. All found their way out of the window and on to the roof of the studio below. One night the room ended up completely empty. I had nothing to do with it, but I just sat there without saying a word, as if this was the most normal thing in the world. The only things that didn't get chucked out the window were the endless bottles of booze.

I don't know why in this business we react to success by being over the top. It's a release, I suppose; a release from the pressure of having to come up with the goods. The pressure was always on. 'Great show last night, Michael.

When's your next one?' I'm trying to figure out at what point in my career it went from 'I can't get a break!' to 'You can't have a break – we need more shows!'

Strike it Lucky was the show that really established me as a force to be reckoned with on TV, and which gave me the leverage to get to the big time. Thames wanted another series, but I wanted to get back to doing what I came into the business to do: comedy. Much as I loved *Strike it Lucky*, it wasn't stretching me. I got so used to it that it was like working in my front room. That was good in a way; the more relaxed I was, the more daring I became in what I said and did, and the more outrageous I was, the more success-ful the show became. Thames would have liked me to carry on with it for ever – and I would have done more, as long as I could have done another series as well, based on my own comedy, without the constraints of the game-show formula. Thames had nothing else to offer me though, so it was time to leave Thames again.

The new head of entertainment at London Weekend Television (LWT) was John Kaye Cooper, and he decided that he wanted to poach me from Thames for my own show. Some people thought I was mad to give up *Strike it Lucky*. 'For what?' they said.

'I don't know. I have an opportunity to work for LWT.'

'Doing what?'

'I don't know. A show called *Barrymore*.'

'And what's all that about?'

'Don't know . . . a bit of this and a bit of that . . .'

Thinking back, John Kaye Cooper must have had some blind faith to sign me up with no more of a format than the fact that I would be in the show, whatever it was!

So LWT signed me, I signed with LWT, we had a title for the show – and that was all. We did a pilot that was absolutely disastrous: I was all over the place. What were we going to do? We all dug deep and decided that the best idea was to keep it very natural and free, not to saddle ourselves with a format, just to base the whole show around me interacting with all sorts of people. Somehow it found its feet and it worked. It was hard work, because you can't fall back on a format – it wasn't like a quiz show, where you just moved on to the next round. We were in constant rehearsal, we had the very best production values available at the time, but it was all dependent on improvisation.

Whatever we did on *Barrymore*, I threw myself into it wholeheartedly. So what if I couldn't tap dance? I'd get up there with the professionals and I'd do it with an insane amount of enthusiasm. I interviewed people using the old two-sofa system, but instead of just asking them questions I'd become part of the interview, mucking around with them, drawing them out. We stuck to the principle that I should never meet anyone before the show – what you'd see on screen would be my first encounter with them. The people who worked best were the ones that initially seemed quite normal, but who, as we got chatting, it became apparent were completely barking. We had one bloke on who called himself The Nutty Professor, and it didn't work at all – everyone knew he was strange, there was no element of surprise. The most successful ones were like the woman who was convinced that she'd been Marie Antoinette in a former life because, as she was passing through Crewe Station, she started to have a strange feeling around her neck, which made it fall to one side. I reminded her that Marie Antoinette had been guillotined and her head hadn't just fallen to one side as the axe sliced through it! She disagreed. She was absolutely convinced – that's what made it funny. We had the Marquis of Bath on once, and I went straight into, 'My Lord, I thinkest thou art off thy trot' –

and he got it immediately, 'Yea, verily I am.' It was quite a dangerous way of working, and it could go wrong, but it gave the show edge and spontaneity. We had the women from *House Party* on as guests – lovely women, very mumsy – and one of them, called Jean, started being a bit arsey with me. So I got arsey with her, it escalated and soon we were having a big bitchy fight. The more outrageous I became, the more people seemed to like it.

Anything could happen. The choreographer was Alan Harding, and he taught me every move, every step I made. I was thrown through the air in mad rock 'n' roll routines. I tapped impossibly complicated routines. Not being a trained dancer my feet at the end of rehearsals would bleed and my socks would stick to my feet with the blood. Worse than that for me was when my legs refused to move any more and many times I would have to be helped upstairs and into a hot bath to recover. At one point, we had so many different numbers in preparation that we used up all of LWT's rehearsal rooms. I have never worked so hard in my life. I would rehearse day in, day out, arriving early, leaving late. I sang difficult songs, played instruments, roller-skated, balanced, boxed Bruno, danced with old dears and young dears and a lot of oh dears. Some of the routines that people did on the show they'd been practising all their lives to get them perfect; I had two weeks to get it the best I could to join them on the show. *Barrymore* was a relentless giant; I had to be all things to all people.

Just thinking about the workload now makes me feel tired. Is that because I've done so much that I now find it hard to be enthusiastic about the business that I once so dearly loved? Or am I just feeling out of the picture? I've spent my life in the frame; it's hard to know how to look into one. I'm sure I've felt like this before, and once I get back to work it'll be just the same as when I left off. It's my old problem: I can't seem to pop in and out of the business. It's all or nothing. I wish it were different, but I can't see that happening at this stage of my life. I'll have to find a different way of doing it. But what?

Did I go off on a tangent just then? Yes, I'm sure I did – and that's part of my way of working as well. Going off on a tangent has become my trademark. I always have the basic skeleton for a show, a rough format – and then I can wander off wherever I want to go. Some of my best-ever moments came about in that way on *My Kind of Music*, a show which came along much later, and which was basically *Barrymore* meets *Strike it Lucky* with extra music. It was the template for *Pop Idol*. In fact, today, they use many of the edit styles we created. How do I feel about that? It's great to know we were the foundation of such a world-wide hit! Good luck to them. Especially Nigel Lythgoe, who always knew what worked for me. He's rare, he's a producer with talent.

I wandered into the audience and found a guy who was wearing a multi-coloured knitted jumper – pure Frank Spencer. I got him to give it to me, I put it on and I looked, to put it mildly, a prat. Then I wandered on and found a winter hat with ear flaps, which I pulled down hard over my head. I found a ladies' shoulder bag, which I wore like a satchel. I took a walking stick off a woman who clearly needed it, and then, when I made her stand up without it, proclaimed that I'd performed a miracle. I stood astride a woman and indicated that she should give me her knickers. She obliged, and wriggled out of her drawers, beach fashion. Seeing this, two other women immediately took off their bras and threw them in my direction. I put everything on and topped it all off with someone's heavy puffa jacket, then asked the audience:

'I don't look a prat, do I?'

They all shouted a mocking 'No!'

What inspired these moments I have never truly known. Something takes over. It's like I'm guided by an outside force and my body just makes the moves. When I look back at the tapes I have the ability to look at him rather than me. Sometimes, as in the sketch I've just described, he makes me smile. Sometimes.

I few years ago I took part in a Channel Four programme about TV rebels. I was deemed to be a rebel because of how I'd changed the way TV comedy is done. I'd never really thought about what makes a TV rebel; all I know is that you can't manufacture one. You can't say 'I am going to do something rebellious'. A TV rebel is someone who does something wrong in the right suit.

The show *Barrymore* ran for eight series, and I'm proud to say it won award after award. And from the National Television Awards, the one that everyone counts as the barometer of what's hot, I have been presented with thirteen separate trophies, all voted for by the public. So thank you.

Why was it successful? Because of the people. The show could be anything it wanted to be from one week to the next, the only unifying factor being that I was in it, and that we had fantastic guests. It was real people performing in front of real people, and that makes for the most exciting, unpredictable TV. One guest said it all: Nobbin the Gnome, a little Irish fellow, whose wife followed him around dressed as a toadstool. For their party piece they just jumped up and down, no more and no less. If you see them, it's enough. She complained to me that they'd wanted to get married as a gnome and a toadstool, but her father said he'd disown her if she did. All I said to her was, 'Do you think your father may have had a point?'

All our hard work paid off when we were asked to put together a slot for *The Royal Variety Performance* in 1987.

We worked up a routine of hand-clapping. Doesn't sound much: just sixteen of us in a line, me in the middle, crossing hands and clapping faster and faster to the music. One mistake and the whole routine would collapse – and because we were doing it on *The Royal Variety Performance*, we only had one chance to get it right.

The director that year was Nigel Lythgoe. John Kaye Cooper was in charge of production again. When John watched the rehearsal of what I was intending to do, he decided that I should go last, as top of the bill. It was a rare honour – and one that I was determined to live up to. Apart from the clapping routine, I was involved in another using soldiers from the Queen's Guards; around forty of them rehearsed over and over, marching in time to 'Will You Still Love Me Tomorrow?', with me singing between the ranks, all of it choreographed by one of the best in the business, Alan Harding. I also did a comedy routine, involving yet another woman from the audience. She sat on my knee and I sang 'Crazy' to her, then gave her all the flowers in the auditorium.

After the show we stood in what's known as the Royal line-up to meet Her Majesty. When she got to me at the end she said, 'That soldier routine was very special. The dancers were very convincing.' I said, 'Thank you, Ma'am, but they weren't dancers. They belong to you.' She turned, gave them a wave, and said, 'Ohew.'

After she left I lost count of how many people threw me up in the air and congratulated me. Cheryl must have been really pleased as she didn't have one note for me on my performance. I can still see her now, standing in the wings, calm and smiling, with everyone else jumping up and down. Whatever I went through with her, it was always so important to me that she approved of my work. Norman Murray walked up to me and said, 'Dolly, that was one of the greatest performances I have ever seen and you haven't even started yet.' I would rate Norman as one of the best agents ever. He had a great understanding of people, especially performers. Not long after this, he passed away. I believe he, like my father-in-law, Eddic, would have been able to deal with the problems that later arose. They both came under the heading 'The Old School'. So that, I suppose, made me the new one. I just hoped I had learned enough from them to deal with what lay ahead.

It was quite a night. Twenty million people in Britain alone watched, with a world audience of over 100 million. It was where all roads in my career had led to. I knew when I'd finished that I'd done well, but I didn't anticipate the reaction I got. It was overwhelming. One television critic, Margaret Foreword, wrote, 'He is the greatest television entertainer of our time.'

Where do you go from there? Well, I didn't sit back and rest on my laurels. Masses of offers came in to do all sorts of things, but, despite that, it seemed harder than ever to find people who could write for me, because it's very difficult to match my individual style. Maurice Leonard had always realised that the key to the success of *Barrymore* was the calibre of the guests, and that the best way to find really great people was to go out and look for them.

Maurice and I have a similar sense of humour. What amuses him has the same effect on me. Such as the Sunday afternoon he was in a cinema in Fulham. At the time, the cinema was predominately filled with people from the gay scene. It was the first showing of *The Exorcist*, still considered by many to be the scariest horror movie ever. The whole cinema was absolutely terrified; guys were covering their eyes, their faces screwed tight in anticipation of what was going to make them jump next with sheer fright. Then one of several classic moments. The demonised little girl is strapped to the bed, her face full green, her eyes bloodshot, her hair a filthy, crawling grey. The priest is splashing holy water all over her, which turns to steam as it drenches her skin and blisters. She pulls hard on her chains to taunt the priest more. The whole house is now shaking, he screams out more prayer. The whole audience holds its breath. The girl projects vile red blood and green vomit at speed and huge volume all over the priest. Then her head starts to turn to the left, the bones crunching, splitting and cracking as it continues to revolve 360 degrees. As the head completes its inhuman turn, she lunges forward, eyes wider than humanly possible, and says in a voice low and gravelled, 'Your mother sucks cock in Hell'. In the silence of horror that followed, an old, grey-haired gay guy turned to his partner and said, 'Ooooo, doesn't seem too bad to me!'

We started a regular slot in the show where I'd go to a town centre and find people in their normal environment, where they could really be themselves – standing outside their local Woolworths or Marks & Spencer's, for example. We reckoned they'd feel more at home than if they were dragged into the unfamiliar environment of the studio. It started off really small – just me standing on a pallet, with one camera, one sound guy and the director. I remember standing in the Bullring in Birmingham, literally pleading with passers-by to come up and talk to me. But before long, the idea really took off, and we'd have thousands of people crowding around. It was a natural extension of what I'd done before, crossing the boundary between the performer and the audience. I'd done it in theatres, going down into the audience to pick people out, and I'd done it at *The Royal Variety Performance*. Now we were doing it on a grand scale, taking the show out to the people.

This little segment grew and grew and eventually

---

became a series in its own right – *My Kind of People*. Of all the shows I've done, I think this was the most popular, and I still get asked when we're going to do some more. It was completely unplanned and spontaneous; you couldn't control a situation like that, you just had to work with it. The best bits were when I'd be talking to someone in the crowd, and some old boy would shuffle into camera and just stand there. You could never create something like that in the studio. It had to be absolutely genuine. It got to the point where *My Kind of People* was so popular that many places wouldn't let us film because of the sheer number of people that turned up, and all the attendant security risks. In a shopping centre in Dublin, for instance, 55,000 people watched the recording. And we were never really very popular with the shopkeepers; they complained that we took away all their business. On some occasions we paid them the equivalent of a day's takings just to let us carry on filming.

As my popularity increased, I was asked to appear on many other shows. I did the first *Saturday Night Live* that was ever shown on British TV; the format was already popular in America, where it still airs today. At the time, it was deemed cutting-edge television, and I suppose it was quite an honour to be asked to present it. On the first night I hosted the show and introduced a young man called Ben Elton, one of a new wave of comedians that were being called 'alternative'. I'd been an alternative comedian myself for years; it's just when you get popular that the title disappears.

A lot of established performers made a huge fuss about alternative comedy, complaining that they thought a lot of the new comedians had no talent, while the new comedians said that the old school was dated and no longer funny.

There was a lot of name calling at any given opportunity. I kept myself to myself and floated unharmed through the middle of it all. I've never been one to slag off other people's work; I don't see what's to be gained from it, or, more to the point, what's funny about it. Comedy is seeing what is funny in how we react to normal situations; that's why visual comedy always has a long shelf life.

It soon became clear that it was no longer politically correct to make jokes about minorities, and that caused a problem for a lot of the older generation of comics. But it was never a problem for me; I didn't do jokes about blacks, gays, women, the old, the young, religion or anything else that was not PC. But you never knew when people were going to object to something. On *Saturday Night Live*, I wanted to do a parody of the Elvis song, 'Are You Lonesome Tonight?' The lyrics, as I wanted to perform them, went:

> Are you lonesome tonight?
> Would you like some tonight?
> Would you like me to come home with you?
> Can you still do those tricks
> When you pull down your knicks
> And thrill me like you used to do?
> Put your hand in my pocket, and what do you see
> Is it a gun or a rocket
> Or the trunk of a tree?
> Is your mother away?
> Is your brother still gay?
> Tell me, dear, are you lonesome tonight?

Now, for some reason, that was deemed un-PC. I can only think that they had a problem with the gay line. My God, were they going to get a surprise in a few years' time!

Breaking the rules, taking chances and pushing the

96

boundaries was part of my make up, like the time I was asked on to a morning TV chat show. The presenter asked what was it like meeting the Queen after a *Royal Variety* performance. I said, 'Well, she is very small and nothing like you would imagine.' The presenter asked, 'Oh, really, in what way was she different?' I said she said to me in a broad cockney accent, 'Hello, Mic, how's it going?' and that I replied, 'Fine, Liz, how are you?' The presenter started to get slightly wide eyed, not sure if I was for real, due to my convincing manner. 'So I said, "How's Phil?" She said, "Do what?" I said, "How's Phil? Phil the Greek?" She said "Don't talk to me about him."' I showed the presenter how she physically became aggressive, hunching my shoulders and lowering my head. I said, 'And then, out of nowhere, she leaped at me and head butted me with her crown! I said, "Leave it out, Liz." My forehead had all these jewels stuck in it – sapphires, diamonds, a couple of rubies, and she came at me repeatedly shouting, "Tiara, tiara".'

Desperate to get to the commercial break, the presenter said, 'Perhaps we'll take a break there, that's if we're still on air.' Cue nervous, 'Ho, ho.'

I said, 'Liz then said, "Sorry, Mic. Fancy coming back to the palace for a coffee?" I said, "Yeah, whatever," so we left the theatre and instead of jumping in the back of the Rolls-Royce as normal, she got in the driver's seat, started it up, hit the pedal hard, slung it into gear and we went flying backwards. I said, "Liz, you're in the wrong gear!" She said, "Leave it out, Mic, I'm the Queen, I can wear what I like!"'

On many of the Royal shows I have appeared in over the years it has always been those surrounding royalty who have a problem with what I say, never the Royal Family themselves. Once, in the middle of a routine in the presence of Prince Charles for the Prince's Trust, I got a ladder and climbed up to the royal box to have a chat with him face to face, apologising on behalf of the management for the terrible seats he had been given and for the fact that he wasn't even in the theatre but, because the council flats had been built so close, he was watching the show from one of the block's balconies. The lady who sat beside him bent over double with laughter, to which I remarked, 'Jesus, love you shot down there quick!' The front pages of the tabloids ran with 'Barrymore in Royal Shocker'. Afterwards, though, Prince Charles suggested I do the same routine to his mother for the next Royal show. I replied, I don't think so. He said, 'Oh, it would be great fun.'

Eventually *Barrymore* lost its way, because it became all-singing, all-dancing, and it lost the rawness that it had in the beginning. But it was the vehicle for some great TV moments, and some routines that will stand the test of time. But by the end, though, it was felt that the show relied too much on me coming up with the goods week after week, so for my next vehicle – *My Kind of Music* – we came up with a little bit of format, so I had something to fall back on each week.

At the beginning of its trial runs, *My Kind of Music* looked as hopeless as *Barrymore* first did – lots of ideas, but none of them good. We ditched the original idea of running up and down on an oversized keyboard, and that didn't leave us with much. We were all looking at each other, thinking, 'Well, this pile of crap is going nowhere. Let's just go through the motions, finish the pilot and make another load of *Barrymore*. But, yet again, fate would decide what was crap and what wasn't. We made the pilot for *My Kind of Music*, and, to my surprise, it worked. I don't know who exactly looks down on me and guides my way, but one thing I do know – they have a warped sense of humour!

Ultimately, the person who was running all my shows

was Cheryl. Whoever was producing or directing had to clear everything with her. She had her own special seat at the production desk, and when she turned up it was like royalty arriving. Everyone knew when Cheryl had arrived, flanked by two security guards and covered in Prada and Gucci, diamonds, but never pearls. If Cheryl liked what she saw, it was in the show. If everyone else liked a particular act and she didn't, there was no way it would get through. The same applied at rehearsals: every routine had to be done in front of her to get approved. In the studio, if there was a debate about whether something was working or not, she would have the last word. When it came to editing, all the master tapes had to be seen by her first. She would give her notes to the director about what bits could stay in and what had to be edited out.

Cheryl's trademark was her long, red, immaculately manicured nails. Maurice had a cardboard cut-out of a finger with a long red-painted nail pinned to the wall of the rehearsal room. A piece of string wagged it, imitating Cheryl when she 'wanted a word'. If Cheryl 'wanted a word' the response was usually, 'Oh God, what have I done?' That was how powerful she had become.

Success brings its own problems. The money got bigger, the house got bigger and we started to go on expensive holidays. More time in between jobs to look at myself, more time not to like what I was seeing. I was still in good shape physically, but I didn't like the person I had turned into. I'd worked hard for stardom, and now I was up there playing with the big boys, but I always felt that it was for someone else, not for me. More and more I craved being on stage; I only felt at home with a microphone in my hand. My performances were getting better and better, while my home life was getting worse and worse.

The money for *Strike it Lucky* and *Barrymore* was so good that I no longer had to run around the south east of England doing three stag shows a night. I didn't have to do summer seasons if I didn't want to; I could do very well out of my TV work, or headlining big shows. This left me with a lot of time on my hands, and I was cut off from the addiction that I really craved – live performance. I'm the sort of person who needs to throw himself into something heart and soul, and I needed something to replace the buzz that live work used to give me. I poured myself a drink to relax, to take away the withdrawal symptoms of not performing. It worked, so I had another one. And another.

Cheryl was taking more and more control of my life, vetting the jobs that I did, where I went and with whom. She was never off the phone. One morning she was on the phone, doing a deal – Cheryl was always doing deals – when she turned to me and said 'What are you wearing?' I said, just the jeans and top I found on the rail. She told whoever it was she was talking to on the phone to hold on a minute, covered the mouthpiece, and said, 'That's Thursday's outfit. Today is Tuesday. Go and put on Tuesday's outfit.' Then she turned and carried on talking to the person on the phone.

I went back to my dressing room, took off the jeans, shirt and socks, put everything back on the rail and put on Tuesday's outfit. To be honest, it didn't look any bloody different to Thursday's outfit, but obviously it made a huge difference to Cheryl. It never crossed my mind to question her.

Cheryl once complained to my agent Norman that she wished I would just behave normally when I wasn't on stage. She was referring to my various 'bad behaviour' moments. For example, the night in Manchester during a theatre season, when, at three in the morning, and several drinks the worse for wear, I thought it highly amusing to run from top to bottom, end to end, door to door, knocking loudly, waking up every single resident at the Britannia Hotel. A local photographer took a flashlight face shot of me that was slapped large on the front page of the *Manchester Evening News*, accompanied by the heading 'Boozy Barry-more Bombards Britannia'. They kindly added a tinge of green to my complexion to enhance the already dreadful shot. But at least she knew where I was that night!

Norman said, 'Look Cheryl, you can't have it all. People like Michael don't behave like, as you put it, "normal folk". It's because of the way they are that makes them who they are. Sensible and safe don't marry with style and stardom.'

So I took up cooking. Cheryl was far too busy, and I loved it. I bought loads of cookery books, and plenty of booze, because that's what famous chefs did – cook, slurp, cook, slurp, and so on. When I started to think that perhaps I was drinking just for the sake of drinking, I moved on to fine wines, cultivating a taste for the decent stuff, just to lend a bit more legitimacy to my boozing.

After I'd cooked the dinner, I'd think, 'Oh, I'll go and relax now', but relaxing never lasted for more than five minutes. I couldn't just sit with myself. I did not like the feeling at all. I would start to go over and over in my head what I wanted to say. Everything was word perfect, in my head, of course everyone understood, in my head. Then all the counter arguments would begin. I said all the wrong words, in my head, no one understood me. I couldn't even say enough is enough to myself, thinking that someone could actually hear my thoughts.

That was the time I discovered one of the most danger-ous places. Inside my own head. Instead of talking to another person and telling them. I felt so scared. In my head I was the judge, the jury, the defence and the prosecution, and I found myself guilty every time. I thought, there must be a way for all of this to go away, so that I can sit with myself, so I am no longer afraid of what will happen to me if anybody finds out that I am even thinking about being gay, let alone actually being gay. God, what would that be like to deal with.

It always made me think, 'I'll just have another drink, she's still on that poxy phone.' Relaxing was boring; it was dangerous, just sitting there drinking on my own. My tolerance of alcohol wasn't that high, and before long I was pissed. Then, of course, I became braver and I'd tell Cheryl what I really thought about things that I didn't like. Cheryl rapidly got fed up with my behaviour, and one day she said to me, 'Why do you have to drink so much? You're not very nice with a drink inside you. We don't communicate well when you drink. It doesn't suit you and you can't take it.' I took the role of a little boy being scolded, huffing and puffing, and I was usually saved by the phone ringing again. That would shut her up. I'd go to the kitchen and pour myself another drink. Her voice in the background would gradually fade away until I passed out – peace at last.

In the morning I'd feel like shit and look it, but I never suffered from headaches. But I knew what atmospheres felt like; they were heavier every morning. No speaking, that look of, 'I'm so cross with you I can't speak'. I hate being told off; it's so degrading. Not like drinking. When I drank it numbed my feelings. It did the job for me: shut everyone up and stopped all the tut-tutting. What did they know? They didn't know what it was like being me. They didn't know how I felt. If they did, they'd know why I had to drink.

'Michael, why are you drinking so much?'

———

'I like it, it stops the voices.'

'Voices?'

Yes, the voice in my head that tells me to do what I want and sod everyone else. The voice that says it's okay to be naughty, to be wild, to let my hair down. The voice that tells me that I've done really well and that I should reward myself. The voice that tells me that people want to know Michael Barrymore, the star, not Michael. Who's Michael?

'Just stop, you're becoming an alcoholic.'

'Okay, I'll stop. I ain't an alcoholic.'

I was determined to show that I didn't need drink, that I could take it or leave it – and leave it I did. I just drank soft drinks, and started taking soft drugs. Even better! Now I could get high without passing out or smelling of booze. Perhaps that would shut up all those people who thought I had a problem. There was just one crucial difference: I could go to the fridge any time and pour a drink, whereas I had to hide the cannabis. I'd keep it somewhere convenient, so I could have a nibble now and again. I ate it rather than having the smell of puff around. It tasted disgusting, but I buzzed along with a smile on my face whatever the situation. Glad or sad, I smiled and laughed. That'll teach them to call me an alcoholic. Pieces of cannabis would get stuck between my teeth, so I was always nipping off to the bathroom to check and see if I could find another little bit of dope to add to my stash. It was expensive, but I was doing well, I could afford it. I deserved a treat.

I was very pleased with my new habit, but that voice in my head kept saying, 'Oh, go on, Michael, have a drink! Have a go at that American stuff, Jack Daniel's! Just get a bottle in; a couple of those would make you feel on top of the world . . .' I still never drank or took drugs before a show, and that way I could kid myself that everything was fine. Work work work, drink drink drink, drug drug drug.

***

Everything in its right place – so why was I ending up in so many other places at any time of night, and who were these people? I didn't remember agreeing to go to a party. Where was I? Why was I there? What was it out there that I craved so much? What was the attraction of these nocturnal adventures, and why did I have to get totally stoned before each new adventure? Why could I only socialise when there were alcohol and drugs around?

The fact is that I'd reverted to a type of behaviour that started in my teens. I was going out to clubs and doing anything in my power to engineer situations where I could spend the night with a man. I was hopeless at chatting people up. I've never been able to chat blokes up; I suppose it's not something you learn how to do. Cheryl must have guessed, I suppose, but nothing was said; at least there wasn't the threat of another woman. There was never going to be, 'Hello Cheryl, I'm going off with your husband, my name's George.' It was all very secretive.

I thought I could cope with that – stay married, toe the line, but never confront the fact that I was gay, never rock the boat. Most of the time I felt terrible about it, and I drank more to deaden the guilt. I drank in order to have the confidence to meet these guys, and then I drank to get over it. I knew I was overdoing it, but I couldn't stand my moods when I was sober. People didn't understand what was getting me down; it couldn't be work, because that was going from strength to strength. But at this rate I was going to end up like one of those addicts who just slump and stare and dribble down their clothes. Why?

I was frightened of being found out. I was a gay man living as a straight in a round world, constantly having to make sure that my image and my behaviour gave no indication of who or what I really was. That is very hard. I can only compare it to being a gay football player: male contact all the time, on and off the pitch, drinking with the team, being one of the lads, going to stag shows, giving out that whole 'I'm a lad, birds and booze' image. Always being the one to tell anti-gay gags, calling everyone else woofters in order to take the focus off who was really gay. God forbid they found out that they'd all stripped off and got into a bath with a gay man, that they'd hugged and kissed a gay man after scoring a goal! They wouldn't give a damn about how talented a footballer you were. What would the crowds say once the papers had told them that you'd play better in stiletto heels, a blouse and hot pants? Better to say nothing.

Imagine if David Beckham was gay: would he have been picked to captain England? Would Victoria keep telling him it was 'just a phase'? Would he be any less of a father to his children?

I'm a gay entertainer. These days it's not such a difficult world to be gay in. Has what happened to me put others off dealing with their sexuality? There are plenty who say, 'I've spent years building up an image, I can't destroy it!' But what is an image in show business, exactly? I never built up a particular image; if I have one, it's in the eyes of people who see me, and now that they know I'm gay, maybe they have a different perception of me – but I haven't changed, neither has my performance. The very nature of my performance has always been camp; I mean, look at me, I'm not exactly butch, am I? Some would say that all performances are camp by their very nature, although not all performers are camp. Look at Bruce Forsyth. He's as straight as a die, but his performance is outrageously camp. I mean, butch men don't stand around with their hands on their hips going 'All right my love?' I heard Elizabeth Taylor saying that if it wasn't for gay men and women, there wouldn't be such a thing as show business, let alone Hollywood – and I hung on to that so much. I wanted to stand up and say, 'Right, there you are! Liz Taylor's said it – it must be okay to be a gay man and work in show business!'

The world I'd worked in up to this point was a strange mixture: the ultra-straight world of the stag nights and the working men's clubs, and the much more 'theatrical' world of theatre and television. During all the years that I'd been coming up through the business, playing those hard gigs, focusing on nothing outside my career, I'd shut off any doubts about my sexuality, I'd got married, gone along with what Cheryl wanted for me and just 'forgotten' all that stuff. But now, with time on my hands and booze and drugs in my system, it started to resurface.

Larry Grayson built his entire career around performing as a gay man, but he never once stated in public that he was gay. With him it was always 'Shut that door!' – he never stepped out of that closet, even though nobody can seriously have believed for one moment that he was straight. That's only my opinion, of course.

I was completely ignorant of the gay world. I heard people say certain things without having the faintest idea what they meant – 'I bet he's good to his mother', 'Is he a friend of Dorothy's?', 'I believe he's very musical', 'Who's the rent he's with?' I had no idea where to find a gay bar. Things are very different now: the gay bars are easy to find, the windows aren't painted over and, if you're a gay man, you don't have to hide it. Show business has become much more healthy. I've never heard anyone say, 'I'm not working with Diana Ross because she's black,' and I've never heard anyone say, 'I'm not working with Michael Barrymore because he's gay.' Thank God there's one business that accepts anyone who dares enter it.

But I was still a long way from finding this out for myself. At the time, I thought I had no option. I tried to blot out reality by drinking more and more; I couldn't face up to the fact that I'd got myself into this impossible situation where my marriage, my career, my entire life, depended on living a lie. And it was the pressure of this situation that pitched me headlong into addiction.

5

Drink, Drugs and Destruction

Problems? What problems? I didn't have any, not when I was on stage – and now, thanks to drink and drugs, not when I was off stage either. So I was either working or drinking, which was the perfect combination for me. I didn't have to worry about my sexuality any more, because I didn't need sex – except, occasionally, when I was on drugs and got a bit frisky. On those occasions Cheryl and I would make love, depending on whether or not I passed out. And when I did pass out, that wasn't because of the drugs, of course, that was due to exhaustion. Whenever the drink and drugs became too much, you call it exhaustion.

'Michael, why are you so quiet, so removed?'

'Oh, I'm just a little exhausted, that's all . . . Don't worry.'

But people were worried, very worried. They could see I wasn't just exhausted; they could see the dead eyes, the dry red skin, the slow, deliberate destruction. Everyone knew I was ill; they knew it before I did. I was an addict, and addiction is an illness, the third biggest killer in the Western world.

'You know what you need, Michael?' Oh yes, they all knew what I needed, and so did I, but the problem was that it didn't include drink and drugs. A good holiday? Oh no, not that, please! That was how bad I had become. The thought of a holiday filled me with dread. I just wanted to carry on working.

Eventually, in 1993, I was prised out of England and taken to Palm Beach, Florida, for four weeks. It's the play-ground of the seriously rich and famous: fantastic homes, all facing the ocean and backing on to Lake Worth, clear blue skies, no humidity, Worth Avenue to shop till you drop from the weight of diamonds. Class restaurants, mile after mile of gold, fishing, saying 'Good morning!' to the Kennedys or the Trumps as you drive open-top past their holiday homes to yours. Classic cars by the hundred, our bungalow right on the inlet where Lake Worth joins the ocean. Beautiful beach, which at night gives itself up for the lady turtles to come and lay their eggs. Staff to attend to our every need, stunning women, tanned men. Three police-men to each resident. Manicured ladies. Money, money, money: as much as you've got, Palm Beach can take it.

And none of it meant anything to me. I managed to be miserable in one of the most beautiful places in the world. I never once laid out in the sun, never sat by the pool, never sat on the beach, never watched the turtles. I fished, because I love fishing, sitting all day and all night with my back towards our stunning bungalow, my legs dangling in the water. Pelicans would sit with me on the teak deck, waiting to swallow my catch, huge things with great long beaks and a flopping sack hanging down, they could swallow any fish whole – one gulp. It took me two, three gulps to swallow a drink, and then, when I'd had enough, I'd fall asleep. I spent most nights flat on my back on the deck, the early morning January sun a perfect blanket. That's when I loved Palm Beach – on those hot, salty nights, all the ones I passed out on.

I kept drinking and drinking. I had bottles hidden everywhere: how was I going to get through a month without work otherwise? Damn these holidays, they just got in the way. I hated being away from work, I couldn't function without it.

Eddie had recently died – the voice that knew all the answers had gone. I remember taking Eddie to the specialist in London and hearing he had cancer. His world crumbled and my world fell in as well. How selfish is that? There's this man, who I love so much, who is reeling and not dealing with what he has just heard, and my first reaction is how the hell am I going to carry on without Eddie? He has to survive. I've taken all this time to find an Eddie and now he's pulling out. I stayed by him for the following two years to the day he died, doing anything either to prolong his life or distract him, buying him whatever he wanted. Like all of us at those times, he didn't want much, only his life. I took him to his treatments and we always went shopping afterwards. Whatever they were giving him was having a spending effect on him, which I encouraged. The best was a November night, a few days away from Remembrance Sunday. It was getting dark from about 4.30. As we passed Jack Barclay Ltd on the corner of Berkley Square, Eddie said, 'That's nice.' He was referring to one of the cars in the brightly-lit showroom. I pulled over and we walked in. Eddie ignored all the other cars and stood staring at one.

It was a Bentley in British racing green and in the middle of the immaculately polished chrome radiator was a single red poppy. Eddie's eyes were full. All he said was, 'It's lovely.' On the following Sunday, at 11 o clock, Eddie stood up in his front room for the minute's silence, as he did every year, remembering all those that had fallen, and what he and others had been through. It was always time to talk again when Eddie did. I took him by the arm to the front door, opened it and let him have a look outside. The smile came back to his face and I gave him the keys to the Bentley.

Eddie was there for me. If I had a problem he would sort it. When things were not so good he took the worry away. He taught me how to conduct myself in business and was the one to start up our first company, putting in his own money to get it going. He also taught me that when you do a deal with anyone you have to be fair. As he said, you can't say I'll take 99 per cent as there is no point in the other person getting up in the morning, however great the job. The saying he reminded me of if others were not dealing fair was: 'You can always stoop down and pick up nothing.' Whenever anyone questioned my ability he would say, 'You are as good as anyone else and better than the rest.' He was the first to tell me I had just made my first million, which was all the more special from someone who was one in a million.

My alcohol intake increased dramatically after he died. None of this was helped by how much I had come to rely on him.

God, I miss him.

How I wished he was there in Palm Beach. He would have loved it and I know he would have been able to accept what was wrong with me, even find a solution. Well, right or wrong, that's what I believed.

Cheryl had brought her mother Kit out with her. I didn't remember inviting her . . . I didn't even remember arriving at Palm Beach. Cheryl said I had to be helped off the plane at Miami. I was getting so bad by this time that I'd convinced myself that everything Cheryl told me was made up. It had to be! I couldn't remember any of these things. So don't tell me how I got off the plane two weeks ago. Jesus Christ, I can't even have a holiday without 'Do this, do that, don't drink!' What else was I supposed to do? There was sod all else for me in this poxy resort.

One of my new little tricks seemed to guarantee attention: picking up a chair and throwing it across the room, screaming 'Happy now? Happy that you've got me into a state? You've made me behave just like my dad used to! You want upset? Okay, I'll show you! Here it comes!' Smash, crash, rage, rage. Out of control, heart pumping too fast. It worked: the house emptied, and I could get my bottle of Jack Daniel's out of its hiding place in the garage. Forget the ice, forget the glass, I'll just sit and look at the water and swig the whiskey, nice, hot and sweet at the back of my throat. I poured more and more inside me and cried more and more outside. I felt it was me who filled the ocean – that's how much I needed to get rid of. Just leave me alone! Leave me alone!

Then, one evening, I really was alone. Cheryl, Kit, everyone seemed to have cleared out and left me behind. I was blearily wondering where everyone had gone, when a guy appeared at the house and introduced himself as Bob.

'Who the hell are you? And where is everyone?'

'Everyone has booked into the Breakers Hotel.'

'What do you want?'

'I want you to come to a meeting . . .'

Bob was the first recovering alcoholic/addict I knowingly met, and we talked until four in the morning. By 10 am I was on a plane to Baltimore, on my way to my first rehab, wondering how the hell I'd got there.

Cheryl had become so concerned about my drinking that she'd phoned Austin Tate, the chief psychiatrist at the Priory Group, and he'd organised for someone from Alcoholics Anonymous to come out to the house and '12-step' me. It's a kind of emergency call-out: another addict comes to see you, talks to you about your drinking, maybe leaves you some literature, encourages you to come to a meeting. All I can remember is that Bob kept saying he had somewhere I could go, somewhere I would be safe.

Father Martin is a Catholic priest and recovering alcoholic who runs a rehab centre in Ashley, near Baltimore. My first experience of rehab – and, I thought at the time, very successful. The only requirement for membership of Alcoholics Anonymous is the desire to stop drinking. Did I have the desire, or did I just say I did in order to keep everyone else happy? Did I go into rehabilitation for me? No. I went because everyone thought it was best for me. I was told that I had a disease of the mind. Well, thanks for that, because now I had an excuse for my drinking. I became a perfect student in the college of addiction. I told them everything I thought they wanted to hear.

'Are you homosexual?'

'No, I am not.'

'Have you ever been involved with gay men?'

'No, I have not.' I couldn't look the counsellor in the eye when I said this.

This was my first introduction to the sad world of rehab. Hearing other addicts telling their stories; telling my own, or at least as much as I thought was wise. For the first time in years I was alone, without anyone who knew me, so I could say and do what I wanted. Anything, except drink. I detoxed for a week, and I cried for a week. Time to get well.

To learn how to live life on life's terms, not Michael's. They picked me up, dusted me off and gave me a chance to start life all over again.

After three weeks I was allowed brief telephone contact with the outside world, no more than five minutes at a time. Cheryl told me she loved me and that everything would be good in our lives. I told her she was right, and that I was sorry for what I had become. Rehab had taught me that it was possible to have a life without drink or drugs, to live my life one day at a time. I wrote a book about my thirty days in rehab called *Back in Business*. It's amazing, reading it now, to see how convinced I was that my life was sorted, that I really loved my wife, my work and everyone around me. At no point in the book did I ever say that I loved myself. The press found out that I was in rehab, and then the shit really hit the fan. I thought my career was all over, but the public supported me and cared about *me*, not about what was being said. My affair with the public seemed to have no strings whatsoever; their love seemed unconditional. Father Martin sorted me out, and I was clean and sober – but only for a while for, of course, I hadn't confronted any of the real issues that were making me drink. Since that time I've had several relapses and been through many rehabs. Over and over again, I promised I wouldn't drink or take drugs any more. I just didn't get it. I couldn't accept that the addiction had more power than me. At the beginning of addiction, I controlled the drink. Over the years, the drink took control of me and never gave me a choice about who was running who.

Inevitably, all of this was taking its toll on my marriage. We got home to our house in Roydon, near Harlow, and before long I was back to my old ways. Cheryl thought that things would be better if we moved to London – she thought living in the country with nothing to do was half the problem, that I'd be better off where we could have all the help we needed, with the doctors and psychiatrists and AA meetings just round the corner. I agreed – well, I would, wouldn't I? If the doctors were just around the corner in Harley Street, then the clubs would be too.

We found a new home beside the Victoria Gates of Hyde Park, and I soon discovered that if I caused a row, I had the perfect excuse to storm out and go wandering off around town. I desperately wanted to find an environment that I felt at ease in – and that's when I discovered Heaven. Heaven is a huge gay club near Charing Cross. In fact, it was the first gay club I went to, and it had a kind, friendly manager called Paul, who took me under his wing. For most of my early trips to Heaven, I just sat in Paul's office telling him how hard it was becoming for me to live this lie. I rambled on for hours, and Paul listened, which was just what I needed at that time. He understood, he never went to the papers, and he always got me in and out of the club unnoticed. Heaven became my gay bolt hole. One night I ran into Boy George. He took one look at me, lifted up the baseball cap that I always wore on my nights out, and said, 'Hello, what are you doing in here?'

'Just enjoying myself, George. Just having a night out.'

But by this time the word was getting around. People talked about me and wrote about me and started to have opinions on what was turning into the very public break-down of my marriage.

My marriage was indeed crumbling; it wasn't Cheryl's fault, but it wasn't mine either. I realise that she had put her whole life into me. She controlled every single part of me and at no time did I complain about this – I allowed it to happen. Why? I'll give you my reasons why. Some of you will understand – those of you who live in a similarly

115

controlled environment will identify with my predicament – the rest of you probably won't be able to understand how any human being can let anyone control them to that degree.

It allowed me to be totally immersed in my work, which I loved, always have and always will. To have to do anything outside my work I considered time consuming and time wasting. I have never kept a work diary, I rarely answer the phone, I don't like to check the front door to see who's knocking on it – I couldn't even tell you with any real accuracy what time of day it is. I can do early or late, but that's only due to light change. I never make appointments, but somehow turn up. I don't know how long it takes to get anywhere. I've never started or finished work at the same time, although, because it's a life thing, I do manage to eat. I never sleep the same amount of hours, ever. I have hardly ever said, 'I am going to bed now,' or, 'Oh dear, is that the time, I must get up.'

I have never added up exactly how much money I have. I don't remember to write or send Christmas cards or birth-day cards, but many people have received them from me somehow. What exactly does it take to sort this situation out?

My visits to psychiatrists and rehabs were becoming more and more frequent, and I certainly wasn't getting any better. Cheryl came up with millions of fixes: start playing golf, go fishing, go, go, go anywhere, as long as it's not out boozing and drugging and clubbing. All I wanted was to be somewhere other than where I was, to be with someone other than the one I was with. But I didn't know *where* to go. Or *who* I should be with.

I was Cheryl's husband, her lover, her child, and her career. More and more I played on the child aspect. I can't remember how or when it came about, but looking at what I've written has made it all the more obvious what was going on. What was the attraction originally? I can only think, looking back, that she took away the burden of responsibility. All I had to do was perform on demand, which was easy, just like extra time in the playground with none of the homework. All I had to do was behave, do as I was told, just like I did when Cheryl came back after a show. Maurice always found it unbelievable that, after a live theatre show, Cheryl would stand in the dressing room, with all the guests coming in and congratulating me on the show and the excitement of the standing ovation, with her note pad in hand, telling me what was good and bad about my performance. One night she included, 'Oh, by the way, what was all the waffling after the swan routine?' I shrugged, blinking like mad from the salty sweat running into in my eyes, 'Nothing, just improvising,' to which she replied, 'Don't waffle or stray into improvising unless I know about it. I don't like surprises.' I was too exhausted after every show to waste much-needed breath. Even on sarcasm such as, 'I was wondering why I started to lose them.' Deep down I think I was frightened to voice my view because she never got it wrong. She was right, I *was* waffling. I just chose the weirdest times to protest, like on stage. Maybe the chemistry of both of us fighting over who was the actual star is what made it work.

I set off on one of my regular trips to the doctor's unaware that my life was about to change for ever. Mike Browne, my PA, dropped me off; he knew the score well enough by now. Wait in the car, another doctor, another pill, another, 'How are you, Michael? Here, take ten of these.' Thanks, swallow, no reaction, back to hell, the hell in my head. I looked at myself in the passenger window.

'I'll only be a couple of minutes.'

'Okay.' Mike nodded; he looked even more worn out than me and he doesn't drink or do drugs.

117

'Don't bother switching the engine off.'

I walked into yet another expensive session, just wondering if the doctor had any pills that actually worked.

'You know what I think, Michael?'

I didn't answer straight away; instead I sat there calculating how much that sentence had cost me, six words, call it £60.

'I'll tell you what.'

That's two 'Whats'. I hope I'm in on the right day, special offer, two whats for the price of one. He starts off on a long sentence. God knows what that will cost.

'If you don't do what you have to do when you leave here, you will be dead by Christmas.'

I didn't answer.

'It's October now. You don't have much thinking time left.'

I spoke at last. 'You mean, now? Right now?'

'Yes.'

'Right now, this minute?'

'If that's what it takes, yes.'

'Okay.' I stood up. 'Thanks.'

'Right.'

'Bye then.'

Silence. I left the room, went down the stairs, climbed into my car and shut the heavy black door.

Mike broke the silence. 'Home, guv'nor?'

'No, Mike. Take me to a hotel and find me somewhere else to live.'

No questions from Mike. Just a very confident, 'Certainly, guv'nor.'

Mike took me to the Sheraton Hotel in Knightsbridge, ringing ahead to book a suite with an open-ended check-out date. As we drove down Park Lane, a sense of real fear began to enter my body. A sense of the start of the war, into battle, not knowing whether I was going to survive. I can't say I had any real feeling of having done the right thing. I just knew that there would be no more denials of my sexuality, no more pretence, no more fear. No more career?

What would people say if I came out on stage and said, 'Ladies and gentlemen, welcome to the show. My name's Michael and I'm gay?' Several possible scenarios ran through my mind. It was all right for that doctor to tell me to go for gold – he didn't have to do it.

Mike left me in my suite at the Sheraton and drove back home to get as many of my clothes as he possibly could. I wished him luck; I didn't envy him walking into my room, packing a case and confronting Cheryl.

'What are you doing, Mike?'

'Oh, just packing a case for Michael . . .'

'Why?'

'He asked me to get some clothes for him. He's not coming back.'

'Is he going away?'

'Yes.'

'Where?'

'Sorry, Cheryl, he didn't say.'

'So how long is he going to be away for?'

'Er . . . for the rest of his life, I think.'

'Mike, is this a joke?'

'He said he'd ring you to explain.'

Mike returned with several suitcases of ill-matching, hurriedly packed clothes, made sure I was okay to be left alone – and left. I sat on the edge of the hotel bed, the lamps low. I rang Cheryl. She asked me where I was and when I was coming home. I told her that I was in a hotel in London, but not which one, and that I needed to be on my own. I told her the doctor's prognosis. She did not agree with it.

'Come home and we can sort this out.'

'Cheryl, you cannot sort this out. No one can sort this out. I have been trying to tell you for years that I am gay.'

Cheryl buried my confession straight away.

'Michael, you're not gay. It's just a phase you go through every now and again, a phase that gets worse when you have a drink. You can't be gay. We've made love together for years. You love me. You know you do.'

I had never been good at dealing with Cheryl when that certain sadness entered her tone of voice. I took a deep breath and backed off.

'Look, Cheryl, I have to have time on my own.'

The way she pleaded for me to come back still pains me today as I write this.

'We can sort this out, I know we can.'

But the only one who could sort it out was me, not we. I ended the call abruptly, the coward's way of dealing with problems. I had to get out of the relationship, out of the hotel, out of my head, out – just to discover what being gay was.

I decided to head for Old Compton Street. I'd heard that this was the most famous gay street in London. It was Friday night, and time for me to find out what it was all about. I changed into some new clothes from my suitcase, took a deep breath, walked with purpose down the street and hailed a cab.

'Old Compton Street, please.'

The cab driver didn't even raise an eyebrow. 'Certainly, Michael. Off out for the night, are we?'

'Yes.'

'Well, good luck to ya.'

Old Compton Street is right in the middle of Soho – one long straight street full of gay bars, restaurants, clubs, clothes shops and sex shops. To the untrained eye – which mine was on that first night – it wasn't easy, apart from the bleedin' obvious, to pick out who exactly was a gay guy, who was in a couple, who was a gay girl or who was straight. I walked down the street; it was a summer evening, and I felt like the king in his new clothes being stared at by quite a few queens. Danny Kaye's voice ran through my head: 'Oh, the king is in the altogether . . .'

Many of the bars were open-fronted, allowing the early evening drinkers to spill out on to the street. I picked a bar that looked busier than all the others, squeezed past one man, past another and made my way to the bar, leaving a trail of comments in my wake.

'That's Michael Barrymore!'

'No!'

'Well, it looks like him!'

'What's he doing in 'ere?'

All eyes were turning in my direction, but somehow I managed to keep mine trained on the ceiling, as if there were something very important stuck on it. Eventually, I forced myself to make eye contact, a half-smile, a half-nod, until I found myself doing it so much that it must have looked as if I had a severe facial tic. Thank God a small group of lads broke the spell.

The tallest of the three lined his face up with mine and cocked it to one side.

'Michael.'

He seemed to me to be shouting it.

'What are you doing in here, Michael?'

I spoke through my fixed smile. 'Just having a drink.'

'And where are you going afterwards?'

I wished I knew! I mumbled out a weak, 'Oh, I don't know, ha ha ha.' I hadn't been this nervous since my first stage appearance.

'Why don't you come with us?'

As if I knew all the places to go, I said, 'Where are you going?'

'We're having one more pint here, then we're going to the White Swan.'

My face must have given away my ignorance. I was the new boy on the block again. 'Oh, where's that then?'

'It's a pub in the East End of London. It's great. Come with us, you'll love it.'

Suddenly I felt calmer in that noisy, smoky bar than I had ever felt before. These were the first three blokes I had ever met under these circumstances, and they had made me welcome in their world. I hesitated for a moment about going with these people I had never met before to a pub I had never heard of. Then I heard the doctor's words again.

'You have to be what you have to be and do what you have to do.'

During the taxi ride to the White Swan, the three guys told me about all the different clubs and bars around London. The gay scene was clearly much bigger than I imagined, full of people from every background. I was on my single man's honeymoon, enjoying all the new sights and sounds, taking it all in.

The White Swan was a very traditional-looking East End pub – just full of men. I remember thinking how loud the music was. One particular track stood out for obvious reasons: Gloria Gaynor belting out 'I Will Survive'. Well, I thought, if she can survive to the end of the track, so can I.

It was dark inside: men dancing with men, men talking with men, some girlie, some butch, some screaming, some looking hard, some looking limp, a few too young, a lot too old, some leaning left, some leaning right, some holding friends' bums a little too tight, lots of denim, lots of shirts, the odd one proud in their sister's skirt, a fat one, a thin one, three in drag, one sitting on his own guarding his mate's bag, a rich one, a poor one, no beggars, no thieves, dustmen, postmen, civil servants, half a dozen punks, and a whole heap of sleaze!

When you squeeze your way through a crowd, people usually do their best to make a space for you. I volunteered to get the drinks in for my new-found friends, and with lots of 'Excuse me's made my way to the bar – and every time I passed a body there was more of a thrust forward than a shift back, which I didn't mind. I was surprised at how relaxed I felt – while everyone else looked totally surprised at seeing me. I was even more surprised at how easily I answered their questions.

'Hello, Michael. Nice to see you. Are you gay?'

'Yes, I am.'

Not too loud so that everyone could hear, but loud enough.

The atmosphere got higher and higher, and I went along with it. I lost count of how many people came to introduce themselves and welcome me. Just before 10 pm I found a small patio area at the rear of the pub; I grabbed a piece of fresh air and sat and smoked. I felt good; I didn't feel as though I had walked into the wrong place. I had no urgent wish to leave. I could hear the DJ talking, announcing the cabaret, so I stood up and found that I could see the small stage without being seen.

The entertainment for the evening was Dave Lynn, a drag act. He came on and said, straight away, "'Ere, what about Barrymore!'

I lowered my head and wanted to disappear in a cloud of smoke. There had been tabloid rumours going around about my sexuality, but nothing had been confirmed. The guys in the pub who had seen me earlier all gave a big 'Ooooh!'

'Well,' said Dave, 'he's not here, is he?'

To this day I don't know why I did what I did. Instead of keeping out of sight, I put one foot on the stage, sprang up on to the platform and announced, 'Yes, I'm here!'

The reaction from the crowd was electric. They seemed to carry me with their applause and warmth. I felt happy, safe and loved for being whatever I was. I burst into song, to the tune of 'New York, New York . . .'

'Start spreading the news, I'm happy today, start spreading the news, I'm gay!'

The crowd roared their approval.

Did I do it to find out the effect on the crowd? Yes. Did I mean what I said? Yes. Was I happy with my decision? Yes. Did I really think through the ramifications of what I had said? No.

Dave Lynn and I continued to improvise our un-rehearsed routine, the crowd laughed, clapped, roared, and I spent the rest of the evening being congratulated and kissed by, it seemed, every man and woman in the White Swan.

I was born again on that Friday night. I was welcomed to the world of live and let live. I was still Michael Barrymore, I was still a comedian. The next day I was walking through Knightsbridge, with my baseball cap lowered to facilitate moving around relatively unrecognised, when I saw an *Evening Standard* poster with the large black type reading BARRYMORE'S GAY. I lowered my cap even further and carried on walking.

'Oh shit.'

Later that day, my PA Mike rang, his usual jolly self whatever the circumstances.

'Hello, guv'nor. Have a nice night?'

'Yeah, I did, as it happens. I went to a pub called the White Swan.'

'Did you indeed?'

'Yeah, and I got up on stage. It's a gay pub, you know.'

'Is it?'

'And I told them I was gay.'

'Did you?'

'Yes.'

Mike continued. 'And I hear that you also took your wedding ring off and threw it into the crowd.'

'No I didn't. Who told you I did that?'

Mike rustled something at the end of the phone. 'Er, most of the newspapers.'

'Newspapers? How did they find out I was there?'

I could have bitten my own tongue off for asking such a stupid question. Mike moved me to another hotel, a small, very discreet one near Kensington Palace. I had a feeling I was going to need all the support I could muster. Not many people stay on a boat that's going through angry seas; most of them jump ship. A few of them have stayed on board, gone below, battened down the hatches and waited for calm waters.

From the moment I sang 'I'm gay' and the press was told, the going got very rocky indeed.

From my hideaway hotel, which very few people know about and which, knowing my life, is probably better kept that way, plans were made about how to deal with my situation. How would the public react? My friends? My workmates? My television company? My wife? Did it matter what people thought?

Yes, it certainly did. Whatever I have done in life, I've always sought the approval of at least one other person, more if possible. I'm not capable of making a decision on my own. I knew one thing: there was a good chance that my career was over. Saying you're gay does not go down well in a lot of households. How would people react when they discovered that a man who had entertained them for years in their own front room, a man who did family shows for mums, dads, brothers, sisters, aunts, uncles, grandmas and grandpas, all ages from eight to eighty, who for years had wanted to be part of their household, suddenly turned out to be gay? Man of the people, my kind of people – was I still going to be their kind of person? Would they leave their doors open to me? Could I have survived if I kept my secret? No! Are some things better left untouched? Yes!

I always manage to get myself into tight corners, and for someone who suffers from claustrophobia that's not a very good idea. Two days had passed without contact from Cheryl. I only spoke to Anne, my agent, and Mike, my PA. We all agreed that in the circumstances, it would be better for me to get away before the press discovered where I was. I rang my producer, Maurice Leonard, and got straight to the point.

'You got a passport, Maurice?'

'Yes.'

'Can you spare a few days?'

'Yes.'

'I'll have a car pick you up.'

'Where are we going?'

'I don't know yet. I need some fresh air – preferably not British.'

Four hours later we were heading for Chicago – I just needed some peace. The most peaceful part was the flight. Who was there to greet us at Chicago? The press. They really are so thoughtful sometimes. I said nothing as Maurice and I pushed our small cases to the waiting limousine. The questions flew about our heads.

'Mr Barrymore, could you confirm you're gay?'

Silence.

'Mr Barrymore, how has your wife taken the news?'

Silence. Click, click, flash, flash.

'Michael, please just give us a statement and we'll leave you alone.'

Silence. Enter car. Shut door. Wind window down.

'I'll give you a statement.'

Pens at the ready.

'Aren't the nights drawing in?'

Limo accelerates away, journalists run to waiting taxis and the chase begins. Later that evening faxes fly into the hotel – and every headline has the word 'gay' in it.

Maurice and I ventured out into the Chicago night and found a small restaurant, nice and quiet and out of the way. The waiter bore a strong resemblance to the builder from the Village People, although he didn't have what you might call a builder's voice.

'Oooh, mmmm,' he said, 'I know who you are.'

'Really?' said Maurice.

Barbie the Builder was getting very animated. 'Look, I've got a picture of you two! Some people came in earlier and gave me this little picture and said if I were to see you guys to be sure and give them a call and tell them you're here.'

Maurice and I just stared.

Barbie became headmistressie. 'So what have you been up to, then?'

'I've just come out.'

Barbie squealed with delight. 'Let's go hide you out back!'

We were seated with two bowls of hot spaghetti Bolognese. Barbie was having a wonderful day.

'The doors are locked. You'll be safe here.'

On the other side of the locked double doors, right across the restaurant, I could make out a crowd of photographers desperately trying to get a picture of us slurping pasta – and it didn't take much imagination to guess the sort of captions they'd use. Suddenly I wasn't feeling very hungry, but, being of a generous nature, I let the photographers have some, Frisbee-style. As my pasta-laden plate spun heavenwards, Barbie grabbed his chest in horror and delight. (Note: simultaneous horror and delight can only be achieved by homosexual men. Not advised for hetero-sexuals, or even bisexuals.) Then he screamed at full throttle and charged at the doors with a heavily-laden sweet trolley. While the photographers picked themselves up and removed the evening's food, Maurice and I left by another exit. Barbie waved us off.

'You boys are so kewl!'

There were no pictures in the papers the next day.

My return to London was the usual routine: disembark, clear passport control, retrieve luggage, clear customs, fight through crowd. There were no photographers, but a lot of journalists, lots of noise. I kept my head down and said nothing as I was guided through the mob, then one sentence rang out above the rest. An Australian accent. 'Is it true, Mr Barrymore? You have Aids?'

Even the other journalists turned to stare in disbelief. I could feel the blood seeping into my mouth from biting my tongue. I can still see that guy's face watching mine being pulled away from making hard contact with his.

I returned to my hideaway hotel to discover that Cheryl had moved out of the Bayswater house and flown to the south of France in an unsuccessful attempt to lose the press who had been camping out on our doorstep. I was asked to join her for a summit meeting in the penthouse of the most famous hotel the south of France has to offer: the Martinez at Cannes. No half measures for Cheryl. She had a girlfriend, Tracey, with her; I took Tommy, my security guard.

The minute we landed, Tom and I were chased by photographers on motorbikes. I know from personal experience just how dangerous a press chase can be; I have lived to write about it, Diana did not. It's so easy to get caught up in the cat-and-mouse game. You get a natural buzz trying to lose them, you get faster and faster. It still happens; and although I should know better, sometimes they press too many buttons and I react by trying to lose them. You knows it's dangerous, but you just think 'Sod 'em.' So I put my foot down, exceed speed limits, shoot red lights, cut corners.

Tommy and I outran the bikes and got to the Martinez before them − but, of course, everyone knew where we were. By the time I was inside, the photographers were gathering in crowds around the entrance; Cheryl, meanwhile, was high above it all in the penthouse. It was the perfect setting for our romantic reunion. Cheryl was looking great; calm and smiling. A bottle of champagne was cooling, honeymoon-style, by the bed. All we had to do was kiss and make up.

We talked, never once mentioning the media circus that was building up beneath us.

'We can make it,' said Cheryl. 'We can get through all this nonsense.'

I said nothing, just smiled. I wanted to say, 'It's not nonsense, it's true that I'm gay and I want to leave and have a life of my own.' But I couldn't. Instead we kissed, went to bed and made love.

There was a knock on the door while we were in bed − room service delivering another bottle of wine. We giggled like newlyweds as the waiter poured the wine with a 'I know what you're up to' grin. It was late afternoon, a small oasis of tranquillity in our lives. So: what do you do when you are about to tell the person you've lived with for eighteen years that you have a huge problem to solve? Simple! You fly to the south of France, book into the most expensive suite, drink champagne and make love. Well, you do if you're Cheryl, anyway. It didn't work for me. I still wanted to get the message across: that I was gay, and that I still cared for her, but I could no longer live with her.

Tommy and Tracey picked us up and Cheryl suggested we all went down to the beach to catch some sun – and to be photographed, of course. The papers the next day said that Cheryl and I had never sat that close before.

Of course, this was exactly what Cheryl wanted, and I realised that. She wanted us to be seen together so that the whole world would know that there was nothing wrong. Later that evening, the four of us ate at a beachside café, Cheryl laying out a plan of how we were going to deal with all this 'press nonsense'. She was back in charge – of her husband, her lover, her child, her career. I felt trapped by my own inability to speak up. I left the table; the child in me reacted as all do, sulked and ran away. Tommy came after me to calm me down. We met up in the suite to talk things over, but there were constant knocks on the door. The press had secured rooms next to us – we were cornered. Tommy had to keep opening the door to say, 'Mr Barrymore has no comment.'

I was about to say, 'Cheryl, this has to stop. We can't pretend nothing's wrong,' when we heard a rustle of paper under the door – and there, in huge black and white letters, still hot from the hotel fax, was the front page of the next day's *Daily Mirror*: BARRYMORE: YES, I AM GAY.

Cheryl's eyes locked with mine. 'What the hell is this? How could you do this to me?'

I didn't reply.

Cheryl held her right hand in a fist. The diamond solitaire, a Christmas present, shone like only real diamonds can.

'You see this ring you bought me?'

I said nothing.

'Well, you wear it!'

It made a perfect cut as she punched it into my left eye. The blood flowed down my face, and I caught a little on my finger.

'Well, that proves it's a real diamond, I suppose.'

A few more kicks and blows were followed by a torrent of verbal abuse. I never hit back, but I had to push her away to stop her from clawing into me. Being tiny, she fell down in a dramatic heap. I have always believed that it's wrong to hit women, but I also believe that just because it's a woman beating you up, she doesn't have the right to use long sharp nails or pointed stilettos.

It was time to leave. Tommy and I booked into a nearby hotel and I flew back to London the next morning. As I left Heathrow, Mike told me that Cheryl had phoned through to say that she wanted to leave right away as well, even though she was already booked on the one o'clock flight from Nice.

'Why are you telling me this, Mike?'

'Because she wants a private jet to be waiting for her at a nearby airstrip.'

'But she's flying today.'

'She wants to go right now.'

'How long till the flight she's booked on?'

'One hour.'

'Why can't she wait an hour?'

'Because she's Cheryl and she wants to go home now.'

'And how much will this private jet cost?'

'Ten thousand pounds.'

I phoned Cheryl and asked her why she was doing this.

'It's your fault,' she said. 'You put me in this mess.'

'But Cheryl, it's ten thousand pounds for an hour's flight. This is ridiculous.'

'Michael, I've only just started.'

Phone disconnects. Cheryl didn't take the private plane. As it prepared for take-off, one of the engines malfunctioned and she had to take the scheduled flight after all. Ten thousand pounds was saved – just as well, as things were about to become very expensive indeed.

6

Out in the World

I moved out into rented accomodation first in Chelsea Harbour and then in Docklands, with drink and drugs as my constant companions. Cheryl wanted me back; she even suggested that I could 'do my thing', as she now called it, as long as we could work it out. I wanted that too: but then, I wanted everything. I wanted to be with her, but not to be 'with' her; I wanted freedom, but I wanted us still to be 'Cheryl and Michael'. I wanted to be gay, I wanted to be married. In other words, I didn't know what I wanted.

It was easy for that doctor to tell me to do what I had to do – but it was never going to be quite as simple as that. Learning to live on my own, to form my own relationships, to deal with the separation from Cheryl and the intense media scrutiny of my life was more difficult than anything

I had ever imagined. Fortunately for me, I had a few good friends who helped me through the hardest parts.

I met Sir Ian McKellen, who spent a lot of time talking to me, giving me advice, always reminding me how hard this was for Cheryl as well as for me. In fact, he offered to talk to Cheryl, to be a peacemaker, but she was having none of it. Ian and I started spending a bit of time round at each other's places – he lived in Docklands as well – and I got to know a few of his friends, including Michael Cashman, who had starred in *EastEnders* as their first gay character and gone on to become a high-profile campaigner for gay rights.

Michael was great: his party piece was to sing *Gypsy*, the musical – every part, every number – after we'd had a few drinks in someone's flat. I was starting to enjoy this new gay world I'd become part of, but Cheryl hated it. She felt that a new group of people were controlling me – and you have to remember that Cheryl and I were still working together. We were making a series of *My Kind of Music*, and it was hell. Our private problems were putting incredible pressure on our professional relationship, and the cracks were beginning to show.

More support came from an unexpected source. I was in rehab at the Marchwood Priory in Southampton, where Austin Tate was the chief psychiatrist. Out of desperation to find neutral ground, I opted to return to rehab on this occasion, using it as a safe house. Austin Tate was now aware of my sexuality, as my spectacular self-outing couldn't really be missed by anyone who read a paper. He believed it was true and not in my mind, and he knew the added problem was Cheryl not accepting the fact. He made the comment that we were very strong people to deal with and, whenever he got us together, almost impossible. He managed to get Cheryl to come to The Priory to sit and referee our discussion. She wasn't in the best frame of mind, as she was used to running the ship. When she had met Austin prior to this, when he was brought in to help with my addictions, she had loved him.

This time, she wasn't smiling much when he said, 'Cheryl, Michael is gay.' She gave him a look which I knew meant, don't tell me what he is or isn't, and replied, 'Austin, he is not gay. This is just his way of playing up.' Austin took a trained psychiatric pause, looked at me and said, 'Well, are you?' I needed extra strength not to back out, because I was doing this without booze. 'Yes I am.'

Cheryl had an amazing ability to change direction. Glaring at Austin, she said, 'You lot have made him like this with all this rehab/AA nonsense.' She hated AA, the ones who had, in her mind, taught me to think for myself – even to the point of saying, not long after my first visit to rehab, 'You're not an alcoholic. It's the whiskey. If you just drank white wine you would be fine.' I, being an alcoholic, obviously agreed and ordered white wine. Cases of it.

Austin took the opportunity to tackle what he thought was another problem. 'Cheryl, do you think anything would be gained by you attending the clinic for a while?'

Another Cheryl warning sign was the deep intake of breath and shoulders rolled back to a balletic position. 'What are you saying?'

I thought, nice one, Austin. He attempted a smile, but it twisted. 'I think you need to deal with some issues, that only you can sort out.' He carried on, despite her now almost hovering above the chair, 'I think it would help matters all round, if the two of you were on equal ground.'

Cheryl did not get into the conversation, it was too near the mark. He wasn't saying what she wanted to hear, he did not agree with her, that I was on a flight of fancy with the gay thing and, worse, he was implying that champagne and brandy every night meant she might have a drinking problem. She stood up, would not look at me and barely at him and said, 'When you are back on course dealing with his problems, then we can talk. And if I need your help, I'll decide where and when. God, I thought you were supposed to be helping me!' Austin let out a heavy sigh, I raised all six of my brows and Cheryl left the room, digging deep into her bag for her cigarettes. I didn't have to see her to know that she would be drawing very heavily on the first cigarette, as she always did when she wasn't best pleased.

I'm not afraid to say that I am one of the few artists who have made a career out of touring rehab clinics. On this occasion, after the Cheryl meeting, I managed to get on with get-well time. Austin was getting some rest-from-Cheryl time under his belt and we were getting to know each other better. Austin was broad shouldered with grey peppered hair. He had kind eyes, and a cricket-playing, tough exterior; he was a soft-centred Yorkshire man who did a mean job as a psychiatrist.

'Oh, hello, Austin,' I said.

He looked at me over the top of his expensive half-moon glasses, giving it that real doctor look. 'I have something for you which I think may cheer you up,' he announced. He then began to read from a single sheet of paper.

My dearest Michael,

I was so sad to hear that once again you have had to be re-admitted to The Priory for treatment. I so hope this time you will find the help to make you well and come back to us all who love you dearly. I have been thinking of you since I read of your most recent news. You have given so much happiness and pleasure to me and my family over the years, as you have millions of others. The least we can do is to be there for you when you need all the love and care you can get.

At the moment I am writing this to you from Majorca, where I am on holiday with the boys. As soon as I return and you are well I would love to meet up and have some time together. The boys send you their very best wishes. Much love from me, and please let me know when we can meet.

Love, Diana.

Austin tilted his head back and gave me a broad smile. It wasn't every day that one of his patients received a letter from the Princess of Wales and I guess he couldn't hide his own excitement.

At first I thought the letter was a hoax – some ruse to try and help make me feel better. After three attempts by Austin to convince me the letter from Diana was real and that it required a response, pins and needles began to lock into the bottom half of my legs to such an extent that I thought I might soon be able to claim handicap benefit.

How would you feel, if you were me – the no-nothing kid from Bermondsey, with not one school certificate, a terrible speller, the skinny poor boy who receives a letter from the Princess of Wales, the world's most famous person?

For a moment, I felt like I wanted to be with my mates in The Lilliput, or The Dun Cow (two of Bermondsey's more renowned drinking establishments), having just come from steering a barge into Butler's Wharf, when you just throw casually into the conversation, 'Oh, have you seen this? It's a letter I just received from Diana, saying she wants to meet me.' Yeah, right, dream on!

I can only say to you, that as excited as *you* may get meeting famous people, I'm not any different. I feel the same nervous shake, and I start talking to them with a different voice that sounds nothing like my own. Making stupid remarks and staring too long into their eyes. It happens to some people who come up to me in the street to talk. But I'm no different.

Then, a few weeks later, Mike, my PA, got a message from Paul Burrell, the man who made all Diana's contacts for her, saying, 'Diana was wondering why Michael hasn't rung.' I sent a message back saying, 'I didn't want to bother you,' to which the reply was, 'Well, bother me!'

The first meeting was arranged by Martin Bashir, who had done the big TV interview with Diana and had become a trusted friend of Diana and myself. He rang my agent, and the arrangements were made. Diana was in one of her 'I don't want to talk to the press' moods, so it was all very cloak and dagger. It was reported in the press the day after that she had left Kensington Palace, changed cars in Cadogan Square and 'disappeared into the night'. In fact, she only drove across the park to my house – at the time I was still living at the Bayswater house. The first meeting place of 'The Princess and the Pauper'. I was still married to Cheryl. Among the stipulations from Kensington Palace was that the meeting between Diana and myself would be at my home in Bayswater and would be just between the two of us. The news was not well received by my wife. Cheryl went along with the arrangement, albeit reluctantly.

Our first meeting was made for 7 pm. When the bell rang at exactly 7 pm I thought that that would be the moment when either the hoax would end or the moment would become reality. Then in walked the Princess of Wales as large as life. 'Hello,' she said. 'How are you feeling?' Up until then, I was extremely nervous, but the moment she walked in she had this amazing ability to put you at ease.

Kiss, kiss, we sat in the front room and started talking about my shows. I was impressed by how much of my stuff she'd seen, and how well she remembered what happened in each one. It was as if we'd known each other all our lives. My housekeeper, Lena, knocked at the door and came in wearing an amazing black and white uniform – amazing because none of the staff ever wore uniforms. She asked if we would like a drink. I was about to ask for wine – but Diana asked for water.

I agreed that water would be a great idea.

'So,' I said. 'What do I call you? Princess Diana?'

'Just Diana. I'm not a princess any more.'

Her eyes were darting around the room, taking in all the details. She pointed at a framed photograph of Cheryl. 'Oh! Is this wifey?'

'Yes ...' This first meeting was just before Cheryl and I separated; 'wifey' was, in fact, four floors up, at the top of the house.

Lena came back in with a tray, her uniform even more starched than it had been before, her eyes wide with terror. Lena comes from the Philippines; I suppose her idea of a royal lady was Imelda Marcos, which is enough to terrify anybody. As she walked towards Diana, her knees were buckling, and with each step she was a few inches shorter – a perfect Groucho Marx impersonation. I thought she was going to faint, but somehow she managed to right herself and get out of the room in one piece. I had to give her a few days off to recover from her ordeal.

I had always thought that Diana grew more beautiful the older she got. What I most remember was the size of her eyes. She looked stunning, and wore a beautiful cream trouser suit.

Bear in mind that this meeting was not long after I had 'come out' in quite a public way. Diana told me, 'I want you to know that you can come through all this – you just have to be strong.' She explained how hard things had been for her, during recent difficult times in her life. How much her own close friends had helped her through. She made it clear that without the support of her two best girlfriends she doubted whether she would have coped with the constant media attention when her marriage break-up was made public. She told me that she wanted to be there for me. It was pretty strange really, hearing that the Princess of Wales wanted to be there for me. I keep asking myself *Why? Why me?* She did try and explain this once. 'Oh, by the way, I have something to thank you for,' she said. 'Every time you appear on the front pages of the tabloids you keep me off!'

When you are sitting on the same couch as Diana, just a few inches away from her, it does take a little while to settle down. It's not that she unnerved me; I was used to meeting royalty. I had done the *Royal Variety* shows and had met Prince Charles, the Queen and Princess Margaret – but that was work. This was so different; here I was chatting to Diana in my house about my own personal problems. She was incredibly gentle with me. That first meeting was all about gaining my trust and helping me understand that she was going to be there for me. I think she truly believed that we were both very similar in personality. There was an immediate connection.

I remember Cheryl opened the door to the lounge where Diana and I were sitting chatting and announced in a firm voice, 'Diana, your car is waiting.' I can't tell you how much I would have loved at that point for them to have got on, but it was clear from my piggy-in-the-middle position that the words 'We must do lunch' weren't about to be forthcoming!

After Diana left my house that night I felt a huge weight had been lifted from my shoulders. Just the very fact of sharing my problems with somebody who so obviously genuinely cared. She was a very special lady. She never once attempted to explain how sensitive our meetings were.

She didn't stress the need for confidentiality, she just knew instinctively that what we talked about would remain between the two of us. As it has and shall remain so.

I felt very emotional when she had left. I felt it took a lot of guts for somebody in her position, who had been through so much, to decide to just drop what she was doing and come and help me. It was very humbling and I felt I was getting advice and immense support from the highest level possible. I will always remember those eyes. Diana had her own air of vulnerability, and I think this showed in her eyes; she was able to show every emotion through them.

All our subsequent meetings were also held in private – no mean feat for someone who was the most photographed person on the planet – and her mate who was quite well known himself.

Not surprisingly, it didn't take long for our meeting to become the talk of Fleet Street. I'm not sure how these things get leaked; clearly it wasn't myself or Diana who let it out. There was much speculation in the tabloids about why we met and what we were supposed to have talked about. It made us both laugh. There were never any rules as to how our relationship would carry on – if at all. Though I have to say, by this time I dearly wanted it to continue.

When she left she gave me her personal telephone number and we soon began to talk on the phone almost every day. Her messages increased in their warmth of tone.

I also began to receive handwritten notes from Diana. They often said for me to call her at anytime if I had a problem. I didn't always ring straight away; I didn't want to bother her. Then one day I was playing golf, my new hobby, at Denham and my phone went off – it was Diana. 'Why haven't you contacted me?' she demanded. I told her I didn't want to bother her. 'I *want* you to bother me,' she replied with a laugh in her voice. 'When are you coming round to see me?'

I made an arrangement to go and see her at Kensington Palace for what was the first of many private meetings. At the time of my first visit I had just taken delivery of a new black Bentley Azure, which I drove to the Palace apartments – I wasn't about to hide or go in some form of disguise. I thought if we were going to meet I should be completely open about it. Diana saw where I had parked the car and, after her comment that it was a bit flash, promptly told me to move it, as Princess Margaret would go mad since it was blocking her space. Needless to say, Diana's apartment was beautifully furnished – though the first thing I noticed were all the photos of the boys.

She always seemed to know what I had been doing and where I had been. I wasn't the only person in Diana's life at the time, but she had this uncanny way of caring for the ones she felt close to. In the end, I suppose Diana became a sort of counsellor to me. I think our talks were good for both of us, but I can only speak from my side. I became very close to her and began to look forward to the next time we would meet.

As time went on, I got to know a lot of her private staff at Kensington Palace – Diana always made sure she introduced me to them. Paul Burrell was one of the first of her inner circle that I met.

One Friday she appeared distant and a little tired. I asked her what was wrong. 'Oh, nothing,' she said. 'I've just been rushing around because I'm going off to Paris tomorrow with Dodi. But I have to be back next week as it's the boys' half term. Do you want to meet next Wednesday?'

'Yeah, next Wednesday would be great.'

In the early hours of Sunday morning I was in a London club when one of the resident paramedics came up to me and said, 'Michael, we have some bad news for you.' They sat me down and told me that Diana was dead.

I just broke down, I couldn't help it. This beautiful woman who had just stepped quietly into my life had been snatched away. Abandoned again for getting too close. That's what my head told me.

For the week or so running up to Diana's funeral I stayed at a small hotel just off The Mall. The few times I did venture out, the sight of so many people walking towards Kensington Palace with flowers, combined with a quietness London had never experienced, took grief and gave it a face. Everyone, whatever their background, had the same look.

The only communication Cheryl and I had was her telling me that we had been invited to the funeral service at Westminster Abbey. Even though we were at war with each other we met at the house to be driven to the Abbey the morning of the service. On a cleared route to the entrance we passed thousands of people that had turned out to fill the streets. As we got out of our car even the motors of the hundreds of cameras seemed to be silenced. The entire *Who's Who* of the world were gathering and none of us did any more than politely nod to each other. Cheryl told me to adjust something with my suit, to which I replied under my breath, 'Give it a break will you.' We were not a couple, we had just arrived together. We were shown to our places inside. I went through the service just following the order, but straight ahead of me was Dodi's father, Mohamed al-Fayed. The lights of the Abbey made his eyes look so huge that I got transfixed. It seemed as if he never blinked, he just stared hard in the hope he would see his son. Elton John sang, the choir sung in perfect harmony and when Diana's brother gave his speech it was incorrectly reported that everyone in the Abbey applauded. In fact, his condemnation of certain media caused an immediate reaction in the public listening outside. The first we were aware of it, was when we heard what sounded like heavy rainfall coming from the back of the Abbey. It was the crowd clapping – a sound which swept up to the entrance forcing all inside to complete the shower of applause.

As the service finished and we filed out, I cried like you do when it actually makes you feel sick. On the way back to the car I broke away from Cheryl to go over to the crowd. It seemed the right thing to do. I don't think Cheryl approved. I wasn't seeking approval from anyone. A few news reporters asked me if I would talk on air and I declined. Mike drove us back to the Bayswater house. I never sat down. I gave into my feelings and asked Mike to get me out of there. The funeral procession was on its way out of London to Diana's final resting place. The TV covered the momentous journey as her car found its way through the endless fall of flowers from the thousands of people who lined the streets. I went to the airport and waited in the lounge while the coverage of her journey was still being televised live. I cried and I'm not sure it was all for Diana.

It's very easy for me to say now that if Diana was still around perhaps a lot of things in my life would not have happened. The strength she gave me during our relationship was only just beginning to change my life. She made me believe in myself and she was one of very few women I could talk to in an honest and open way. What she taught me about myself had begun to take effect.

When certain people have gone out of my life, that's when I have been on very rocky ground. I tend to invest a lot of my emotion in a reliance on other people. As bad or weak as that may sound, it's true. When Diana died I began to lose it again – and go back to my old ways. I missed Diana that much, I just couldn't cope with a future without her at least being around.

The press have always said that 'I chase and adore public attention and that was my undoing'. But that's what makes me tick and what makes me work. So if you move that on logically to a time when, five years ago, I was led to believe that the mass of people was taken away from me, it's not surprising I felt completely empty. It becomes a huge loss. Just like Diana was a loss to so many people. The press has always accused me of not being able to exist without an audience. It's more than that; I have a relationship with my audience. Rightly or wrongly, I have invested my entire life in having a relationship with my audience. Diana was one very special part of my audience.

You never realise how much people mean to you till they have gone. Diana had this amazing ability to be able to sift through other people's lives and help them. It was the special gift she had and wanted to give to the world. She gave it to me and I think the truth was I began to fall for her the first time we met. She knew that too, and I will never forget her.

As soon as Cheryl and I had stopped living together, I started going out a lot. I felt that I'd done what the doctor had ordered, I'd made my decision and come out, so the drinking and the drugs would no longer be a problem. I'd sorted myself out, and if I went out and had a drink it was just because I was having a good time. What I didn't realise was that I was in the grip of a disease, and that it was pulling me further and further down.

I enjoyed going out on the gay scene, not least because there were always loads of drugs around in a hedonistic party atmosphere. I had a couple of boyfriends as well – the first time that I'd been able to see anyone for more than just a one-night stand. It was early days for me, and I wasn't ready to handle a relationship; after being married for eighteen years, I couldn't just suddenly step into a gay life without there being some problems. I wasn't promiscuous – I wasn't with a different man every night. Once I'd got used to someone, that was the person I wanted to be with.

One of my boyfriends, Steve, moved in with me, and I found it very difficult to adjust to that, not least because he was about twenty years younger than me. I was always moaning, 'Don't make me feel like your father!', but you've got to allow people to act their age. I wasn't very forgiving at this time, and of course I was always drinking, which makes it very difficult to carry on any kind of relationship at all.

I found it hard to introduce Steve to people as 'my partner'. It felt strange and embarrassing; I preferred to say, 'This is my mate, Steve,' and leave it at that. When I finally plucked up the courage to say, 'This is my partner,' Maurice used to take the piss out of me mercilessly. 'Oooh, your partner, is it? You mean your shag!' And I got very nervous about being seen in public with a boyfriend. If we were coming through the airport, for instance, I'd pull my cap down over my face and try to disappear into the crowd. I'd always be going, 'Are they looking at us? Are they looking at us?' It was ridiculous: of course they were bloody looking at us! I'm 6 foot 3 inches for Christ's sake – how did I think I was going to hide from anyone? But I couldn't face that. I wanted all the nice bits of being gay without any of the shit that went with it – and that ain't reality.

The awards season was upon us, and I was nominated in three categories for the 1997 National Television Awards. Instead of taking Steve, it had been arranged that I would go over to the Bayswater house and that Cheryl and I would travel to the Royal Albert Hall together. Cheryl had it all arranged. I still managed to maintain a level of 'Do as you are told', for the sake of the business. As Mike drove us across Hyde Park, Cheryl went into manager mode.

My first school photograph at St Joseph's RC. Even at the age of eight, I was happy to be in front of the camera

One of the rare times the family was all together and dad held me in his arms. At my sister's confirmation, from left to right, brother John, my sister Anne, mother Margaret and my father George

21 Darnay House (3rd Floor) Bermondsey, my birthplace and childhood home

Brush with a Body, in 1966, my first amateur dramatic role playing the Irish chimney sweep. Here I am making my exit with the sack!

Rock band Fine China at the K52 Club, Frankfurt 1968. I'm the one with the long hair, not smiling! From left to right, Johnny, Rob, Mike, Bob, Alan, and me at the front

Butlin's Clacton, aged 17. Would you wear a jacket like that for £7 per week?

My first publicity shot. The suit was in fact bright yellow and purple with a velvet bow tie. Pure class!

Doing impressions my way on the TV show Who Do You Do? in 1976

MICHAEL BARRYMORE

Management:
TREVOR GEORGE
A. T. P. M.   E. A. A.
42 Marldon Road, Torquay
Tel: Torquay 63752

"R"

The first publicity shot of Cheryl & me for the London Evening News

Our wedding day, 10th June 1976

My first big break at the Showboat in the Strand, London, where Cheryl and I first met in 1975

*Performing the GI Routine on
The Michael Barrymore Show,
Thames Television, 1983*

*Russ Abbot's Madhouse 1981-2.
As the Weatherman. Well, my
version anyway*

A magical child on another magical day filming My Kind of People. My favourite format

The very first National Television Awards 1995 – the only time they ever used this award design

Filming My Kind of Music – I just don't understand why some people don't take me seriously

Royal Variety Performance 1993.
A memorable night for me, as this
took my career to another level.
Cilla wasn't quite sure what to do
with the Queen's hand

My Kind of Music.
It's no job for a man!

Taking a break in Florida. You would think, after spending 4 hours getting this kite off the ground, I would look a lot happier!

The only problem with fishing back then was that it gave me too much time to think, probably not the best idea

THE AWARD WINNING

MICHAEL BARRYMORE *Laid Back* **ON TOUR**

SEE REVERSE FOR TOUR DETAILS

My live UK tour in 1998 that also went on to tour NZ in 1999. Without those feet that position was not possible!

National Television Special
Recognition Award 1999 – I think
the look on my Mum's face says it al...

Press shot during rehearsals of my live
tour in God's Country – New Zealand

The morning of my 50th birthday in New York 2002. It looks as though the little man knows something I don't. From left, Mike Browne, Morgan, Maria Browne, me & Shawn

On the set of Bob Martin in 2000. My first TV film acting role and I was proud to be surrounded by some of the best in the business. From left, Denis Lawson, me, Keith Allen & Stephen Fry

StarJam Stage Show in NZ, 2005. Acting the fool at a magical evening supporting children and young people with disabilities

Majorca 1998. Mike & I enjoying the beginning of my downward slide!

My life long friend and neighbour from heaven, Jean Swetman

My good friend & NZ legend Gray Bartlett in rehearsals for my live show in NZ

JD & Sprite were trained to bark if I got anywhere near the cask! JD on the left, Sprite on the right

Tina Cross and I at the end of our tour with Chicago The Musical, 2005. One of the greatest performers I have worked with

Mexico 1999. Shaun about to start on his drink, me having just finished mine. Obviously funny at the time

Kevin, Russell & Maurice. The team responsible for producing and directing most of my TV shows. You can see why they got the job!

*Playwright &
cartoonist Tom Scott.
A true NZ icon and
a true friend to us*

*This tiny lady played a huge part in
turning my life around - our very good
friend Chrissy Smith*

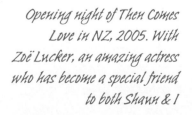

*Opening night of Then Comes
Love in NZ, 2005. With
Zoë Lucker, an amazing actress
who has become a special friend
to both Shaun & I*

John Cleese during his live tour in NZ. It's rare to meet one of your comedy heroes – and even rarer to find out they are really nice as well. From left, me, Alyce Faye, John Cleese, Garry Scott Irvine & Shaun

New Year's Eve, Paris, 2005. On the secret route to the Big Brother House. From left, my agent Karen Kay, Shaun & me

One of the most memorable moments of my life.
Leaving the Big Brother House, January 2006

The skiing resort of Queenstown NZ. The magic of NZ,
where you can be on the beach in the morning and skiing in the afternoon

'Look, Michael, we can make this work, I know we can. Just keep your cool and watch how much you drink, then when you go up for an award, which I'm sure you will, keep it very simple, and don't mention anything about recent events. If we are seen to be happy together, it'll squash all this nonsense. There will be millions watching. Don't throw it all away.'

I didn't say a word. I couldn't. I wanted to explode into a thousand pieces just to escape all of this. I'd had enough of being told what to do, how to do it, what to say, how to dress, how to think. Are these thoughts ungrateful? As far as the journalists were concerned, yes – but what do journalists know about how someone feels? They were all there waiting for the story – whatever story suited them.

We posed for the army of photographers as we walked into the Albert Hall. I didn't feel right; nobody needed to accuse me of being a fraud, I knew it all too well. Madeleine Pallas, the press officer at Granada Television, had the pleasure of looking after me that night, trying to keep some kind of control over the events that were unfolding. I tried to keep it together, but the too-many-glasses of red wine I'd drunk at the pre-awards reception were beginning to kick in.

'Mr Barrymore, are you and your wife back together?'

'Mr Barrymore, what do you have to say about all the reports about you?'

'Mr Barrymore . . .'

'Mr Barrymore . . .'

I grinned inanely and tried to pretend that everything was all right. But I'm not very good at pretending. As soon as we were safely inside, past the press throng, I made my way through a sea of famous faces, people I knew from film and television, people who waved and smiled in our direction but felt, for some reason, that it was best to keep a distance. I felt safe with my team around me: Maurice; Kevin, my associate producer; Russell, my director; Mike and Cheryl.

There were 5,000 people sitting in the Royal Albert Hall, with the front rows saved for the nominees and VIPs. I heard a few shouts of, 'We love you, Michael!' which made me feel better. We were shown to our seats, but Cheryl wasn't happy – she hadn't been placed next to me. So there was a lot of shuffling around until she'd got where she wanted to be.

As the various awards were announced, I started to feel more and more depressed. The first category in which I was nominated came up, and I froze. All I could hear were Cheryl's words: don't do this, don't say that, do this, do that. I thought I would throw up at the least provocation.

'And the winner is . . .'

For the first time in my life it didn't seem such a great idea to be a winner.

'The winner is . . .'

Please let someone else have it this year, please . . .

'It's . . .'

Oh God, I want out of here.

'Michael Barrymore!'

I stood unsteadily and walked towards the podium. I was completely empty of any thoughts. Applause and cheers all around me. I thanked the public for all their support, and then I started to cry. I cried because of all the love that so many people have for me, I cried for all the mistakes I had made and I cried for what I had done to Cheryl.

Then I just blurted out, 'Thank you. At last I am happy with my life.'

The audience applauded and I left the stage with a hostess who led me towards a press room where the photographers and journalists were waiting to ask each winner how they felt. I never got that far. Cheryl had stormed out of the ceremony and was waiting in the outer corridor. I walked towards her as Madeleine, the press officer, tried to get me into the press room.

Cheryl's face said it all. She screamed at the top of her voice, as if we were at home.

'What's up? WHAT'S UP? How could you do this to me? I have never been so humiliated in my life.'

The award hung limply in my right hand.

'What?'

'"I'm happy now! I'm happy now!"'

And here came the boys from the tabloids, on the scent of tomorrow's big story: THE BARRYMORES BATTLE IT OUT AT THE ALBERT HALL.

I tried to calm Cheryl down, saying that it would probably be better if we continued this in private, but she was getting hysterical.

'That's it, we're finished!'

Madeleine tried to help. 'Look, Cheryl, calm down ...'

'You can fuck off! You're just as much to blame! It was you who made the seating arrangements.'

Madeleine defended herself. 'Cheryl, it's got nothing to do with the seating ...'

'You've been behind all this!'

Madeleine started to cry; I defended her. 'You can't talk to her like that, it's not fair.'

'Fuck you and fuck her! Get out of my sight. I'm going to Raymond Tooth in the morning and I'm filing for divorce.'

Not many things are like a red rag to me, but the name Raymond Tooth is one of them. He is a divorce lawyer, well known for taking husbands to the cleaners.

'If I hear that name one more time, I will take it that anything we had in our relationship in the last eighteen years counts for nothing. If you go to Raymond Tooth, then as far as I'm concerned, you never existed.'

'I'm going to Raymond Tooth and I'm going to do you for every penny.'

I tried once more. 'Let's work this out . . .'

Cheryl's last words were, 'I made you, and I'll break you.'

She turned and walked away.

I would have liked to have been one of those very few people who manage to get divorced amicably, but it was not to be. Cheryl went ahead and engaged the services of Raymond Tooth, so I had to find someone equally formidable. That person came to me in the shape of Fiona Shackleton, who numbered among her previous clients the Prince of Wales. Before our first meeting, I had a dream . . .

'Hello, Mr Barrymore, lovely to meet you (£100) . . . Do sit down (£200) . . . Would you like tea? (£300) . . . or coffee? (£400) . . . I must say I'm a great fan (£500) and so are both my daughters (£600, £700) . . . So you want a divorce (£1000) . . . Such a shame this has to happen (£2000) . . . Yes, it is a nice brooch, isn't it? The Prince of Wales gave it to me as a thank you present (£5000) . . .'

But when I turned up I was greatly relieved to hear Fiona say to her assistant, 'God, I'm exhausted. I must dash – I've got lunch at the Savoy with Gazza.' At least, that's what I think she said, although with her impeccable Sloane accent it could have been something quite different.

I took it as a personal slight that Cheryl had taken on Raymond Tooth because what that basically said to me was that I would not behave honourably over the divorce. Now, I have never, ever had my honour questioned before. I am honest and generous, and if I give you my word about something, you can rely on it. I was angry, and that made me uncooperative. During rehearsals, I'd start contradicting Cheryl, refusing to do things that she suggested, just to have a swipe at her. It was ridiculous, really, that we were still working together while this huge, messy, expensive divorce was about to get going – this was anything but a clean break. So I'd stamp my foot and say, 'No, Cheryl, I'm not doing the show like that, or any other way you suggest.' Pointless and childish, but it was the only way I could get back at her for hurting me. This was very hard for the production team; they were used to Cheryl making the decisions and me going along with them. But now I'd suddenly found my voice – and I was abusing it, saying things for the hell of it.

We were both kidding ourselves for a while that we could carry on working together, that she could be my manager and my friend but not my wife. Of course, that was never going to work. Cheryl wanted all or nothing: she wanted me back as her husband and her protégé. I couldn't get across to her the fact that I was gay – and by this time our relationship was becoming so bitter that neither of us was expressing ourselves well. I wanted to say, 'Come on, Cheryl, we're the best of mates, we get on great, we've laughed together so many times, we've created a great business together, we've carved out a piece of this life – why destroy it all?' But I wasn't saying it right, and she wasn't listening, and before we knew it the only communication between us was conducted by lawyers.

Once Cheryl realised that I was never going to come back, she seemed set on destroying me – not just financially, but professionally too. I began to think that she wanted to make sure that nobody would ever want to work with me again, that I would have no career. Her attitude was that she'd made me and that she could could break me. She'd created the perfect showbiz professional, always there on time, always smart, never causing any trouble, and now she was going to turn me into the villain. She was going to show the world that I was not the man they thought I was, that I was a drug fiend and an alcoholic and an all-round monster. She played to the crowd; stories started to appear in the press about how much I drank and drugged, about how I had 'boxes of drugs' in the house. If I had boxes of drugs, I wouldn't be an addict – I'd be a drug dealer. The more out there it was, the more Cheryl played it.

It's true that I was out of control. I was having a hard time finding my feet in a new world. I was going out a lot, running around, having fun, overdoing it – but was that so bad? I was finding out that I could be a bit of a Jack-the-lad if I wanted to; I'm only human. I was suddenly doing everything that I should have done at nineteen – which, I admit, sits a bit strangely on a man in his forties. So yes, I did go mad. Instead of being tucked up in bed ready for rehearsals in the morning, I was going out clubbing all night and then going straight to the rehearsal. In some ways it might have enhanced my work, but in other ways it wasn't doing it any good. The addiction had full control of me now.

The divorce settlement was severe. It cost several million. But in the end we went for a clean break. We'd got stuck in a lot of arguments about the property and the chattels, and I felt that I was starting to be controlled by lawyers – at very great expense to both Cheryl and me. It wasn't just a question of who was going to get the sofa, who was going to get the hi-fi – we were talking about a lot of very expensive gear, antiques and such-like. At one point the judge looked at my counsel and said, 'Look, how much will it cost to settle this argument over the chattels?' My counsel looked at her counsel, they muttered a bit and said, 'About five hundred thousand.' So the judge turned to me and Cheryl and said, 'Mr and Mrs Barrymore, you are eating into your own money. You're going to have to let go.' So I did. I paid the settlement in three lumps. Cheryl got the house in Bayswater. And that was it: over and done with. No further contact.

I have been married once and divorced once, and that is enough experience for me. The marriage vows end, 'Till death do us part'; they ought to add on, 'or till divorce doth tear us to pieces'.

Fortunately for me, I didn't have to go through all of this alone. I had someone else in my life by now – someone who's stuck with me through an awful lot over the last few years: Shaun.

We met during the divorce. I'd had a small affair with a guy named Paul, and I'd just split up with Steve, who I'd been seeing for about a year. I was getting used to being out as a gay man; the public always gave me their full support, and now I was starting to get feedback from a lot of younger guys whom I met in clubs and pubs, thanking me for making it easier for them to tell their parents that they were gay. It usually went something like this.

'Mum, Dad, have you read the papers today?'

'Yes, son.'

'What do you think about the news on Michael Barrymore?'

'It makes no difference to us, son, we still like him.'

'Well, that's good, because I'm gay too.'

There was something else I'd discovered on the gay scene as well: Ecstasy. I was given a tablet in a pub one night: I took it and immediately vomited. I hate being sick at the best of times, so self-induced chuck-up didn't go down too well.

'Oh, that's all right, Michael,' said the guy who'd given it to me. 'That always happens. It's afterwards you get the buzz.'

And I did. Half an hour later I was watching ticker tape falling against a sea of lights as the Carpenters sang 'Calling Occupants of Interplanetary Craft'. It was ecstasy: pure ecstasy. I danced for hours. I smiled. I was in a living dream – a dream which thousands of people drift off into every weekend. For this addict, one ecstasy was too many – a thousand could never be enough.

One night Mike said, 'You're not staying in tonight, are you?' There's always a tone in Mike's voice that tells me he has other ideas.

'I'm knackered. Yes, I'm staying in.'

'Why don't you go to The Fridge?'

The Fridge is a huge, predominately gay club in Brixton; I'd been there once before, and Mike managed to persuade me that it would be a good idea. A taxi took me down there, but by the time I got to the club I'd changed my mind: I was really tired and just wanted to be on my own. I talked to a few people I knew, then made an excuse to go to the toilet with the intention of leaving and going home.

I queued for the loo – girls, guys, it's a gay club, no one minds. A girl with wide eyes and huge pupils was washing her hands.

'Is this toilet for boys or girls?'

The guy to my left was standing with his head hung at half-mast, looking down at his shoes, so I answered her, 'I don't know, love.'

She cocked her head. 'I know you. You're the woo-woo man!' I think she was referring to the sound that was made when anyone hit a hot spot in *Strike it Lucky*. If not, she had a terrible stammer.

I ignored her, confident in the knowledge that whatever it was that had made her pupils so huge would probably make her believe that everyone was the woo-woo man.

'Ooooo, would you like my phone number?' Before I gave her my answer, she planted a scrap of paper with her scribbled mobile number on it in my hand. A loo became available and, as I headed for it, I passed the scribbled note to the guy to my left, saying, 'Here you go, there's the number of a nice girl for you!'

I entered the cubicle, turned to close the door and smiled back inanely at the guy with the half-mast head, who had still not managed to raise it to the full Queen-in-residence, top-of-the-mast position.

I left the loos and went to the bar for a short while, planning my exit, when the guy who had been standing in the queue for the toilets walked past and asked if I was okay? He looked just like the sort of guy I like, so I delayed my departure slightly. 'Yep, I'm okay.' He said, 'What you up to?' and, instead of saying I'm off home, I said, 'Oh, I'm just going downstairs to dance.' We walked without conversation down the stairs on to the dance floor and leaped up and down to 'Feel it' by Tamperer. I thought two things: one he's a great dancer, and two he looks great. I can't say what he thought, except he leaned over and shouted in my ear, 'I won't be a minute,' and left the floor. My first thought was, 'Well, whatever he dances like and looks like, that's the last I'll see of him,' and I carried on dancing with the space that he had left behind. Shaun had left the floor to find a friend of his. After squeezing through the crowd he went to him and said, 'Will you come with me and stand on the side of the dance floor?' His mate shouted through the club volume, 'Why?' 'Well, I'm dancing with this guy and I know I'm pretty stoned, but I think it's whasisname!' Shaun rejoined me on the floor, danced and, after a while, looked across to his friend, who was observing from the side. He mouthed very slowly 'BARRYMORE!'

Shaun, recalling our first meeting, said two words entered his head. 'Oh shit.'

Something else good came out of the divorce: I got back in touch with my mum. Cheryl blamed her for the bankruptcy and was always pointing out all the bad things about my family. When Cheryl and I separated, I was driving home with Mike, my PA, from filming an advert, and he said, 'It's Mother's Day on Sunday. Please call your mum.' I wasn't sure, but he said, 'She's much older now, and if she dies and you haven't got back together, you'll regret it for the rest of your life.' There was a pause. 'I'm going to dial your mum's number now.'

Mum picked up the phone. I very nervously said, 'It's Kieron . . .'

'Kieron who?' How sad that it had been so long that Mum didn't recognise my voice. I could hear her shock as she realised it was me.

It was Thursday; I said I'd be over for Mother's Day.

Sunday came; I knocked on the door. When she answered she hugged and kissed me as if it had only been a week since we last met, not eight years. We talked. She never asked me once why it had taken me so long, she never blamed Cheryl. Only a mother could have such a unique, in-built quality. After that, we talked every day. At first, Mike had to keep reminding me, because I'd completely lost all sense of my priorities and the routine of ringing Mum. After that, it became a habit that lasted for the rest of Mum's life.

Initially, I wasn't too keen on having a relationship with Shaun. I'd tried two that didn't work out and, being in the middle of a divorce, it felt better to go it alone for a while. We started going out for a bit, and I told Shaun on many occasions that it would be better if we didn't get involved; he always looked so sad when the conversation took that turn. Eventually I gave in.

Drink and drugs were very much part of my daily routine at this time, and we spent a lot of time going out – and eating very little. Shaun worked for a City firm of stockbrokers and was not an addict, so it was hard for him to keep up with non-stop partying, sometimes running to four solid days at a time with no sleep. I was turning into a different person – sicker and sicker, obsessed by the idea that I had to be permanently high and that nothing would satisfy the addict in me, no matter how much I drank or swallowed.

At times I was so ill, the thought of dying came as a relief from my self-inflicted torture. My skin dried from lack of moisture. I started to smell as the toxins spread through every vein and out through my skin. That's the deal you make with the devil when you become an addict.

I put Shaun through hell. I put a lot of people through hell, and some of them – the ones that love me – have stuck around. I loved Shaun then, and I love him today, the difference being that now I know that I love him. At the time, I was too far gone in the addiction to know what was going on.

Today, Shaun and I are truly happy. Was I ever truly happy with Cheryl? Yes, I was, for a while. Could she have continued to be happy with me if I had carried on denying what I was? Well, if I had kept my mouth shut, none of what Cheryl had to go through would have happened. If I'd kept my mouth shut, Cheryl would have been happy.

There's only one thing wrong with keeping your mouth shut. You stop breathing.

7

All Time Low

I would love to be able to say that with my divorce all my troubles melted away and I embarked on a new, calm, happy period of my life. In fact, the reverse was true. I had a bad reaction to the divorce. I was angry and ashamed at the way it had turned out. I'd wanted to do what was right: I'd done what the doctor told me to do, I'd tried to have an honourable separation from Cheryl – and it had all panned out very differently. I became depressed and despondent and more than ever dependent on drink and drugs. Before long, I was caught in a spiral of addiction that dragged me down with terrifying rapidity. A lot of bad things happened that just seemed to make things worse. I was always ready to point the finger of blame – whatever happened was always someone else's fault. But the fact is that I was in the very worst phase of my addictive illness, and when you're an addict, bad things happen to you. I've always said that when I see insanity, I don't run away from it, I run towards it. But by now, I was running towards it open-armed.

In 1998, on the final day of my divorce, I left the Royal Courts of Justice and walked down The Strand with Mike and Fiona Shackleton, my lawyer. I was officially free of Cheryl. I was relieved that the case was closed, but I also felt lost. We found a pub, I ordered a round to thank Mike and Fiona for all their hard work and support, and then drove over to Sloane Avenue, where Maurice and Kevin were working on an advertising campaign at Leo Burnett's, the advertising agency. It was a beautiful spring day. We sat in the office with the sun streaming through the windows, then decided to go out for a drink. We used my chauffeured car, and went to Compton's, a well-established gay bar on Old Compton Street.

It was about six o'clock when we got there; the pub was busy, but not heaving. We went to the upper bar and chatted about work; a few guys passed and said hello, asked me how I was, wished me luck. My decree nisi had been reported in the *Evening Standard*, so everyone knew what was going on in my private life – as usual. Most of them moved on after a few words, but there was one who was determined to barge in. He was about 5 foot 8 inches, his eyes were reddened from drinking, darting from side to side.

'Hello, Michael, how are you?' He had a strong Welsh accent. 'You're my hero, you are. Can I be with you? I don't want you for your money. I've got my own money, I have.'

People have said all sorts of strange things when they first meet me, but even I was thrown by this one. I just said, 'Oh, good,' trying to be polite, and carried on talking to

Maurice and Kevin. The guy went over to the bar and kept staring at me.

Kevin gave me a smile, 'Who's your friend?'

'I haven't the faintest idea, but he's certainly off his trot.'

Maurice joined in. 'Don't they all flock to you? Come on, who is he?'

'I don't know, Maurice, but at least he's got his own money.'

'Well, that'll be nice for you,' said Maurice.

'What would be nice would be if he stopped staring at me.'

Maurice and Kevin were ready to go home by now, and just before they left a group of three lads and a girl came over to say hello. 'You won't remember us, Michael, but we met at a club about a month ago.'

They were right; I didn't remember.

'We're all going down to Brief Encounter, do you want to come?'

Maurice and Kevin made their excuses and left, asking if I'd be okay on my own.

'I'm sure I can cope. I'll just go with this lot for a drink at Brief Encounter and then I'll go home, probably.'

Maurice reminded me that the car and driver were waiting for me, gave me a theatrical kiss on the cheek and left. I turned and joined the group that were waiting for me, and said I'd be delighted to come for a drink; if nothing else, it would be a good opportunity to get rid of the Welsh guy, who was now heading straight for me.

'Hello, Michael! Remember me? I've got my own money.'

I said nothing in reply, just asked the three lads and the girl if we could leave now, as this nutter was starting to annoy me. But this nutter wasn't giving up that easily: he followed us down to Brief Encounter, a bar on St Martin's Lane. No matter how fast we walked, he kept up, shouting after me.

'Michael! Michael! You'll like me! I'd be good for you, I've got my own money!'

We made our way into the back entrance; it was far too packed for my taste, and the Welsh guy was still in tow.

'I've got my own money, Michael! You'll like me!'

I was very polite. 'Excuse me. I'm just going to the toilet. Won't be a minute.'

'I'll come with you!'

'No, you stay here. I won't be long.'

I squeezed my way through the crowd and up the stairs leading to the front exit. It was now about nine o'clock. The two security guys on the door said, 'Hello, leaving so soon?' I turned out into the street, trying to get away as quickly as possible before he realised that I was gone. Two policemen sprang into view.

'Hello, Michael. What are you doing here on your own? The streets are packed tonight. It's a bit dangerous for you.'

I wasn't sure what they meant, but I accepted that perhaps it would be a good idea to get away from the madding crowd and the guy with his own money! I'd forgotten which street my driver was in, so I borrowed their phone and rang Mike to find out where I needed to be. The policemen were very helpful, and gave me a lift to the Groucho Club on Wardour Street. My driver was waiting outside. One of the coppers asked me for a signed picture for his children.

Alone at last, I walked into Groucho's for a drink, feeling completely knackered – after all, you don't get divorced every day. Then the driver took me home to Docklands. I walked in and fell on the bed fully clothed. As I started to drift off, the phone rang: it was Shaun, asking me if I wanted him to come over. I did. He arrived, asked me how my day was. I said I'd just got divorced. Night, night.

The following morning I was wandering around in my shorts, not particularly thinking of anything. Shaun had already left. The Thames was quiet, just a few rowers stroking its back. My eighth-floor apartment gave me a perfect bird's-eye view. I looked down to the left: all quiet, just a couple of men sitting in a Volkswagen. On the other side: two or three people standing around chatting. Just another Saturday morning. I made a coffee and reminded myself that I was single again.

The phone rang. It was Ernie, the porter.

'Mr Barrymore . . . there are quite a few journalists outside wanting to speak to you.'

'Tell them I'm not here.'

'I have, but they said they'd wait.'

'Thanks, Ernie.'

I checked the VW again: this time the two men were standing outside it, and one had a camera with a lens as long as a missile launcher, pointed straight up at me. I pulled away from the window and phoned Mike.

'How are you feeling, guv'nor?'

'I'm fine, Mike, except there seem to be a lot of journalists downstairs. Can you find out what they want?'

'It's probably to do with your divorce.'

'That was yesterday. There are too many people out there. It doesn't add up.' The crowd downstairs was growing – and a boat had just pulled up, to cut off any ideas I might have had of escaping by water.

Mike called back later. 'I've had a ring-round, guv'nor, but I haven't heard anything.'

I looked at the answering machine; it was flashing up one message.

———

'Hello, Mr Barrymore. I urgently need to talk to you about a serious matter. If you could ring me back, my numbers are . . .'

I switched the machine off, not interested in the numbers. My first reaction was that everything the tabloids want to talk about is always serious; this would be no different. I rang Mike back and asked him to find out what they wanted.

'Give me five minutes.'

The editor called back; I didn't pick up the phone. The crowd downstairs had grown even bigger.

Mike rang. 'I called the editor and he said he can't talk to me about it, it's too serious.'

'Well, ring him back and tell him that if he can't say what it is, he shouldn't bother me.'

Five minutes later, Mike was back. 'He says it's with regards to an incident that happened last night at the Brief Encounter. He said it was very serious and that the police were involved.'

I paused for breath. 'What incident?'

'I don't know, mate. Look, perhaps it's best we get you out of there while we find out what's going on.'

'Why?'

'Because even more journalists have turned up and I don't want you trapped in there while we find out what all this is about. Unless you know, of course.'

'I haven't got a clue!'

'Okay. The porter can get you out by a side entrance into the next building. I'll have a car waiting and we'll take it from there.'

I packed a few things and rang Shaun, told him that something was going on but I had no idea what it was. As I left the apartment, the phone rang again. So much for being ex-directory.

I left in the getaway car, escaping the posse of journalists who were still waiting for me to come out of my block. The sun was still shining, but as the day wore on, even that would darken.

I rang Anne, my agent.

'Michael, I don't know what this story is based on, but they are saying that you were involved in a sexual assault on a man at the Brief Encounter last night.'

Pause.

'Who is saying that, exactly?'

'A newspaper.'

Pause.

'And what is that allegation based on?'

'They have a statement from a man who claims you sexually assaulted him.'

Pause.

'A statement? What man?'

'Don't know. Apparently they have a picture of the police going into the club this morning.'

'The police? What for?'

'Don't know.'

'Anne, is this some kind of sick joke someone's playing on me?'

'I don't know. Did you see anyone last night?'

'Yes. Maurice, Kevin, Shaun, a few other people, a Welsh guy who drove me mad ... and the chauffeur who dropped me home around eleven.'

'You met no one else?'

'No.'

'Did you have much to drink?'

'Look, Anne, amazing as it may seem, I just had a few drinks and an early night. I was tired. And I can't answer any questions the newspaper may have because I don't know what the hell they are talking about. And if the police have any questions, I'm sure they would have contacted me by now.'

'Well, let's just see what they write and take it from there.'

The headline on Sunday was: BARRYMORE IN SEXUAL ASSAULT.

There was a picture of me, and another one of the police entering Brief Encounter. I had the same sick feeling that I have had on many occasions when reading news 'about' me that is news to me.

Telephones rang the whole of Sunday. Mike allowed Shaun to get through to me.

'What's it all about?'

'I don't know, Shaun. All I know is that the only police I've seen in the last couple of days were the two I met outside Brief Encounter at 9.20 on Friday night who helped me to find my car.'

By Monday, Anne, Mike and I were all sitting in Anne's office with Nicki Paradise, who handled all my legal affairs with regard to libel. Nicki had brought a colleague with her, and I asked who he was.

'This is David Corker. He deals with criminal matters.'

'But there is no criminal situation . . . is there?'

Silence.

When David spoke, I did not like his choice of words. 'The thing is, Michael, although the police haven't contacted you yet, that doesn't mean that they won't. Later on they may arrest you.'

'What do you mean, arrest me? What for?'

'I've made contact with the officers in charge of the case—'

'Case? What case? What's going on?'

'Basically,' said David, 'this gentleman says that you raped him.'

My head started to spin the moment I heard the word 'rape'. It's spinning again as I write it. I think, for me, it's the worst word in the language.

'Now,' continued David. 'The best way to deal with this is for me to phone the detective in charge of the case and explain that you are willing to go along to Charing Cross Police Station to be interviewed. I'm sure they'd prefer that to arresting you and the press having a field day photographing you being taken in.'

I started to feel very sick. I stared at the floor to get my balance back.

'I haven't done anything! I don't know what this is about!'

Uneasy coughing in the office.

David said, 'I'll call them and ask if they will see us.'

He made the call; a lot of silence, a lot of, 'Yes, of course, I understand that.'

'Well?'

'The police have agreed we can go to them. They want to interview you. They won't tell me any more on the phone, but when we get there they'll explain what it's all about.'

David, Nicki and I went to Charing Cross Police Station; I was put in a waiting room until two police officers came to take me down below. Chairs on either side of the table. On the wall, two tape machines were fixed. The only time I'd seen a room like this was on *A Touch of Frost*. But this was for real: no rehearsals, no actors, and only A Touch of Reality.

Two male detectives sat opposite me. David Corker and Nicki Paradise sat beside me. The door to the interview room was closed.

Two box files were placed between one officer and myself. Both were marked in thick felt tip. One read

BARRYMORE in black ink. The other was marked in red: RAPE.

The officer opposite me started to talk. I heard something about taping the interview, something about procedure, 'Do you realise why you are here?' . . . and all I could do was stare at that unfamiliar red word.

The detective spoke to David. 'Do you realise why your client is here?' David nodded. 'And you, Michael . . . May I call you Michael?' I nodded. He pushed a button; the tape recorder spun into life.

'My name is Detective Blah Blah . . . With me is Detective Blah Blah . . . Also in the room is Mr Michael Barrymore, Mr David Corker, Miss Nicki Paradise. The time is blah blah . . .'

I continued to stare.

'Mr Barrymore, it is alleged that on Friday night at around 9.02 pm you and three other males raped a Mr . . . in the toilets of the Brief Encounter club in Soho.'

'What?'

It was the first clear word I'd said. My breathing was heavy.

David spoke up. 'This is the first time I have had notification of this.'

I took a deep breath. 'Is this a sick joke?'

'No, Mr Barrymore. This is a very serious matter. The gentleman—'

'Does this gentleman by any chance have a Welsh accent?'

The officer turned to his colleague, who nodded. 'Yes, I believe so. He is with a rape counsellor at another station.'

'Being counselled for what?'

'He claims that three of your friends held him down and that you sexually assaulted him against his will.'

This was certainly sick – but it was no joke. The

interview continued. I told them about the Welsh guy, how I'd left the club to get away from him. I could not get my head around the fact that he was claiming I'd raped him. All I can remember saying is that they shouldn't believe anything that this lying bastard said. I was fast discovering that anyone can say you've raped him or her; they get rape counselling immediately, and you become the rapist – until you can prove otherwise.

The interview ended. I was cautioned to be available for more inquiries. I was taken downstairs to a doctor's room, where blood and swabs were taken for DNA testing.

I never spoke again that night. I went back to my apartment and drank heavily. I lay beside Shaun and cried all night.

That night. That nightmare.

The nightmare finally ended when, after a long investigation, the police turned up CCTV footage of the Welsh guy going into the toilets of Brief Encounter on his own. There was no DNA match – not with me, not with anyone. He still protested that he'd been raped, but the only part of him that had been raped was his conscience. My instinct at the time, when the case was dropped, was to go and find the git, but it was much easier to pray for him. Just another sicko.

One thing that always puzzled everyone about this case was where this lad was getting the money from to pursue a private prosecution. Despite his claims that he 'had his own money', I was later informed he was completely broke and living in a hovel. How could the photographers have known to be at the club before the police even arrived? Where could the money have come from? How come the journalists always seemed to be one step ahead of the police?

Fortunately, I was really busy performing around the

country with my live stand-up tour. I was just about to go on stage one night when Mike gave me the news that the police were satisfied that everything the Welsh guy had accused me of was fabricated and that the case was closed.

Despite this, things started to spiral out of control, and I reacted by retreating further into my addiction. I wasn't getting on well with Shaun; the way I was when drinking and drugging was becoming too much for him, and he was coming to fewer and fewer events with me. Then I had a row with two of my closest friends, Maurice Leonard and Kevin Hubbard, whom I've worked with for years; they objected to the way I'd been behaving during the making of a series. Who was right and who was wrong is neither here nor there — but the row ended with me dismissing them both from their jobs on a Monday morning.

Not only had I lost two valued colleagues, I'd lost two treasured friends as well. I decided to cheer myself up by inviting my neighbours and their children over for dinner. My plans did not go down well with Shaun.

'What's that face for?'

'Can't we have some time on our own?'

Without thinking, I said, 'Look, Shaun, I've lost two of my best friends, two of the best people on my team. I want the house to be busy so that I don't get miserable.' My tone was harsh — fuelled by the bottle of white wine I'd drunk. I slammed the door and went back to the kitchen.

The family came over; I stayed in the kitchen, cooking and drinking. The phone rang; Shaun answered and passed it over to me.

'It's your sister, Anne.'

'Hello, Anne?'

'Hello, Kieron. You know that ulcer Mum's got? Well, it's not an ulcer, it's cancer.'

I said nothing.

169

'She doesn't know what it is, so if you ring her, don't tell her I told you.'

I just said quietly, 'Okay, I'll ring you soon, leave it with me.' I carried on cooking.

Shaun asked, 'Is everything okay?'

'No. I'll tell you later. Let's eat.'

I finished cooking, everyone sat down and ate. I carried on drinking. The kids went into the front room to use the Playstation. We stayed at the table: Gary, their father, to my right, Shaun straight ahead.

'My mum's got cancer.'

Ohs and sorrys filled the dining room.

'Are you going to ring her?' asked Shaun.

'No, I am not.'

'Why not?'

'Because I don't want us both crying on the phone.'

'Well, I'd ring if it was my mum. Why don't you go over and see her?'

'It's Sunday night, Shaun. I want to ring Mike, tell him, then we'll get the best specialist we can and, once that's in place, I'll pick her up and take her to see whoever it is. And not before.'

'Then you should ring her.'

The temperature was shooting up. I leaned forward to face Shaun closer. 'I have said what I am going to do and how. That's it.'

Yet again he came back for more – not a good idea in an addict's company. 'She's your mother—'

'Shaun, for God's sake shut up! Jesus Christ, you never know when to back off.' I wanted to strangle him; the madness boiled my blood, made my head spin. Saliva rushed into my mouth. Gary jumped in to stop me getting closer to Shaun. I stormed off into the kitchen – my beautiful, brand-new, all-stainless-steel-and-black-granite-

and-French-slate kitchen, threw anything possible at it – and raged. Shaun ran out of the house in fear for his life, got into the car and drove off. I sent Gary out to stop him; too late, he was gone. We had rowed before, he had left before, and we'd always made our peace. This would be like any other time.

The next morning, I hadn't really calmed down. I felt all alone – without my two friends, my mum, Shaun. It seemed like everyone in my life was checking out and asking for the final bill. Hotel Barrymore was being vacated, emptied of people, to leave space for more booze, more drugs, more medication.

I met Mike and he helped me sort out a specialist to see Mum. Then I saw Anne, my agent, and we got working on finding some new producers. As the day progressed, there was no contact from Shaun. I started to worry that he had crashed the car or done something stupid. Mike said he'd drive down to Shaun's father's place to see if he was there.

About an hour later, Mike phoned me to say that Shaun was fine, he was just not answering his phone. I reacted out of relief and anger. "Then sod him. Tell him to stay there.' I'd had enough; I couldn't stand any more of our non-stop dramas. I don't know if I was being selfish, but after losing two of my best mates and being told that my mother had cancer, I couldn't cope with my partner running off just when I needed him most. My anger pushed me deeper into drink, deeper into the addiction. I raced without brakes into insanity. Shaun rang, but it was just to retrieve some clothes. I wouldn't have him near me. I found out that during one of my recent trips away, Shaun had been moving his clothes over to his dad's place, laying the tracks for his escape.

I asked Shaun to come to the house. He never looked me

in the eye. It made me so sad: it seemed that the only option for anyone who got close to me was to abandon me in the end. Am I really that bad? Can nobody stick with me, for richer, for poorer? It seemed hopeless at the time, and I didn't see Shaun for a long while.

I drove Shaun away with my ranting and raving, but of course I wanted to blame him for abandoning me, like I blamed everyone else. Mum was fighting cancer, and there were whispers at work that I wasn't very together. All my dreams of having the life that I wanted and needed, of being free from Cheryl and in control of my own destiny, were turning into a nightmare. I had to get back on course, to get happy again, but the only time I ever felt happy was when I was drunk or stoned. So I took more; I had to. Just to achieve normality, to function, would take several drinks. I got out of bed to start the process again, and carried on until I passed out. I hated being on my own. I lived in permanent depression, only smiling on request. Surely it couldn't get any worse?

I was still seeking treatment at this time, but I'd learned to be very wary. For me, Alcoholics Anonymous could never be anonymous; that's true for a lot of people in entertainment. The press takes photographs of you going into meetings, and they'll even record what you say in the rooms. When I was going to AA meetings in Chelsea, I'd see things that I'd shared at the meetings printed in the papers the next day – so I stopped sharing. The whole point of AA is that you get well by sharing, by developing a sense of belonging and trust. You've been through it all on your own, you think you're the only one, 'Poor me, poor me . . . pour me a drink,' and then you find yourself in an environment where you belong. You learn to trust people. But if you then read what you've said in the papers, you

172

stop trusting. So I stopped sharing. And who gets ill? Me.

I was drinking too much, taking too many pills then getting panic attacks. I'd lie in my bed thinking, 'I'm going to die, I'm going to die, please don't let me die like this, let me get my breath back ...' Then the feeling would fade, and half an hour later I'd be going off to take another tablet. That's the disease of addiction for you in a nutshell.

By the end of 2000, I was completely out of control. You know when you get hold of a child and you start spinning them around in the garden? At first the kid finds it funny, and laughs and screams. Most parents would put them down at this point, because if you go on any longer, the child will feel sick. But I kept getting spun round and round. At first I got a buzz out of it, then I got an extra-ordinary buzz out of it, then I got sick, and when I was put down I couldn't stand up. I had nothing, nobody, no one to hold on to. And then I hit a brick wall.

I broke my rule about never drinking before going on stage. I was doing a charity event at the Hilton Hotel for the Wish Upon a Star Foundation, and I figured that as it was for charity, it wasn't really work, and so I could have a drink. All I had to do was get up in front of an audience and explain that there was going to be a raffle, and ask them to dig deep into their pockets. Sort of thing I'd done hundreds of times before.

I'd had a few drinks before I went on, and I was feeling very hyped up. I started into my spiel, 'Hello, ladies and gentlemen, thanks for coming,' and I could hear this mumbling coming from one of the tables.

'Please could you be quiet, I'm trying to explain what the raffle is.'

Mumble mumble.

'Would you mind being quiet? I've asked you once.' No smiles coming from me.

They looked at me then, trying to figure out if I was joking.

'Now, ladies and gentlemen . . .'

Mumble mumble.

That was it. 'Would you shut the fuck up?'

Ooooh! That got a reaction.

'I tell you what. Let's forget about the poxy raffle. Why don't you all just put twenty quid in the pot, we'll go up to my suite where there's plenty of booze and drugs and we'll all get fucking stoned.'

Someone started a slow handclap.

'How dare you? How dare you do that? You come here in your poxy designer clothes, you drink all the booze and we're struggling to get twenty fucking quid out of you. Do you go and see these kids? No, you do not. I do. You just turn up here once a year and take the piss.'

Well, that certainly shut them up. But I'd only just started. The evening was sponsored by a lot of mobile phone companies, so that set me off.

'And what do you lot do? You make poxy mobile phones, which you've now made so small that when they ring you can't find them in your pocket or your bag, so what do you do, you make them vibrate. Now when anyone rings you can't find them at all because they've been sat on by all the women!' I went on in that vein for some time.

The whole place erupted. I walked off, and I saw Richard Branson coming towards the stage. Now for some reason I'd got it into my head that Richard Branson always ignored me at these dos, and so I laid into him. 'And if you ever ignore me again, Branson, I'm going to fucking sort you out.'

And on that note I stormed out of the hotel and went next door to the Met Bar for several more drinks.

*

The next day it was all over the papers, with outraged comments from the charity. I called Mike.

'I really said that, did I?'

'Yes, guv'nor.'

After that, it was just one thing after another. The papers picked up on every slip, making sure the whole world knew that Michael Barrymore was falling to pieces. And I was. Which reminds me, I must apologise to Mr Branson, the truth is he has never to my knowledge knowingly ignored me, and it wasn't him who needed sorting out at all, it was me. That's where the out of control head takes you. Believing it's everyone else, when all the time it's you.

For all that I've said that I never took anything mind altering before a performance, the truth was that it was now getting so bad that, in my mind, I was always thinking of ways to get the job over and done with quicker, so I could get back to the next drink. I was always willing to turn up to rehearsals earlier, so they could finish earlier. And I lived in hope that they'd be cancelled, so that I could go off and get shit-faced. I put incredible amounts of energy and ingenuity into my habit. Have I got enough? Am I going to run out? Do I need to go and see someone? How can I get some time off? I became very devious and manipulative. That's the disease: it's very clever. If I can put as much effort into my recovery as I put into my addiction, I'll be fine. It would have been better if that hadn't just been a passing thought.

After Shaun left, I met a guy called Jon (Jonathan Kenney), who was very quiet, very laid-back, easy company; Geordie accent, thirty-one years old, worked as an estate agent in north London. He was good for me. We all like the ones who say nothing – what I should have said there was he was good for my addiction. I enjoyed his company (my addiction loved his company) and he started to spend more and more time at the house, although he had his own place. It helped, too, that he was a little bit older than my previous boyfriends. I liked Jon, we got on well. We had an on/off friendship. I'm not that good on my own and I suppose I craved company. Although I had begun to feel that Jon wanted a closer relationship. He appeared to want more than I did. I also believed he got off on being with Barrymore rather than Michael. That statement could, of course, be based on total paranoia! He also started to become possessive and controlling.

I was still drinking and Jon was beginning to make comments about it. The more people tell you not to drink, the more you push them away. You tend to believe that the best, and sometimes only, conversations you have are with the bottle. You start to believe that you can have better conversations with your addictions than you can with any human being. And the addiction is always right.

I was fairly depressed during this period. I wasn't happy with anything; I wasn't getting any joy from my work. I suppose I didn't really think I was an alcoholic then – but I realise now it was the drink that was making me depressed. When you get success, it breeds its own unemployment. I had spent my whole life making everybody else happy and I never thought I had time for myself.

I was also missing Shaun, but I wouldn't admit it. I was never a morning drinker – it was a half past five in the afternoon start that soon became half past four, then half past three. A mistake a lot of people make is that they look at the dosser with the bottle of cider in the street with no shoelaces and think, well, I'm not him. Well, you're not, not yet. Drink kills you mentally first.

Right then, I think I was trying to find the equivalent of Shaun, but I knew I would never replace him. So I needed to be with people; I didn't want to be on my own.

Maurice Leonard, one of my best friends, gave me a little advice on this one – and, he being such a saint, I just had to listen. 'Why don't you go out with someone a bit older; they don't come with so much baggage.' Well, it worked up to a point; Jon went out to work every day, came home around six or seven, I'd cook a meal and we'd spend the evening together. Sometimes we went for a weekend in the country, just getting to know each other; sometimes we entertained at home. For a while, it was a nice, settled existence. My neighbours, Gary and Denise and their kids, were round almost every night; I couldn't be on my own. (There is something not quite right with that last statement: It was a nice settled existence, followed by, I couldn't be on my own. See that, that's the disease of addiction working, saying everything is as it should be and then total contradiction; I couldn't be on my own. Proves that even sober the mind still thinks, talks and writes like an addict.)

One evening Jon rang me up and said, 'Fancy going for something to eat tonight?'

'Okay. Where we going?'

Jon had arranged with Gary that we'd all go out to the Indian restaurant in Broxbourne, just down the road. At around six o'clock a people-carrier turned up to collect us all, kids included, and we had a really nice time. A few drinks later, I felt better than I had in ages. We went home and said goodnight to the family – but I didn't want the good feeling to stop.

'Shall we go to a club?'

I wanted to carry on, I didn't want to be alone. The driver who took Jon and me to the Indian restaurant told us about a club, The Millennium, and I said I knew where it was in Harlow. The Millennium is a straight club, so it was just spur of the moment. You know how people just want to carry on having a good time – that's how it was. Or is that just me?

I'd already had a fair bit to drink at the restaurant; I was drinking my favourite tipple, Jack Daniel's . . .

I wasn't dressed to go out. I looked scruffy, not even casually smart. I had an old jumper on. It wasn't exactly a 'let's go pulling' outfit. Everything was a deflection; if I could deflect attention away from myself, I would. In many ways, drink was also a deflection. The club would be crowded, so I knew that I wouldn't have to think. It was another way to get through another night of not sitting around. I'm not good with my own company.

There were a couple of guys I recognised from the village; it was my area so I felt comfortable and everyone was really nice. There was quite a mixed crowd and lots of people offered me drinks.

The manager welcomed me, told me he'd make sure that I was looked after and safe. The place was packed and buzzing; groups of girls and guys came up to shake my hand, groups of lads shouted out my surname, I gave out autographs. I felt so relaxed. We went to the bar, drinks were ordered, security stood either side of me – all good and safe.

I talked to a lot of people – among them a man called Stuart (though I had no idea of his name at the time). With all the background noise in the club, I couldn't really hear what anyone was saying to me; mostly it was, 'What are you doing here?'

'Oh, just having a night out, just enjoying myself.'

I don't know if Stuart asked me the same question, or, indeed, what we talked about. He was just another happy smiling guy, out to enjoy himself.

Jon went for a roam around the club. I talked to people all around me.

'My mum will go mad when she finds out you were here!'

'My mum loves you!'

Hand-shaking, smiling, laughing, trying to have a drink. Someone offered me champagne; I refused, I don't really like it. But I do like people, so it never bothered me getting what others would call pestered. If I'm willing to talk to people, there's no problem going out to public places. It's a great way to meet all types of people, and people is what my business is all about.

When the club was closing I wasn't with Jon – he'd wandered off. I guess it was early days with us and he wasn't used to people being around me and giving me attention all the time. Shaun learned to get used to it, but Jon hadn't . . .

Most people have the luxury of walking into a place or sitting in the corner with nobody bothering them. If you've never been with someone who attracts attention, signing this, signing that, wanting a photo for their mum, dad, sister, themselves – I suppose it's hard. Right from the start the management put two big blokes around me because the crowds were getting heavy and blocking up parts of the club.

Time flew by, and I made my way to the exit. The security guard told me he'd get me a taxi, but as I walked up the stairs a tall, bald guy approached me and said, 'It's okay, Michael, I'll be your security, I'll get you back home!' I didn't think, I just said, 'Yeah, okay.' It was nice that someone cared that much. A taxi pulled up and I got in. I asked where Jon was. The tall bald guy seemed to have everything sorted.

'Don't worry, he's coming. He'll follow us. This is my sister – can she come along?'

'Yeah, yeah, why not!'

He climbed into the front, she got in the back. Another

guy climbed in beside his sister: I still did not know this guy's name was Stuart. I just assumed he was a friend of the bald guy or his sister's boyfriend.

Just before we left I saw James, a guy I knew from the village. I said, 'What's happening?', and he said he wanted to carry on with the night. It was no big deal – people go out, they want to carry on and go back to someone's place.

'Are you having a drink back at your place?'

'Well, it looks like it!'

'Can we come?'

I wasn't too sure if I had seen his mate before, but I said, 'Yeah, whatever.'

The cab drove us to my house, the only conversation was me giving the driver directions. We arrived at my house and I got out to put the code in so the gate would open. I can't remember who settled up with the driver, but someone did and he drove off and we went into the house.

I opened up the front door. I turned off the security and started turning on the lights. I hadn't really talked properly to Stuart up to this point. He said it was a nice place and I showed everyone where the drinks were. I opened some wine, then more people started to arrive. There was another car behind ours with Jon and the other girls in. We were in the kitchen and the music was on and the bell rang around the front, it was James and his mate (Simon). Jon hadn't said anything to me but apparently he was upset that I'd left him at the nightclub.

There was a bottle of After Shock, which Stuart had a glass of, and he seemed very happy, chatty and enjoying himself.

Apart from Jon and James, I didn't know anyone else's name. I went into the front room and showed the girls how the sound system worked. People were moving around the house just to have a look. It was just another impromptu evening, like the thousands of others all over the world that happen every Friday night.

'Can we go in the swimming pool?' I can't remember who asked.

I said, 'The pool's heated, but it'll be cold outside. Have a go in the Jacuzzi at the side.'

How many of you reading this story have ever invited some people back to your home after a night out to carry on the happy atmosphere? And how many of you have been invited back to a friend's home where it transpires you know hardly anyone there? Or just joined on to a crowd and partied the night away in a strange house where you don't know anyone?

It's human nature not to want the evening to end, and any rules you may normally have about who you invite are soon relaxed once you have had a drink. I think we all want every night we have to be the best when, in truth, they all turn out to be just another late night. We all get scared that we might miss the big one. This was far from big – nine people were at the house.

That includes me. I am sure that every showbiz do must be as glossy as the shine that reflects in your face every time you read a celebrity magazine. I don't suppose it's every day that those you read about are suddenly standing right in front of you giving you a chance to become part of the glitz and glam of this make-believe world. I suppose that's what happened on this night.

There is nothing like the feeling of sharing your home with other people. The music creating an atmosphere, the flow of wine to help ease the conversation along. Every person present at my home that night had made their own choice about wanting to be there.

Much has been made about the fact that Stuart was the

father of two young children. This, combined with the fact that he was in his early thirties, would suggest a man who is more than capable of deciding how much he wants to drink, how late he wants to stay up, where he goes and what he chooses to do.

I declined to join those that headed for the Jacuzzi and went to have a joint with James. He wanted to see the new house extension, and his friend Simon came too. As we walked along the corridor, I looked out to the garden: there were the girls, Jon and the bald-headed guy (Justin Merritt) enjoying themselves in the Jacuzzi, and Stuart walking towards them. I showed James and Simon round the extension by torchlight, as the building wasn't finished, then one of the lads rolled a joint and we had a smoke. One of the girls popped her head round the door, said, 'Sorry!' and left us. We carried on smoking and decided it would be a good idea to try the Jacuzzi, so I took them down to the master bedroom at the other end of the house to get them some shorts to change into. Jon and Justin Merritt were in there, sitting on the bed in dressing gowns. I asked them what it was like outside; they said it was a bit cold, but the Jacuzzi was nice.

We got changed into shorts and I led the way outside towards the Jacuzzi, which sits adjacent to the left-hand side of the pool. Everyone who had been in already was now back inside. Outside the air was cool. I looked down at the pool lights, shining a brilliant blue against the night.

Lying at the deep end of the pool was a man's body. Face up, arms hanging by his side, not moving. You see a man lying motionless in your swimming pool. In crystal clear water with the underwater lighting and however still the body may be there is still movement. Small even waves ripple the body. It was his eyes that I fixed on. For some reason they gave the illusion of being wider than they should be and staring through the water at the night sky. My mouth wanted to form the words, '*Oh, my God*', but nothing came out. Just how much your body goes through in those first few seconds is a time frame unique to the human being. For me, and those of you who also can't swim, it's that moment that can't possibly happen to you, because you never put yourself in that situation, because of your inability to swim.

Oh, God, surely he is just resting in that position? was my only thought. Any second now he will spin in on himself, pull himself out, start to swim back to the edge and climb out of the pool. My body starts to tighten, in slow motion, frame by frame.

James and Simon jumped in immediately to pull him up. I ran back into the house to get Jon, who was still in the bedroom talking to Justin.

As I ran along the corridor to get Jon hope started to stir inside me. Thank God I had met someone who is a trained lifeguard – he will make it all come right. Surely Stuart could not have been lying there that long. All three of us ran back outside. Jon took control, pumping Stuart's body, trying to revive him.

Jon pumped his chest hard in between giving him mouth-to-mouth. Fluid flowed from Stuart's mouth, tinged red and alarming in colour (identified later as the After Shock drink he had been consuming). As I went to move forward my legs carried me nowhere.

A voice shouted, '*Get an ambulance . . .*' I went to carry out the request but, as I did so, another voice told me, '*It's done. It's on its way.*'

I was still glued to the same position. Two of the girls emerged from the lower end of the garden and immediately let out the kind of scream that only girls can make. My head held one sentence that was on an endless loop and, unlike the music, it did not stop. *'Please don't die, please don't die.'*

My movements were out of sync. Nothing was in sync. Heartbeats became heavy dull door thuds. Whatever all the others were shouting at each other became piercing sounds and made no sense. I didn't even say to myself, 'This isn't happening' – I had to believe it wasn't. And any second Stuart would come round and BREATHE. It's only at times like these that you can really have your eyes wide open and stare full in the face of absolutely nothing. It became obvious that he was not reacting. No movement, no colour in his face. The girls started to scream hysterically. I froze to the spot. This couldn't be real. How could this be real? All I could think as Jon pumped at Stuart's body was, *Live, please live.*

James broke my empty consciousness; *'Michael, Michael!'* I made contact with his eyes without any expect-ation.

'Michael, come with us.'

No reaction from me. He upped his volume.

'Michael there is nothing you can do here. The ambulance is on its way.'

Another voice joined in, but I couldn't put a face to it. All I could hear was, 'Come on, come on. Come to Simon's flat in the village.'

I spoke for the first time. 'I've got to tell Mike what's happened.'

It seemed like everyone was moving around in slow-motion circles. Simon and James ushered me with urgency towards the front door. I picked up my jeans and started to walk down my drive, pressing the number on my mobile to tell Mike what had happened and that I was going to be at Simon's flat in the village. I was not in control of events;

they were in control of me. This was purely reaction, not thought-out action, however stupid it turned out to be. We are responsible for our actions, not our reactions. People burst out laughing at funerals, but that is not a response to how they truly feel.

I started to seize up; a panic attack changed my breathing into gulps. When we got to Simon's, he made some tea. I sat staring at the walls.

Mike arrived with two police officers. One of them, a WPC, sat on a stool and took a statement from me. I kept asking, 'How is he? How is he?' Her radio crackled, she mumbled a few 'Yeahs' and 'Okays', then told me that Stuart had been pronounced dead at Princess Alexandra Hospital in Harlow. My stomach tried escaping through my mouth. I said 'Jesus' over and over. I just remember thinking, *Oh, no – this can't be true*.

That's all she said. I felt sick, somebody had lost their life. Somebody had died. He'd come along, jumped in the car to go somewhere and have a drink and the next minute he's pronounced dead at the hospital from drowning.

Simon was being interviewed in the other room, so Mike went back to the house to see what was happening. His father-in-law, Brian, came and took me back to Mike's place; there was no way I could go home. The house had been surrounded by the press already.

I tried to take in what had happened: a guy had died. A guy whose name, at that particular point, I didn't even know. Who was he? Was he married? Single? Did he have kids? A man I knew nothing about had lost his life. How did he get into that situation?

Why was I one of the first to discover him, when I'd been inside all that time? How long had he been lying there under the water?

I did not run away from the scene, as has been reported.

185

James and Simon suggested that I go with them to Simon's flat a few minutes' away because there was no more that could be done. I had hesitated, but they had said to go with them. Was that the right thing to do? No, of course it wasn't. Do I regret leaving? Of course I do. I am a human being and who knows how we will react to any trauma. I was not trying to avoid anything. The first thing I did was to ring Mike and tell him what had happened, and where I was. I did not ring my PR (Public Relations) man as the papers put it. I didn't have a PR man. Mike had worked for me for eighteen years and he was my PA (Personal Assistant). There is a vast difference.

The next day my lawyer, David Corker, came to see me, and we went to Brentwood Police Station to give a further statement.

Two detectives interviewed me and, from the outset, they took an aggressive stance; they made me feel I was a prisoner under their control. One asked all the questions, whilst the other slumped in a chair to my right, swayed his legs to and fro and chewed gum the entire time, staring at me menacingly. His hands hung on to the edge of his trousers.

During the interview, another policeman entered the room and whispered to the one interviewing me. Both David and I were then told the whisper. The interviewing detective said, 'Michael, I'm afraid this inquiry has taken on a different angle. We are now holding a homicide inquiry.'

I just stared at him and said, 'What do you mean?' He said that the pathologist had found injuries to Stuart's body. I heard what he said but they must surely be talking about somebody else, it just did not fit with my recollection of the evening. Who was I to argue with the two officers? I resolved to give every assistance possible.

*

When you hear the word murder, your brain says how, what, who and when? I thought, who was in my house who could be a murderer? Was it just circumstances that prevented me being murdered? How could someone have planned a murder – how is that possible? It doesn't fit; I couldn't make sense of it. I certainly can't make sense of it the way the media would have liked me to – the orgy that didn't actually happen, the wild party that never was. There was just no sense to any of it.

One of the officers, the stockier of the two, seemed very hyper about the whole situation. There was a feeling that once they knew whose house it was, it became a celebrity murder-mystery.

I felt uncomfortable with the policemen; one in particular seemed to be very scary. I thought to myself, 'Please tell me that this isn't happening.'

David took over the questions. 'What exactly are his injuries?'

The detective answered, 'We've been told that the post-mortem revealed severe wounding around Stuart's anus. The severity was such that the pathologist said that Stuart would have been in agony and have bled profusely.'

I interrupted. 'Well, the last thing I saw, he was walking towards the Jacuzzi.'

'Pathologists get it wrong sometimes,' said David.

With confidence the detective said, 'I don't think so. He's the best.'

David answered without looking at him, 'We'll see.'

The house had now been closed off as a crime scene. When I had left to go to Simon's, there was no suspicion of foul play at that point and why would there have been – there was nothing in the pool, no discoloration of the water, nothing on the poolside tiles where Stuart had been lying, we would have noticed if there was anything. The police were there, the paramedic team worked on him there; if something wasn't right surely they would have noticed.

The cause of death was drowning. There were no injuries mentioned in any reports from the medical team at the house or from the hospital at all. It was only afterwards that these injuries seemed to appear.

There has never been an explanation as to what happened to the body when the police signed off at 8.30 am, as noted in their log books. If there was any suspicion either at the scene or at the hospital, wouldn't the police have stayed with Stuart from the outset until the pathologist got there?

There is a gap, where he was unattended from 8.30 am in the morning until 4.40 pm that afternoon, when the pathologist arrived. When questioned, no one gave any indication as to whether the body had been guarded or not. The phrase 'horrific injuries' comes from other sources. The pathologist's report does not say 'horrific', it merely describes the injuries in medical terms. The word horrific found its way into news reports later.

Another pathologist's report concluded that there may not have been a sexual attack; that the injuries could have been inflicted by a blunt instrument. Any reports subsequently are based on the original report that has photographs and it seems odd to me that if there was a suspicion why no mould was taken of that area of his body to establish if it wasn't physically done, and what the shape of the supposed instrument actually was. How could this have taken place with no thorough investigation?

Jon and I were in a state of shock. We couldn't stay at Mike's, so we rang Austin Tate at the Marchwood Priory in Southampton, and were taken down there to be under the close surveillance of psychiatrists and nurses. They sedated me heavily – but not enough to block out the constant flashbacks of seeing Stuart's body floating in the pool.

As the stories outside got wilder and wilder, I was barred from seeing newspapers, but occasionally the odd nurse would slip up and I would catch sight of my name in heavy black type on a front page. I blinked rapidly and walked in another direction, feeling the eyes of all the other patients staring at me.

I realised then what a feast the media was going to have, every homophobic/anti-Barrymore angle. As time went on they did not let me down: BARRYMORE: BODY IN HIS POOL AT GAY BOOZE ORGY; BARRYMORE THE FACTS: DEAD MAN SUFFERED SERIOUS SEXUAL INJURIES; DROWNED GUEST MAY HAVE BEEN SEX VICTIM; BARRYMORE POOL VICTIM TESTED FOR DATE RAPE DRUG. It was open season. The press started an orgy of their own. All in the belief that if some journalists say a thing that they know isn't true, if they keep on saying it long enough it will become so.

Now I was supposed to believe not that only Stuart had possibly been murdered, but also that a sex orgy had taken place – all seemingly in the time that it took to smoke a joint with James and Simon. According to reports, Stuart had taken part in sexual activities so violent that he wouldn't have been able to walk. So where was all the blood? Kylie Merritt said he was happily dive-bombing into the pool, asking her to join him. What were the other girls doing during this time? My whole house is glass on the side that looks out on to the pool – there is no way something like this could happen without being seen. The music wasn't loud; if there had been screams, one of us would have heard them.

All guests at the house that night had their DNA taken and there was no DNA link to anything that had happened to Stuart's body. His body was intact, his boxer shorts were not torn in any way – the paramedics would have noticed if there was anything suspicious; it would have been in their report.

Back at The Priory, hundreds of cards started to arrive with messages of support. A few less friendly ones found their way past the censors: my face cut out from a newspaper, heavy red felt-tip pen drawing horns on my head, red pen in my eyes, and the words 'devil' and 'evil'. I had constant nausea. I couldn't stay still or sleep. I tried to focus on getting well, but I was in no fit state to get well. I knew from experience that, in order to get better, you need to be a little bit well in your head, and that was the last place that felt good. No booze, no drugs to take away the pain. Asking me to pray to God didn't go down too well either: I wasn't sure what his part in all this was. I know now I should have trusted him, but I couldn't. Photographers tried to hide in bushes or dig their way in to see just how sad a picture they could get. Why bother? The one that was being painted was tragic enough.

One of the senior counsellors, David, came to see me. 'Michael, could you pop into my office for a moment?' There was Mike – and he did what he had to do.

'Michael, you need to take an HIV test as soon as possible.'

I sat down and stared at the floor. My head started to spin and I wanted to cry, but my eyes just stared, wide open. I must have thought out loud, 'I can't be HIV!' Mike said, 'You need to confront Jon and ask him if he's HIV positive, because the papers are threatening to print the fact that he's got Aids.' I already knew the story about the sex orgy; now they were trying to make it even more sinister.

'Mike, you ask him.'

Mike confronted Jon, no messing.

'Jon, are you HIV positive?'

The slightest of pauses. 'Yes.'

He said he hadn't told me before because he was frightened of rejection. It was a situation I'd never had to deal with before. I couldn't speak to him, I just thought, 'Thanks for telling me, mate.' This particular story was not fiction. I began to panic – you would wouldn't you? I was devastated.

Jon left Marchwood the next day. There was no point in him staying, really: he wasn't taking part in any rehabilitation, he was just keeping himself to himself. Under normal circumstances, they would never treat two people in tandem like that, and the doctor thought that nothing was being gained by Jon staying – and that suited him because he didn't like being there at all.

I was tested for HIV later that day. A doctor took a blood sample from me at six o'clock in the evening, and told me that I would have the results within 24 hours. He asked me how much I knew about the disease. I know only what most of us know – that it's life-threatening and still has a stigma attached to its name. The doctor told me about the various treatments, and that with the new medication available most people can live a full life. He didn't say don't worry, but he did say it was very hard to contract. I missed a lot of what he said; all my mind was saying was that after everything that's happened in my life, I might find out in 24 hours that I was HIV positive. I could only think the worst. I was going to die. I couldn't stop talking to myself, talking to God, asking him why. Not once did I say to myself, 'Hold on, you haven't done anything to get HIV!'

No sleep that night, just thinking about how I would deal with this. What was happening? Any resolve I had was dissolving. I was closing down. I don't think I've ever felt as lonely as I did that night.

After what seemed like only a few seconds, the doctor

walked back into my room and said, 'Your test is negative,' followed by a polite 'Okay' as he left.

We hear all sorts of things throughout our lives, some good, some bad, and no one ever reacts the way you think they will. When the doctor left, I carried on staring at the wall, wondering if what had just happened had actually happened at all. I must have fallen asleep. I woke the next morning fully clothed on top of my bed, and reminded myself that I had not dreamed about the day before. And I thanked God.

I spent about six weeks at The Priory. It might as well have been six minutes for all the good it did me. It wasn't their fault. 'Fault' and 'blame' are two words that, in the future, I would have to learn to take out of my vocabulary.

I went over and over what had happened, and never seemed to reach any conclusions. I tried to find some answers, some reasons, but I just went round and round in circles – ever decreasing circles as the weeks went on. I started to feel as though I was actually going mad. Mentally I started to die. I never slept for any amount of time, just catnapped through sheer exhaustion. My room became smaller and smaller as I spent more time in it, desperate to be on my own. The investigation into Stuart's death was going on, but I wasn't told what was happening. His death was taking on a life of its own; the stories in the papers were out of control.

I left The Priory by being taken out in the boot of a four by four, hidden from the press. I had nothing to hide: I just knew from experience that it's not a good idea to let them take any more photographs than necessary. So many pictures of me have been tampered with to make me look just how they want me to look, depending on the story at the time. Years earlier, when they were hounding me for looking too skinny, they took a photograph of me on the beach without my knowledge, then shaded my ribs to accentuate the bones along the side of my body. They stuck my head on the top of a Coke bottle; the headline read, 'The Real Thin'. If I had been ill at the time – which I wasn't – imagine how that would have affected me. How caring and nice, and all justified as being 'in the public interest'.

Back home I couldn't settle down at all. It was too soon. Seeing the pool for the first time since that night brought on flashbacks, and I reached for the bottle to deal with it. So I had gained nothing from being in rehab. I found a comfortable corner in my kitchen and stayed huddled up there for a week, pushing against the walls with my back. I can't remember much of anything that was said to me. My head had blocked all conversation. The press was camped out at the gates of my house; small planes and helicopters flew overhead, trying to get the shot that no one else had. I was trapped inside my head and my house. They knocked on neighbours' doors and offered them money to use their gardens to get a photo of me. No one let them in or talked to them, and I thank them for being what neighbours should be.

Mike saw that my depression was making me worse, that being cooped up in the house with all the rumours flying around wasn't doing me any good at all, and so he got me out of the country for a week. We stayed at a secret location in Dubai, and halfway through the week Mike told me that David Corker, my solicitor, was flying out.

'Why?'

'He has to talk to you.'

'Why?'

'Because on your return to England, you're going to be arrested.'

Arrested for what? I had been told that Stuart's death was definitely now the subject of a murder investigation. I had been told I was not under any suspicion of murder myself. I was going to be arrested on suspicion of possession of controlled drugs.

On my return to England I reported to Harlow Police Station to be arrested. I have to say that some of the detectives treated me well, not that I deserved to be treated any better or worse that anyone else. It was clear that some of them found it difficult. What does it feel like to look at someone and think that, until you know different, they could be guilty? Some of those officers found it hard to hide the fact that they did not enjoy reading me my rights.

The desk sergeant, very stern, late thirties with cropped hair, looked me in the eye and told me that I would be bailed to reappear in two months' time, pending more tests and more inquiries. As I left the police station under heavy escort, a crowd had gathered to swell the usual throng of journalists, TV cameras and news crews. As we sped out, heads craned around us at all angles. Some waved, some stared, and I stared into nothing. I became a nothing. Anyone could have said turn right, turn left, walk straight ahead, jump, and I would have done. I had to get sorted before life sorted me once and for all. The next day I flew to Arizona.

Jon and Justin were arrested on suspicion of murder. No test has shown that Stuart had any kind of sexual contact with anyone in the house. The police tested everything, including the bed sheets, for evidence of the supposed orgy – and none of the tests bore any relation to what the pathologists had said took place.

A thorough investigation (their words not mine) by Essex police followed, while the tabloids put me on trial with false rumours and statements, trying to make out that

I had personally taken part in whatever was supposed to have happened that night.

I had nothing to do with Stuart's death. I did not see anyone else have anything to do with his death. I can't imagine the pain his family went through at this time. Although I felt as if my life was turning into a nightmare, it was nothing compared to what the Lubbock family must have been going through.

8

Coming Home

I was bailed until August, and so in June I flew to the States and checked into Sierra Tucson, Arizona, which is known as one of the toughest rehabs in the world. Now, I know my rehabs. I've been to several. Been there, done that, got the T-shirt. Rehab, for me, usually means a short period detoxing from drink and drugs, followed by a pretty rapid relapse. So what was going to make this place different?

I talked about what happened to me. I cried and cried until I couldn't cry any more, and just when I felt I couldn't go on, they made me go over it all again, and again. It empties you of self-pity, it takes away all your fears and it removes your paranoia so that you can start again. They make it abundantly clear that if you look at all the shit in your life, all the bad things that have happened, a drink or drug was never far away. Your problems are drink and drugs, and you deal with them by taking more drink and drugs. The problems get bigger. This was the first rehab I had been to where you got busted for eating sweets, for turning up late for classes, or for skipping duties such as cleaning out the smoking area, known as the 'butt hut'.

I became 'mayor' of the Tucson community within a week of arriving – a fact that alarmed my counsellor, Pete. 'It worries me that you were elected mayor within a couple of days of arriving, Michael. It worries me how you achieved that. So I want you to wear this badge for two days.' He pinned a sign to my shirt which read: CONFRONT THE CHARMING BEHAVIOURS.

He wanted me to stop using my communication skills on people – in effect, to stop doing this thing that I do for a living. He knew I was trying to do what came naturally: keep everyone else happy and hide how I really felt behind the usual clown mask. He wanted me to learn that it was okay to be seen with a sad face, if that was how I felt. I had to learn to be responsible for myself first; other people came second. He latched on very quickly to what comedians do. This joke is a perfect example of how a comedic statement is hiding what a comedian is really feeling. 'I was so depressed I went to the library and asked the librarian if he had a book on suicide. He said, "Sod off, you won't bring it back!"'

The Sierra Tucson day starts with a wake-up call at 6 am. For the first couple of weeks I was always the last to bed, and was surviving on two or three hours' sleep. I was frightened of sleeping. Every time I closed my eyes I saw Stuart's body lying in the pool. I kept myself awake as long as I could to avoid it. I sat awake every night wondering what was going on back at home. During the four weeks I was there, I had no contact with anyone outside rehab. I had to concentrate on getting well. It felt like my last chance – and, looking back, I think that if I hadn't got away from the persecution, the witch-hunt that was going on at home, I might not have survived. If I'd read the reports, the way they were portraying me as some devil, I would have crumbled. I couldn't handle that kind of onslaught; who could? Horrible things were happening.

Looking back, some of the paragraphs I have written read like a very sad novel, not real life. But they are real, and it's hard to face that.

So here I am in yet another rehab, and a minimum of one month's trial to try once more to get my life back on track. The amount of times my life has derailed, my chances of being cast as Thomas the Tank Engine are getting much thinner. Which nicely leads me to my train of thought.

At Tucson the therapy revolved around psychodrama – the re-enacting of scenes from your past with the other patients playing the role of your father, mother or whoever was involved in the traumatic moments that you think helped get you there. The acting ability of the others was Oscar-winning, but then we would all make good actors had we actually experienced what they had. When the subject of my childhood came up, I was made to sit opposite one of the other guys who I had selected as being most similar to my dad. I had to describe what he was like. The person imitating my dad took on his posture. I was made to talk to him, which became frighteningly real and increasingly intense as the counsellors told him what to say, making him non-caring then introducing the woman playing my mother. As the anger at him and myself rose, they encouraged me to beat a paddle as hard as I wanted on a large square cushion to release the anger. If you were ever passing one of the rooms at this time, the noise, and an occasional chair flying out of the window, would indicate there was therapy in session.

I hit that cushion so hard, and in the end realised that it's what you believe that gets you where you are. The answer is to deal with what happens without asking someone else and without having a drink to help make up your mind. I had to take responsibility for me. That meant letting go of the boy and becoming the man. Easier said than done. That boy had been very successful – it was a hard call to hand the business over to the man.

The basic rehab setup is that you are cut off from your surroundings with no television, radio, newspapers – practically anything that will distract you from your recovery. The first time you get to see family or close friends is towards the end of your treatment. Obviously there is an emotional reunion and, as in my case, you sit in a circle with those you have been recovering with, plus their families and yours, with a counsellor in attendance to steer the meeting. This is used as a method to tell each other personal details that have previously not been aired for fear of your family's reaction. Hard as it was, I was actually glad I went to Sierra Tucson. Of all the rehabs I have been to, this one had the desired effect. I have been well, clean and sober for over five years now.

I was one of a community of seventy people. Anorexics, overeaters, bulimics, obsessive compulsives, compulsive gamblers, manic depressives, self-harmers, drug addicts. A mixed bag of mixed-up people. In this environment it is easy to isolate, to shut down and just stare into the desert. If you do that, they deal with it by making you walk around with a giant teddy bear, which has to be by your side at all times, including lunch and dinner – the bear is your baby and you have to show that you can be responsible. Do you feel foolish walking around with a giant fairground prize? Yes you do. Does it work? Yes it does. One of the men in my group had to look after teddy. He hated doing it and protested that it was ridiculous. But even though it was just to complain, this was the first time he had spoken to anyone in two weeks. He would stand in line at lunch with teddy, making sure that he always had a seat beside him and he made no comment about everyone looking at the grown man with the giant teddy. For my part, I felt only respect for him for doing the teddy caring. That lunchtime another man was being shown to his seat. He was blindfolded. He ate his lunch blindfolded and attended all his counselling classes for the next two days blindfolded. Why? So that he had to learn to ask another human being for help and trust that they would see him around without walking into walls. I took him for a walk, he said he needed to get back to his bedroom. I took him to the stable yard and left him holding on to one of the horses. For that I was given a pink slip. Sounds nice, but it is not one you wear. Get too many pink slips and you get shown the front door, however ill you are. This was a strict place. I never heard that much laughter, but there were plenty of tears.

Millie (not her real name, for obvious reasons), a young girl from LA who I had been in treatment with, started the session. Her mum and dad looked stressed. Strangers, such as myself, are mixed into these most private of moments. Tearfully Millie explained the reason for her behaviour over the last year, which she dealt with by drinking and drugging. I looked at her mum and dad, their eyes darting from side to side, trying to search for their part in all this. A silence called for all of us to adjust in our circle of chairs.

Mike Browne, my PA, was to my left. He was representing my family as Mum wasn't up to the long flight. The counsellor broke the uneasy silence by saying to Millie, 'Millie, are you up for saying what you need to say?'

Millie's tears were flowing, her mother's eyes held water without flow and her father's eyes held a point in the room that contacted with nothing and nobody. After several attempts to speak without success Millie explained what was so secret. Her mother pulled her daughter's face to squeeze against hers so that their tears could join. My heart sank to its lowest beat ever. Mike adjusted his legs to deal with the unease and the father's eyes stayed in contact with the nothing space he had fixed on. Whether he knew that I was looking at him or not he stayed locked on to his emptiness. Millie was sixteen years old. Before any further reaction, the counsellor talked across everyone's reaction to what they had just heard.

'Now,' said the counsellor, turning to Mike. 'I believe you have something to say to Michael.'

'Yes.' For some reason he did not make eye contact with me. I allowed my body to relax slightly in the knowledge that whatever he had to say could not have quite the impact of Millie's statement.

He spoke. 'Michael, I have given a lot of thought to what I am about to say, but feel just to say it is perhaps the best.' He hesitated, 'I just wanted to say . . .'

I gave him a slight crease of my eyes to visually say, it's okay, Mike – whatever. He said, 'Michael, the real reason your mother did not attend this meeting was not because of the flight, it is because she only has six weeks to live.'

I lowered my eyes to find my own focus of nothingness, like Millie's father opposite, and the heaviest flow of tears I had ever experienced joined Millie's to form a river of sadness. Up to that point, I truly believed that mothers lived for ever.

*

I learned that writing letters to people was a good way of dealing with how I felt. I wrote a letter to Mum. In writing this letter, I was trying to face up to how I would deal with her death.

1 July 2001, Sierra Tucson, Arizona

My dearest mum,
I hesitate to start this letter, which at some point has to have an end. If anything in this world has a start, it has to come to closure – except for God. I'm not sure that I can deal with handing you over to someone I can only see in my mind . . .

One day I will join you and we can spend the rest of our eternal life doing everything we missed. Over and over, again and again, in health, without disease, with me asking God if he can turn the wine back into water. All those days as a small boy I just wanted the screaming and shouting to end, not you. I am so, so proud of you. Despite what you were given as a life, you came through to a wonderful age with the dignity of a queen. A queen with jewels in her heart, so warm . . .

My mind has gone back to a day in the 60s: I was ready for school, you were in the front room hoovering the carpet. Your head bowed to avoid eye contact . . . I looked at the dark green carpet and locked on to a small puddle of tears darkening the wool.

'What's wrong, Mum?'

You looked at me with such sadness and croaked, 'John Kennedy is dead.'

I left for school and cried not for him but for you. I didn't want any more upset for you – you had been through enough already. Now I realise that you were crying at the thought of another war, the thought of losing the family that you had struggled to keep together.

Thank you for my life, thank you for the laughter, thanks for all the tears you soaked away for me and thanks for the memories. Sorry about the water stains, they are dripping from above. I really will always love you.

Michael Kieron

I also wrote letters to my brother John, my father-in-law Eddie, to Stuart – each of them an attempt to sort out feelings, to unload my grief. None were ever posted.

After four weeks at Sierra Tucson, I went into aftercare at another rehab centre in Malibu. It was less tough – a way of easing you back into normal life. Sierra Tucson is very institutionalised, and it would be hard to go from there straight out into the world. A lot of people don't want to leave at all, because they feel safe in a totally controlled environment. They drag you in there kicking and screaming, and then they drag you kicking and screaming out.

During the month I spent in Malibu I had to deal with the thought that I had been bailed to reappear at Harlow Police Station, not knowing what was really going on at home. I also talked to my mum every day knowing that she was slowly slipping away from me. I'm not sure who kidded who; knowing Mum, she probably put on a brave voice saying she was doing well and for me to concentrate on keeping myself well.

I kept a diary during my month at Malibu; it was a way of recording not only what was happening in my life, but seeing how rehab worked on a day-by-day basis.

17.07.01, Tuesday pm
My sponsor (a person with long sobriety, who helps the

newcomers or constant relapsers), who for anonymity I will call 'Rewind', took me to a meeting last night. I enjoyed it. Great atmosphere. One of the guys – Jesus, I'm getting so American! – said, 'Hi, I'm Bob and I am an alcoholic.' From the rear of the hall the fellow addicts shouted in unison, 'Who gives a fuck?' Definitely my kind of recovery! I was asked to share, so I walked nervously to the platform and nervously shared, and they all confidently clapped. In AA you are taught to listen. It doesn't matter that I can't understand half of what they are saying, I listen. At tonight's meeting one of the addicts spoke of his hope and vision, elongated with fifty-four 'fuckings'. I mentioned this to Rewind. He stared at me and asked, 'Why were you counting?' I said I was only guessing, and he seemed to accept that. I was relieved; I was also lying.

Now I am back at Funny Farm headquarters, on my bed, writing up my diary as prescribed by the almighty Rewind. I have to put my shoes under the bed – Rewind's idea – so that when I bend down to retrieve them in the morning I'm in the kneeling position to say my prayers. This is only my second day. God knows how many pairs I will need to get through this. I rang Rewind this morning, as he said last night, 'I want you to ring me again tomorrow. If you don't, then don't bother ringing me again because it will mean you can't be bothered and you're not serious about your recovery. Read page eighty-six of *Alcoholics Anonymous* before bed and I will be asking questions tomorrow.' Rewind doesn't mess around. He's got eyes in the back of his head; that must be why he wears his baseball cap peak to aft.

It's now five past midnight, my forty-second day of sobriety. My eyes are closing; I've had a busy day. Must pray for Mum and I suppose it would not cost too much to throw in one for Rewind. Lights out!

18.07.01, Wednesday am
My 43rd sober day. Woke at 7 o'clock, turned over, rewoke at 7.30. The sun is up, the sky is blue. Not a thing to do except what I am told. Put on yet another beach shirt. I am really getting into this sober thinking, which includes dressing half my age. On my first day Rewind said, 'All I'm interested in is keeping you sober. We'll talk about the clothes at a later date.' I haven't got a phone card, so I'm debating whether to call Rewind collect. It's now 8.30 and I'm sitting on the balcony overlooking Malibu beach. A weak cup of tea, American style, with Carole King singing in the background.

Wednesday pm
First group of the day was lively. One of the members wanted attention. In his words, 'I get no fucking attention. I've been here over two weeks for fuck's sake. Everybody hates me. I'm never told what the fucking hell is going on around here. All of you are against me!' Two others interrupt. 'That's because you're in bed all day and never come to the meetings!' The screaming addict continues, 'Fuck you, I do come to group!' The two others reply, 'When?' 'I came to one two days ago, you shitheads.' I sat in the middle watching this perfect display of recovery, with my head lefting and righting, tennis fashion. The screamer got satisfaction when told everyone really loves him. Another one reacts to the word failure. 'Don't say that word. I am not a failure, don't say I'm a fucking failure.' Another rehab hang-up starts screaming about the use of the word failure.
I listen, not getting involved.

20.07.01, Friday pm
Not feeling too good at the moment. My neck is really
hurting and I feel like I want to throw up. I was at an
AA meeting at St Aidens. Obviously he's not the patron
saint of cures. The neck seems to have dominated the
day. I kept dozing off in the group. Found it hard to
focus. I was late ringing Rewind. 'Where the fuck have
you been hiding all day?' I say, 'My neck hurts.' He
replies with a dismissive, 'Oh, really, no shit. Now
let's get on with more important things. Have you read
your book?' 'Er . . . yes,' I say. He doesn't sound too
convinced, nor am I. So I go and do what I was
supposed to do twice, to make up for the one I lied
about and read page eighty-six twice. I think that I've
got my dates mixed up and today is my forty-fifth day
of sobriety. Or then again, it could be my forty-sixth.
Oh, I don't know. Night, night.

21.07.01, Saturday am
To be brutally honest, I haven't read page eighty-six
because I was late getting up and I feel rushed. Still got
a neck, not so bad this morning, it's just killing, so at
least some progress. I have a new roommate, Ked I'll
call him. He's from Texas, so he doesn't open his
mouth very wide when he talks. Nice guy – sorry – man!
He's not that tall, so he fits his bed really well. I've
got the same size bed: when I lay down my legs stretch
out beyond the edge. From a side view I look like
a wheelbarrow, you know, full of shit. Just need
somewhere to dump the shit, know what I mean?

23.07.01, Monday am
It's Monday morning, my eyes are sore, and it's coming
up to the time for me to plan my return home. Rewind

has offered to come with me and help me through my first sober six months to a year. My tea is ready, my pay phone is ready to ring Mum, Mike and Rewind, and I'm ready for another day.

It's taken forty-nine years, a lot of pain, masses of worry, heartache, etc. to find out and finally understand what telling little lies leads to. It may be obvious to a lot of people, but it sure as hell passed me by. I lied a little yesterday by not telling anyone that Jackson had relapsed seven days previously, and I engineered it so that we could be around each other like everything was fine. Now some people who are not of the suppy-suppy, drinky-drinky, druggy-druggy, more more more, shove-down-throat brigade, of which I am a fully paid-up member, may wonder what is wrong with this. Well, imagine your child is learning to climb mountains. You leave the child with the most-experienced instructor, with a fine record of mountaineering, you watch with pride as the child climbs to the top, you watch as your darling hangs on to a razor sharp rock, you look round to show your admiration to the instructor, only to discover he is ninety-three years old in a wheelchair and has senile dementia. It is the little lies that I have grown to live with. They have to go, my old way of thinking has to go, and it's frightening giving up my way of doing, my way of surviving, worst still without a drink or drugs.

25.07.01, Wednesday am
My forty-eighth day of sobriety. The tragedy of Stuart's death is floating around in my head. I did think to correct the word floating, but realised I can't correct every detail that comes genuinely from my mind. I have to learn not to edit what I say to suit other people. He was one of my guests in my house and treated equally.

What isn't equal is the fact that his life came to a close; I need to deal with his death. I would never wish for anyone not to have life. I've prayed for my own often enough. Do I wish it had never happened? Yes. I wish so much that it has all been a sick dream that's gone on far too long, far too many hours of sleep, a sleeping hell, just like I wish so much that all the years of being an addict will end and I find out it's all been a dream. Screaming myself out of nightmares, waking up with a shudder, alone in bed, alone in what I have dreamed. Which is actually my reality. Everyone pointing at me. Tabloids making judgements, everyone's opinion. People in the street saying, 'You didn't have anything to do with his death, did you?' How sick – how am I supposed to deal with such a question?

28.07.01, *Saturday*
Long lie-in. Phoned Mum, she sounds well. Typical Mum, she's in hospital fighting cancer and the first thing she says is, 'It's too hot in London.' I hope when my time comes I am as brave as her or at least as brave as she seems. Morning group, Day fifty-one of sobriety. Feeling a little anxious about going home now that the time to return is drawing closer. Had art therapy this afternoon. No point asking me what it was all about, I slept through most of it. When I did wake I drew a lot of toys on a sideboard. Went back to sleep, woke up, said what they meant to me in my life and went back to sleep.

31.07.01, *Tuesday*
Day fifty-four. Just received a fax from Mike – Mum's not doing very well. I ring, she sounds good, but a bit vague. I've left group to get my bags ready in case I have to leave quickly. I hope that God is kind and Mum is

not in any unnecessary pain. Must ring Rewind to give him an update.

01.08.01, *Wednesday*
Overslept slightly on this first day of August; fourteen more days to the police station and fifty-five days of sobriety. I must be getting some balance in my life because fifty-five days clean and sober is more important than fourteen days to the police station. Had an early trip to the chiropractor, click click, $45 please. I'm sure he short-changed me by one click. Mike rang; said Mum is doing as well as can be expected. Mr Tobias, her consultant, said he'd located another tumour, which explained her health decline, and that with treatment he could fix it so that she would last a bit longer. It's just crossed my mind, all the years you have together, Mum gave me life and a stranger is giving life extension to her, and we are both in treatment fighting for our lives. Who has the choice? I do, so therefore I must always remember on this day, the first day of August in the year 2001, when Mum has no choice and yet is so grateful for her life, and I have choice and I am so grateful to her for giving me life, for getting my sanity back – and all she asks to make her happy is that I am well and able to say no to a drink or a drug. For the first time in my life it is so simple. Why was it so hard to learn?

02.08.01, *Thursday*
Got to morning group. The discussion is about leaving the boy behind and becoming the man. It is something I have been fighting for a long time – for as long as Eddie, my father-in-law, hasn't been in my life. I only have myself to ask permission if it's okay to play or not and when it's time to be responsible. I also have to

decide who I play with. All this time I have relied on others to either make decisions or help me make them. Why did my dependency not get a hold till relatively late? Was I so addicted to my work?

My favourite time of day is five o'clock till sunset; also the most dangerous time for me. I got what is known as euphoric recall yesterday. I sat up on the work surface in the kitchen talking to a couple of the other insanities and told them how this time of day, with the sun setting, was perfect for my alcohol intake. The other two joined me in the recall. Within twenty minutes all three of us are out on the balcony writhing with withdrawal symptoms, myself to the point of my skin crawling. We calm down, reminding ourselves of the aftermath we leave behind on such nights.

04.08.01, *Saturday*
Kov, my roommate, said today, 'I suppose the first thing you will do after spending over two months in rehab will be to book into a hotel and hire a hooker.' I didn't disappoint his observation and let out a nudge-nudge, knowing wink, followed by a false, quick short laugh, 'Ho ho.' Actually, I have no intention at this moment of getting involved with anyone because I'm leaving on a jet plane.

Back home. David [Corker] just called. He's talked to the superintendent, who said that tomorrow I will be rebailed for ten weeks due to fresh information. He wouldn't tell him what it was until they talked to Stuart's family. It's made me feel lost again: my head is like pins and needles and my body is wired. I realise how much I will need all the resources I have learned at rehab to keep me centred. I really have no power over this situation.

We tried to work out what this mysterious new information is, but didn't have to guess for long as one of this morning's newspapers proclaims that the police will be making another full search of my house. I am thrilled that the press has the information before my lawyer or me. Makes me wonder why I spend all this money when, for the price of a paper, I can get all the information I need. I've been away for over two months. They've decided in that time that maybe they missed something. If there is new evidence and it involves me, I want to know.

9

Ticket to the Future

Mum was very sick when I got back to England. I'd already been prepared for the worst. Mike had called me just before I left Malibu and told me that she only had two weeks to live. If there's such a thing as a good place in which to hear that news, I was in it: I had plenty of support around me, and I wasn't going to reach for the nearest bottle or pill. Instead I sat with a few of the other guys and cried, rather than trying to blot out the pain. I think that meant I was able to deal with things a lot better when I got home. When I arrived back, storms were raging all around me.

The police investigation, Mum's declining health, the press coverage, worries about my career – if I ever had cause to draw on the resources that I'd gained from rehab, now was the time. But I felt confident, even calm. For the first time in my life I felt mentally well. Not running, not plodding, just walking. Neither the tortoise nor the hare. At last I had learned to be content with who I am. I started attending AA meetings in Essex, and one old boy recalled how his wife and daughter had been away for the day, leaving him on his own. He made no plans to do anything that day. No housework, no thinking about how the next day should be, no levels of expectation. By the time evening came he thought back over the day and realised he had just had an ordinary day. For someone with the disease of addiction, that is as remarkable as someone else going out and having a great night with a drink.

Rewind thought it okay to go to the papers and tell his story about me. Because he was seven years in the fellowship of AA I felt that I could trust him when he suggested that he should sponsor me. I paid for his flight to London and he stayed at my house. When we arrived back home the first thing he hit me with was that he was missing £1,500. That it must have slipped out on the plane. I wasn't too sure I believed him and I am not going to give him too much page space explaining why I thought, 'Oh dear Michael, this guy is a wrong one.' When I confronted him with the fact that I did not believe his story of the missing money he said, 'Are you saying I am a liar?' I replied that even if the airline said that they had found the money I still didn't believe him. He said, 'Well, I better leave then.' I agreed and dropped him off at the local hotel. The next time I saw his face was on the front page of a newspaper slagging me off. I was right – the man was wrong and better off gone. I know that a lot of people in AA don't like the fact that I am not anonymous, but it's my choice and right to break my own anonymity and talk about myself.

*

I attended Harlow Police Station to be told that on the same day the police would be conducting a surprise swoop on my house to search it for more evidence. Such a surprise that one of the newspapers that morning ran the front page BARRYMORE'S HOUSE TO BE RE-SEARCHED. If it was at all possible there were more press than police at the gates of my house for the surprise swoop and a surprisingly huge white lorry trying to back its way up the drive to my house with ESSEX POLICE SPECIAL INVESTI-GATION TEAM embossed on the side. This was a blockbuster for the press, seeing as they were writing the script. The lorry couldn't get in, though, so urgent calls organised another smaller one – more delight, more pictures. I sat with my solicitor David Corker in the garden and watched the search being conducted. The police wanted me out of the house, I refused to leave. I was not going to let them have free reign of my home. David Corker sought to know from the police what it was that they were looking for, so that it could be found and immediately handed over. In my opinion, the two-day search of my house was staged entirely for the benefit of the media. They were now looking for an instrument that they believed could have caused injury to Stuart. I'd been away for months, during which time they could have searched the house and the grounds inch by inch. They could have put together all the evidence they needed to come to a satis-factory conclusion about what happened that night. The whole search seemed absurd, seeing that they were coming back for a second bite over four months later. What did they seriously expect to recover? Looking in my wardrobes, under my chairs, in my shoes. What?

A young police officer was standing at the gates trying to turn the press away, but they knew their rights better than he did and called his bluff. His response was to well up with tears.

Then the search got under way. Here's how it's done. Wait till four months after the incident in question has taken place. Gather together about twenty very young police officers, make them put on dark blue overalls with POLICE printed on the back, just so there can be no confusion for the press. Check that their boots are as heavy as possible, especially on a warm August day. You need the ones that mark carpets and wooden floors. Take about six girls, get them to wear white silky overalls not only with POLICE on the back but also with SCIENTIFIC DEPARTMENT, just in case some of the other ones in the blue overalls get jealous and say they want one. Then add a few very senior policemen who don't have to wear anything special, just plain clothes. Break everyone up into teams and let them search outside: walk up to a bush, give it a quick once-over to establish that it is indeed a bush, part it with the palms of your hands, peer inside for four or five seconds, no more and move on to the next one. Ignore anything on the other side of the fence.

Inside the house more teams prodded and poked. They took photographs of the master bedroom – a room that didn't even exist on the night in question, as the extension hadn't then been finished. One of the senior officers announced that this bed had been moved, and they started to get quite excited. Painstaking tests were done on the mattress, then everyone froze, specks of blood had been found. One of the team was elected to go and tell the Very Important Policeman in Plain Clothes. The mattress was seized, its cover, the sheets, pillowcases, duvet. This was major. I could have told them that I have psoriasis on my elbow and that it sometimes bleeds, and that this was my blood.

At the other end of the house another team was looking up the chimney. No torch: just a hard look with specially trained eyes. Nothing was found. They carefully put back a basket of logs – small, about one foot long, two inches wide! Were they checked? Sadly, no. By this time I actually wanted them to find something. I wanted an answer. I wanted to know what had happened to Stuart. My faith in the police – and I did have plenty – was fading fast. The next discovery was under a rug in one of the bedrooms – a trap door. It's there to access the bathroom pipes. After a very short time, Mike offered to find some tools to assist them but they said don't worry, we are going to leave it. Another team in the kitchen asked for a senior officer to look at what they'd found in one of the drawers – a box of candles. They didn't want to touch them in case they were evidence. Brand new candles in the box, unmelted, unstained, unbelievable.

The house has a housekeeper who cleans thoroughly every day. It appeared to me that the search was being conducted and spun out with an eye to giving the media a big story in the middle of what is known in media terms as 'The Silly Season'. More like 'The Stupid Season'. Either way, it wasn't funny.

The Very Important Policeman said they would have to go through all my video tapes because they had had a call from an anonymous person saying that a recording was made that night. I told him it was a waste of time, no recording was made, but of course he ignored me and two of his officers spent the next two days watching all my old shows. I only hope they were fans.

The Very Important Policeman gave an interview to the press and, quite coincidentally, the science department walked across the back of the shot so they were seen on camera. As soon as they were out of shot, they took their overalls off.

––––––

Later on that afternoon, they started to search outside the house and Mike walked around with them. At one end of the pool there was an electric pool cover that rolled under a slate cover that was level with the rest of the patio. The cover was held in place by a number of bolts and Mike showed one of the officers to the pump house to find the allen key. To Mike's amazement, the officer stuck his head inside the door and said, 'Leave it. It's okay. There is no need to open the cover.' Mike replied that it was no problem and would only take a few minutes but he responded by saying, 'no, it's fine.' This was surely one of the places that should have been searched.

By the end of the second day I was starting to lose my patience. I told David Corker that enough was enough. I'd watched them prying and poking into my personal belongings which we'd already agreed were not part of the investigation and this was well overstepping the mark.

In the three months before Mum died, I saw her every day. Even though this was much longer than the two weeks she had been given to live originally, she became a little more distant every time. We never spoke about her illness; it never came up, despite the awkward silences. I'd got over the initial shock of how ill she was and I just had to support her in the last few weeks of her life.

Mum died on 20 September 2001, aged eighty-six, in the same room that I was born in – that corner room in the flat in Darnay House on the Dickens Estate in Bermondsey. I'd offered to move her into a nice big house, but she was happy there: she had all her friends around her, she had everything she needed. Towards the end she was heavily sedated, and she had her sisters, my aunts Rose and Cath, taking care of her and comforting her through her final hours. My sister Anne was there too. She said she found it hard to cry. Her face said it all: she looked lost.

Aunt Rose managed to get Mum to open her eyes. 'Look', she said, 'it's Kieron. Your favourite is here.' Mum turned and looked, her eyes straining to recognise me, then she quietly sighed like a newborn baby, smiled at me and closed her eyes.

I didn't see Mum die. I left at the point that I wanted to remember her at – when she could still turn round and smile at me. I said goodbye and told her I wasn't coming back. Then I waited around until I was told she'd passed away. I like to remember Mum as she was, to lock that memory of her into my mind for ever.

I didn't cry until after the funeral at St Michael's Church in Bermondsey. They offered a full mass for Mum, and when I came out it really hit me. That was when the press were there taking photos of me, and on the front pages the next day there was a big close-up of my face, crying my eyes out. That was really horrible. People were trying to make sure that I didn't see the papers, but I had to know what they'd done. I realised then that there's no line left. There are no more boundaries about private life. And the reports implied, somehow, that I was turning on the tears for the press, making a play for sympathy. I didn't get involved, either to complain or to deny anything. One thing I learned in rehab is not to blame people, not to feel resentment. So I let it go. Revenge is an indulgence of the weak.

I was called up to television centre; the bosses admitted that they were not sure what to do. I was still not fully aware of just how much the press had taken the route of fantasy journalism rather than facts. Even so, I did not think their suggestion that I give an interview to Martin Bashir, to tell my side of the story, was a good idea. They said, just do this interview and then we can get back to work. WRONG. The only reason I did not want to do the interview was that I did not see what I had to explain, the facts spoke for themselves, but the facts had not been told. So under extreme pressure from the network, and backed up by my agent Anne, I caved in and said I would do it. I had no idea what he was going to ask. Some of the questions I had no idea what he was talking about. He referred to certain newspaper articles that I had not read. When he started to get more hostile with me I became very uncomfortable and it showed on screen. Realising that all the fingers are pointing at you for something that you haven't done is bad enough, it is even worse with a camera in your face. Bashir was charming to me before the interview. I trusted him because of knowing him as the guy who set up the first meeting with myself and Princess Diana. We had met several times before and he always called me mate. As an interviewer he has a job to get to the truth and show a balanced view, but his interview just made a mess of me, particularly given the fact that, just after it, the police decided that they were discontinuing their investigation and that there would be no prosecution of anyone present that evening.

The press, however, were determined to continue their 'destroy Barrymore' mission. Renowned columnist Lynda Lee-Potter said that she would rather stick needles in her eyes than watch Barrymore on television again. My response to that statement was that I couldn't wait to meet her! At a later date Lynda and I did meet and she was one of those rare journalists who had the courage to admit that her statement was unfounded; we remained good friends till she sadly passed away. One of the tabloids paid Justin Merritt £30,000. Soon after, quite coincidentally, he suddenly remembered how he'd seen me rub cocaine in Stuart's mouth. In his original statement to the police on 1 April 2001 he said, 'During the evening I was drinking continuously, during the evening I did not take any other form of drug. I didn't see any drug-taking taking place.' I find it amazing what money does to the memory!

In October 2001, I was cautioned for the possession of cannabis and allowing it to be used at my home. The charges against Jon Kenney and Justin Merritt were dropped, without any explanation at all.

I have never been charged with anything connected to Stuart's death, but the rumours continue. One of the bosses at ITV told me that in any one day he was hearing three to ten new rumours about what I was supposed to have done. The following day, for example, I was supposed to have removed a large sum from my bank to be used as hush money. This was just one of the many, many malicious stories circulated by people hell-bent on destroying me, but which only ended up hurting other people. Whilst I felt angry and deeply upset, what must it have been like for the Lubbock family, being fed every day on a diet of falsehood and innuendo? So small wonder that they turned against me and gave the media machine what it wanted – more weapons to use against me.

ITV told my agent that until the case was resolved, they could not continue to pay me, that they had shareholders they were responsible to. Only two weeks earlier, they had said they were completely behind me, whatever happened, even if I had to do time in prison. Prison? For what? It seemed to me even they had made up their minds that I was somehow to blame for what happened. But now they were talking about 'relaunching' my career when all this was over. Relaunching?

Despite all of this the television viewers voted my series *My Kind of Music* most popular entertainment show at the 2001 National Television Awards. I was asked if I would mind my award being picked up by Sir Trevor McDonald on my behalf. I agreed but of course it saddened me, as this would be the first time ever that I hadn't picked up an award personally.

After Shaun left, I thought about him all the time and, unlike the others, it really bothered and upset me that he wasn't around. I realised Shaun had done the right thing. Addicts are hell to live with (though clean and sober you couldn't meet a nicer bunch), and the only way to deal with them when they are using is to leave them. It's called tough love by the partner, tough shit for you. When I returned from the States, I found myself wondering more and more what he was doing, so eventually I put in a few calls and told him how I felt. It was awkward at first.

Our relationship started when Shaun came back to me. I had sobered up, and I could concentrate on the relationship. Unlike before, I'm not always desperate to go out and get drunk. I'm happy just being with him – a contentment and peace that I've never had before, except in brief snatches, and never enough to sustain me. Shaun never really wanted all that other stuff, all the running around and the clubs and drugs; he'd got that out of his system by his early twenties. Maybe I needed to do that as well. It's a bit weird being told that by someone younger than you, but then age doesn't mature you. Life does. Shaun had that life when he was younger, and I've had enough of it now to know that I'm happy where I am. The danger was that Shaun might not be able to handle this version of me. It's happened many times before – the partner spends all her/his time trying to get the other one sober, and when they are they find they can't live with sober, they were actually addicted to the addict.

Shaun phoned constantly from New Zealand, where he

had gone to make a new life for himself. When I heard his voice on the phone, I realised just how much I missed him and many times his calls would make me tearful. I am not someone who can be by myself for very long, but you can't live with friends. Shaun said he would come back and we agreed to meet on neutral ground at the Gleneagles Hotel in Scotland. The minute we saw each other we knew it was right. Despite all the continuous press-hounding and the non-stop bad mouthing, he has remained a rock and I am so proud of him, even though this is the first time I have said it. I find it easier to write how I feel about him than say it to his face, but I am sure he knows how I feel, I hope so, because I'm still having to learn about having a relationship with another man; after all those years of being married and of sneaking around, it's not something that comes easily to me. Take away the gay thing, and basically you've got two blokes with blokes' mentalities. If two men are having a go at each other, it comes down to 'Sod you!' 'Yeah? Well, sod you!', which is very different from having a row with a woman. A woman will play off her feminine side against the man's masculine side; she'll break down and cry, if needed, then the man will comfort her. It's not like that with two men. And when you're brought up to believe that a man takes the lead, that a man goes out to work – well, what happens when there's two men? Who does the cooking and washing up? Luckily, I'm quite domesticated, so I do the cooking. I love cooking and Shaun doesn't; he loves cleaning and I don't. So that's all right.

But it's difficult in the emotional sphere as well. Even though I've known Shaun for a few years, I can still be shy with him because he's another bloke. You won't see me and Shaun walking hand in hand down the street, and if we have company around I won't sit on the sofa cuddled up to him. It wouldn't seem right to me, nor to Shaun. If we see a couple of guys walking down Old Compton Street holding hands, it makes me uncomfortable, even though I really admire them and I know it's the right thing to do. Some people are much more relaxed about it than I am. If I pick Shaun up from the airport, I tend to just shake his hand or give him a quick hug. If Cheryl had been away somewhere – not that she ever really left my side – I'd have run up to her, picked her up and swung her around. It doesn't quite work like that with two blokes. When you look at what God has created in man, it is probably just as well. A very good friend of mine, aware of his looks, said that if he was gay he would be a very lonely man!

Some of my friends still can't get their heads around the fact that I'm with another man. They ask, 'Michael, are you sure you're fully gay?' They can't quite accept Shaun and me as a couple in the way they would if we were a man and a woman. They'll take the piss in a way they wouldn't dream of doing if they were talking about my wife. So, even though they might see us coming out of the same bedroom together, it's still 'Shaun' and 'Michael', two individuals, not quite the same thing as a married couple. Some people think that I 'suddenly' became gay, and that I might one day go back to being straight. Someone in AA said, 'You talk about Cheryl a lot: don't you ever miss her?' Well, I was married to her for eighteen years, she was a very big part of my life. How can I truly answer that? I miss what we were, not what we became. I can give several answers that would all lead to, yes I miss her. Will I ever go back to being straight? No. I never was.

I was back on TV for the first time in over a year in February 2002, with a new series of *My Kind of Music*, and for the first time in my life I concerned myself with the viewing figures. They were good, starting off with

3.5 million and peaking with 7 million. Normally I just make the best shows I can, and don't worry about how they're received – but this time a lot of people were waiting to find out if the public still wanted to see me. The figures seemed to suggest that they did, while the papers were determined to put an end to my career in a snowstorm of rumours and lies. So it seemed the future of my career depended on who the people in power listened to: the public or the papers? If they listened to the papers, they'd believe that I had been out drinking again (I hadn't), that the audience at the studio heckled me (they didn't), that I booked myself into another booze-and-drugs rehab clinic (I didn't), that I went out one night picking up various men from various clubs (I didn't). To repeat all the stories would take up a lot of paper. None of them were based on any fact.

ITV said that they wanted to see how it went. First of all they wanted to see if I could still make shows and if people would still turn up. Well, I could and they did; hundreds were turned away at the door, and I worked better than I had for years. But no further shows were commissioned. At one time I would have worked myself into a frenzy over this, blaming everyone left, right and centre – I know the boy in me might not agree, but the man knows, they just have to do what they have to do.

A lot of people have asked me whether I was nervous making those shows. I think a lot of them thought that because I did not have the crutch of a drink or drug that I would find it difficult to make shows. The fact is that I have never needed any Dutch courage to make shows. I was always stone cold sober when I worked. My problem has always been living life away from an audience. If I had a permanent audience I could sail through life easily, but that just ain't gonna ever happen, so dream on. I had been offered a few live concert dates in Australia and New Zealand. I just prayed that I would feel better about doing them, as at the time my confidence was not heading in the right direction. Oh God, I felt like I was hanging on by my fingertips, and if I let go I wasn't sure I would have been able to climb back. All the energy that had sustained me for all those years seemed to have been sapped out of me. I felt like nothing was in my control any more.

So what was I going to do? Well, first of all I was not going to get caught up emotionally; I had to start using the things I had learned in rehab to keep myself well. If I didn't end up with a job, I was the only one that was losing, and I felt I could deal with that. So I asked those concerned just to leave everything: not to make any calls, not to remind anyone. Life will go on for the people who run the TV companies, and for the editors of the newspapers. I had to remain calm and let go if necessary. If I push my will into what's happening and it doesn't work out, I won't survive. If I adhere to the belief that I'm powerless over people, places and things, then I'll get through. It's only when we stick our noses into how we want our lives to pan out that it all goes wrong. Just let go and let god.

I decided to go back to school and train as an actor – properly this time – so I signed up for a course of method acting at the Lee Strasberg school in New York. I looked forward to studying; for someone whose performances seem so undisciplined, I really like discipline. The Lee Strasberg Institute runs tough courses. It's on the East Side of New York. The application forms asked, 'Any previous stage experience?', which made me laugh. It teaches method acting – the technique used by Marlon Brando, Robert De Niro, Al Pacino, James Dean – which is all to do with looking into your own life to bring reality to your acting. Well, I had plenty of material to be getting on with.

225

So I went back to school. I've done it all back to front:
I got married when I was too young, I did my running
around clubs when I was in my forties, now I was going to
be a student in my fifties. With a bit of luck, the nursery
school years should be really sensational.

Emails from America

Dear Shaun
My first letter from America – just waiting for Brownie
[Mike Browne] to get some cards printed up, so
I thought I would play with this machine. I really do
miss you and I am keeping busy to stop from getting
homesick. I am sure once I settle down I will be fine.
I went to an AA meeting last night and lunchtime today.
It's 3.20 am and raining. Me and Mike had ribs and
smoked chicken last night at a restaurant that's right up
your street. Barbeque sauce over everything!! Bought a
new mobile phone so that I can use it just from here!!!
. . . should have the laptop up and running soon.
Till we talk, all my love, Michael

Dear Shaun
Well, it's Good Friday, well is it? I woke up at seven
o'clock this morning, got dressed, then loaded up my
satchel and headed for the immigration dept. I used
the subway yet again. I tend to get rather a lot of 'that
can't be Michael Barrymore using the subway' looks. I
really am getting good at it. Downtown train or uptown
train there ain't no going sideways in New York. On
my arrival at immigration I joined a queue. That was a
new experience for me. You don't see many smiles in a
queue – they are probably getting over the strange smell
from the train. It was a new smell to me, I think it's

called stinky people. I really felt the odd one out because I had taken a shower.
I need a meeting. See ya.
love Michael

Hi Shaun
Felt strange today. I had to deal with phone calls from home. Nothing too taxing, but a reminder that there is life outside New York. One of the students, Carlo, an Italian, came in late to class shouting flick clock – nice to see he is grasping the language. The teacher Erma was in a good mood so she let him stay. Today Erma, the Yoko Ono lookalike, had on a long, lilac outfit, with a side-split right up to her Yoko, about an inch from her Ono. During the warm-up I let out a really loud Ahhhhhhhhhhhhhh! Erma was impressed. 'Very good Michael.' She likes me, I don't ask questions. She called me and a guy called Rich over to sit in front of her. 'Michael, when you were stroking your material did it ever become an item of clothing?' I looked at her confidently and shook my head. No! 'Good, now what I want you two to do, every day for the next week, is imagine there is a mirror in front of you, and a basin below. What you do is shave, but see your reflection in the far wall.' Oh yes, this is heavy method we are getting into here! I repeated what she said in my head. Mirror just in front, but reflection in far wall. Yep, got it. Rich wanted to know something? Please Rich, just accept what she says.
    Rich spoke. 'So is the mirror . . .'
    She interrupted, 'Don't question the mirror, just shave! . . .'
    'He asked more, 'But do I look at . . .'
    She came back in, 'Acting isn't about where

227

something is, it's where you perceive it to be . . .'

'Yeah, but . . .'

Oh dear Rich, you are treading on dangerous ground.

She had one final thing to say, 'Look, either do as I tell you or get yourself another class.'

Dear Shaun

Went shopping tonight – got guests arriving, so better have a little more than a loaf for one, coffee for one, one egg, one sugar lump. I really enjoyed the experience. Oh that looks nice, and that, and that. Oh hot dogs or franks as they call them. American squeezy mustard, fresh spinach, got to have that in Popeye land, donuts, milk, semi-milk, half-and-half, full fat, skimmed, buttery, goat's, cow's, organic, free range, home grown. A quart, a pint, a gallon, a vat . . . Which one? Oh sod it, I'll get the blue one. Got completely carried away, full basket, turned a corner and there was a whole other part, serving everything I had . . . but ready-prepared. Shit, now what do I do? As I slid my way through the checkout, God looked down on me as the cashier asked me if I wanted it all delivered. Thank you, God, there was no way I could have carried what I had bought. I paid, walked back to my apartment and as I arrived so did my shopping. 'How much?' 'No charge, sir.' I tipped him. Oh, all right, if you must know, $5. So tonight my guests have olive loaf, cold roast beef, baby spinach, vine tomatoes, chopped egg in mayonnaise, crusty bread, fresh strawberries with lemon sherbet. And coffee with er . . . er . . . blue milk!!??

Caught my usual taxi ride home – anyone who loves theme parks has to try a New York cab. You get in, shout through the prison-like partition which number and street, and POW! You are thrown back in your seat and there is a grab handle which I recommend you use as you fly past 3rd and 36th in seconds. As you fly off a pre-recorded tape plays through distorted speakers. 'Hello, this is Mary Wilson, and I'm asking you to STOP in the name of . . . safety. Buckle up please!' The cab driver, who says nothing but 'fuck' to every other car seems to be part of a competition. First there gets their green card.

I wish we didn't live in such a sterile world. I've always wanted to get a hot dog from a corner stall in New York, but I just can't bring myself to do it. They are just like they look in the movies except the vendor isn't an extra playing a part. I nearly went for the hot dog seller who wore plastic gloves, but I could not get it out of my mind that he may not have taken them off on his last pee break! Below in the subway I could hear a guard shout, 'This is Thirty-third street'. Only his version had a thyroid in it, say it fast, it works. I tried explaining what a lot of the people I have seen so far look like; a guy at AA last night gave his version, 'Too many dogs on the same bitch'. For some reason this was followed by the statement, 'In NY it's not being a prostitute that's the problem, it's the stairs!' To finish my day off two old gay guys on one of the other tables at lunch had a loud row. One of them assumed the part of Katharine Hepburn (*On Golden Pond* style).

'Look at you, you're drunk!'

'Oh just shut up, speak when you are spoken to, I'm paying the check . . . you wizened old witch!'

'Oh, oh, I didn't realise I had to Paff . . . fom!!!'.

'. . . !It's perform!'

'OH, I'm Sooooooo sorrrrryyyyy Mr Producer!'

He then went into 'I'm just a Broadway Baby'!!!!!!!!

I have heard it sung by various artists, but sung by a

pissed Katharine Hepburn gave it a New York quality!

Back to another day's drama, it's Erma's turn again tomorrow.

Email over laptop off!

Michael x

My diary tells of a landmark birthday away from home:

I am fifty years old today. It's 1.30 am and I can't sleep. I'm trying to be as quiet as possible because everyone else in the house is asleep, and I am the first person to wish myself Happy 50th. I'm not young, I'm not old, so what am I? Maybe a little confused, definitely a little out of focus, because my glasses are back in the bedroom, and if I go back to get them I'll wake up Shaun. I hope I'm writing in a straight line. Mike and his wife, Maria, are in the next bedroom with their two-and-a-half-year-old son, Morgan. They said that we had to get to bed early, to get a good night's sleep, because it's an early start to my birthday celebrations. We all have to go somewhere at 8 am. I don't know where: it's part of the surprise, and I haven't tried to guess what the surprise is. We're in the middle of New York, so there are some restrictions: I can't see us walking into a room and everyone from my past jumping out at me. I'm not sure I'd like that, it might make me feel even more homesick than I do.

I just can't sleep. I've been like this for a few days now. It's a new kind of staying awake for me – as if I'm trying to piece together all the little bits of my life to make one big picture, like a jigsaw puzzle. Other bits of the puzzle come when my friends tell me that it's all going to be fine, I should just wait, wait, wait. But my mind wants to play with the puzzle. Which bits fit where? Do I fit in, staying in New York? Or is it just a distraction, something to occupy my mind? I ain't fitting in age-wise – I don't feel middle-aged – and that's another part of the puzzle. All I've done, everything that's happened to me from the day I was born has brought me to this precise place. It's like being at Grand Central Station. I've reached the place in my life where I can take whichever route I want – no restrictions, no barriers. I've got the ticket, I've paid so much for it – every mile I've come, I've paid for every joy, every nice thing I've had in my life. I'm fifty, I'm in Grand Central Station and I can buy any ticket I want for the rest of my life. And that's my birthday present to myself – fully paid for with my first fifty years.

There's a smile in my eyes that's never been there before. It's a wonderful feeling, to make your eyes smile. It's just a little tug of the muscles and you light up inside. I'm doing it right now and it's making the whole room light up in the dark house in New York.

As it was, I didn't complete my acting course, because I had to go back to England to attend the inquest into Stuart Lubbock's death. Things had begun to quieten down, but second time around would turn out possibly worse than the first.

10

An Inquest

I have enjoyed the benefit of my surname. But at what price? Well, as far as the media are concerned it's been open season on Barrymore. Is that fair? I could say why me? Others could say why not you!

Reams of newspaper print have been written about the events of that tragic night, each carrying the version of the events that fitted their style of reporting. Some people want to believe that I am some sort of monster, that Stuart died after a night of gay orgy and suffered horrific injuries. But the injuries did not take place at my house, neither did any sort of sexual activity.

My lawyer, David Corker, has said to me many times that he doesn't go out on the spur of the moment to a club and then invite strangers back to his place. Well many people do, every week. In fact, in the Irish culture that I was brought up in it is commonplace to invite people back and strangers tag along. At the time I craved company, to cheer myself up. I did not want to be on my own. I wanted to have a good time, and just that.

The inquest into the death of Stuart Lubbock took place on 12 September 2002. The facts of the case were discussed and everyone who was there that evening gave evidence, including me.

Kylie Merritt, Justin's sister, said that shortly before the alarm was raised Stuart was having a good time dive-bombing into the pool and had thrown a baseball cap at her, calling for her to get into the water. So how could he have been brutalised in any way?

The truth is there is no witness, or forensic evidence, despite two exhaustive police searches of my house, which in any way supports the theory or lends any weight to the belief that he was attacked at my house. An examination was carried out to determine if there was any scientific evidence of Stuart having had sexual relations before his death. The forensic scientist, Patricia Lucinda Kenny, concluded that, 'in my opinion, there is no scientific evidence to indicate that Stuart Lubbock had sexual relations immediately prior to his death.'

It is important to deal with the issue of drugs. According to the toxicologist's report, Stuart had taken drugs that night. Apparently, he had taken drugs in the past. These are not my words, but the words of Claire Wicks (Stuart Lubbock's ex-partner) and Karen Harris (another girl-friend). In her statement to the police, Claire Wicks said the following: 'In the past, Stuart has taken Es, but not in front of me, I found out through a friend of both of ours. When I found out, I contacted the local police and told them. I did this as I did not want Stuart to be hooked on drugs, and secondly, I did not want him hooked on drugs around my children.'

During the inquest Karen was asked the following:

Q. Now, you say in your statement that about a year ago someone had actually told you that Stuart was taking drugs?

A. Yes.

Q. Is that right?

A. Yes.

Q. You say he said, or you think that they were Es. Is that Ecstasy?

A. I don't really know a lot about them, but that is what he told me he was taking.

Q. He called them Es, did he?

A. Yes.

Q. Did you get an impression from him how long he had been taking them?

A. Well, I didn't actually ask him when I first found out. I kind of left it. I would say a few months before I asked him.

Q. Can you remember – I know it is difficult, going back over the last year or so – but can you remember more or less when he actually told you that he was indeed taking them?

A. Previous to me asking him, about probably nearly a year before I asked him, he did actually tell me somebody offered him a pill, and he said he didn't take it.

Q. Are you saying that for about a year you think he was taking them?

A. No. Longer than that.

Q. Longer?

A. Yes.

Q. Can you remember when he actually admitted that he was taking them?

A. Probably a year before he died.

Q. A year before he died. You say you never saw him take any pills; is that right?

A. No.

Q. You did not. But he told you that when he had money, he would take as many as four?

A. Yes.

Q. That is right is it?

A. Yes.

Q. I mean, think about that. Was it four, or . . .

A. Well, he told me at first it was just maybe one. He actually told me he took half of one and he gradually went up to four.

Q. So, he told you first of all half, and then he said one, but then he actually said he took four?

A. Yes.

In an article published in a Sunday newspaper dated 30 April 2006, Louise Holland said she had spotted Stuart at the Millennium in Harlow where she was having a drink with her boyfriend. She heard Stuart blurt out, 'I am completely fucked – I have just taken five pills.'

I am not judging or criticising Stuart for using drugs, I have had my own problems. The suggestion that I or anyone else forced him to take drugs is untrue, I have never resisted questions about whether I supplied drugs to Stuart. I will repeat what I said when asked. 'I never supplied or encouraged Stuart to take drugs, in particular the suggestion by Justin Merritt, that I rubbed cocaine into Stuart's gums, is a lie.' At the inquest, Kylie Merritt told the coroner: 'I saw Barrymore put some cocaine on his finger and rub it on Mr Lubbock's gums.' In February 2006 Phil Taylor, associate editor of the *News of the World*, carried out his own investigation into the allegations made by Kylie Merritt at the inquest. Kylie agreed to take a polygraph (lie detector) test and as a result the truth was exposed. She was asked several questions. When asked, 'are you certain that Michael Barrymore put cocaine on his fingers and tried to put them into Stuart Lubbock's mouth?' Merritt answered, 'No.' 'Did you see Michael Barrymore rubbing Stuart Lubbock's gums?' Merritt answered, 'No.' The polygraph expert Jeremy Barrett said: 'Having carefully analysed the charts I can state categorically that all these replies were truthful. It is clear that for whatever reason she did not tell the truth at the inquest.' Jeremy Barrett continued with a second set of questions: 'At the party did you see any form of sexual activity take place?' Merritt answered, 'No.' He asked, 'To your knowledge, was Stuart Lubbock assaulted in any way?' Merritt answered, 'No.' Phil presented me with the results of the test just before I was due to fly back to New Zealand. I was completely overwhelmed.

I decided that if I was asked questions about drugs that I wouldn't go beyond what I had previously said. I had already confirmed to the police that I had never given drugs to Stuart and never did. Entirely as I thought, the moment I exercised my right of silence in return to the questions about drugs, anyone who was part of the anti-Barrymore campaign jumped for joy. My silence was the basis for their announcing that I was holding back on information which, if revealed, would, as far as they were concerned, establish that I was responsible for Stuart's death and for the injuries he suffered. This of course is nonsense. For example, the front page headline on the following edition of a Sunday newspaper, with my picture next to it, was YOU ARE A

KILLER. How would you feel seeing that about yourself when it is completely untrue? You can call me a lousy entertainer, but you cannot call me a killer.

In response to my complaint about that outrageous headline, I received a letter from the editor which included the following:

> It is unsustainable to suggest that the article means that your client murdered Mr Lubbock. However, your client should be held responsible for Mr Lubbock's death because of his actions and inactions on the night Mr Lubbock died. The words in quotation marks beneath the headline justify the use of the word 'Killer'.

This letter rambles on about how it is justified in using the headline YOU ARE A KILLER from the above paragraph. I presume that the reader is expected to read the paper from the bottom of the page upwards!

In advance of the inquest I was given a copy of all the witness statements obtained by the police during their investigation. What immediately struck me were the statements of the hospital staff dealing with Stuart in casualty after the ambulance had taken him from my house. I was astonished that none of the nine A&E staff claimed to have seen any sign of injury on Stuart's body. One of them, Nurse Stuart Nairn, stated that he had taken Stuart's rectal/anal body temperature by inserting a thermometer on about sixteen separate occasions. Nairn, however, said he saw no injury in that area. This was amazing news, because all along the police had said that the injuries could have only taken place at the house. This is what they told me and the media continually from April 2001 to the inquest in September 2002. Yet in June 2001 they had in their possession convincing evidence that the injuries could not have taken place at my house. I hoped, perhaps naively, that once all this came out at the inquest and was placed on record, the truth might at last be told.

I looked forward especially to the evidence to be given by Nurse Stuart Nairn, which was scheduled to be given on the final day of the inquest. When that day arrived Nairn never turned up. According to the police, they had made extensive efforts to find him, but he had disappeared without trace. His statement was read out to the coroner, but no one seemed to take any notice. To make matters worse, the coroner in her conclusion at the end of the inquest also appeared to ignore this evidence, and assumed that there was no doubt as to where and when the injuries had been inflicted: '*No witness has given an explanation as to how Stuart Lubbock should be found in a pool with a significant level of drugs and alcohol and with significant anal injuries.*' (My emphasis added.) What she was saying was that there was no doubt that those injuries had been inflicted at my house. If Nurse Stuart Nairn had read out his statement she could not have concluded as she did. Fairness and justice would not have allowed her to have reached such a firm opinion. In turn, I might have avoided the character assassination that then took place. Despite her earlier comments that an inquest is not a trial and does not apportion blame, her opinion led the media to report that, unquestionably, a vicious gay sex attack took place upon Mr Lubbock.

Could things get worse? Enter Cheryl, with a cleverly targeted attack. The issue she chose was perfect. And what was this issue? Whether I could swim or not and that I had lied at the inquest.

Over the next few days, I was both the killer of Stuart Lubbock and a perjurer. In the ensuing weeks, the Cheryl bandwagon would provide individuals who claimed that they had seen me swimming. Just for the record, I cannot swim. Cheryl's campaign swiftly led to the publication of her book, *Catch A Falling Star*.

However, a glimmer of hope had suddenly appeared. Nurse Stuart Nairn, whom the police had said could not be found, had been located and was willing to be interviewed by my solicitor, David Corker. Impossible to trace? Hardly, he was a university lecturer then working in the Midlands and a simple internet search revealed his whereabouts. David Corker interviewed him and came back with a statement. Here it is in its entirety:

Statement of Stuart Nairn, 24 September 2002

I qualified as a nurse (RGN) in 1988. Thereafter I worked in this capacity for the next eight years, principally at the Princess Alexander Hospital in Harlow, Essex. I then enrolled at the University of Essex as a PHD. I was a bank nurse at the Princess Alexander Hospital. In this capacity I was on duty on the night shift in casualty on 30/31 March 2001. Presently I am a lecturer at the University of Nottingham based in Derby. I teach various courses to students of nursing. I have already made a statement to Essex Police about my involvement in treatment administered to Stuart Lubbock during the period when he was in casualty at the hospital. This statement is dated 1 April 2001. I have reread that statement before making this one and confirm that everything in that first statement is accurate and true. If I had given sworn evidence to the recent inquest into the death of Mr Lubbock, I would have confirmed the veracity of that first statement.

Accordingly, I do not repeat the content of my first statement here. I make this one in the context of

consenting to see Mr David Corker, who says that he
acts for Michael Barrymore. Mr Corker has acquainted
me with the evidence given at the inquest, by the various
experts. He has drawn my attention to the presence
of anal injuries found on the body of Mr Lubbock and
described in general terms what those injuries
apparently consist of. I understand that they include
bruising, lacerations and dilation of the anus. Mr Corker
has also described the images of Mr Lubbock's anus as
photographed immediately prior to commencement of
the post-mortem. Mr Corker has particularly asked me
to comment upon my recollections of the injuries, if
any, I recall seeing during the time Mr Lubbock was
in casualty. Mr Corker has stated that according to the
expert evidence at the inquest, the injuries caused to
the anal area were extensive.

When a patient is unconscious and is receiving
resuscitation treatment, if information on the body
temperature is required, the most appropriate method
of obtaining a reading is via a rectal thermometer. This
is inserted into the anus and placed against or in contact
with the patient's rectum or rectal wall. In the case of
Mr Lubbock, who apparently had drowned and was
hypothermic, taking his temperature was essential to his
treatment. In broad terms the medical strategy adopted
was to seek to raise his temperature to 35 degrees. This
to create the best chance of his survival. Accordingly,
taking his body temperature and supplying this
information to the doctor was essential. It would enable
the doctors to assess what progress was being made and
measure the success of their treatment. Measurement
of the rectal temperature was a crucial part of
Mr Lubbock's treatment. For no particular reason
I assumed responsibility for the taking of the rectal

temperature in exhibit SJN/I. The first attempt to take
a reading was probably about ten minutes after
Mr Lubbock was admitted to casualty.

I recall he was lying face up on the bed. To gain
access to his anus I needed to lift one of his legs upwards
to an angle of about 45 degrees. Holding his leg up,
I then (wearing gloves) separated the buttocks. I recall
the anus was closed and that, using my fingers, I needed
to prise it open in order to insert the probe. I then
inserted it. To gain an accurate adequate reading of
temperature the probe needs to remain in contact with
the rectum for approximately thirty seconds
continuously. I thus needed to ensure that this contact
was maintained during this period. Having gained the
temperature I then relayed this to the doctors.

I believe that I had a very good uninterrupted view
of his anus in good light for a significant period. I saw
nothing unusual or untoward about it. It was completely
normal. If it had been dilated and significantly bruised
I am sure that I would have noticed this. Moreover I
would have reported this to the doctors.

After the first reading, I believe I repeated the
process every five to ten minutes thereafter. If the body
was wrapped in a blanket when I needed to take another
temperature, then this would be removed in order to
undertake the task as mentioned above. In each instance
I needed to separate the buttocks, prise open the anus,
etc. On several occasions I recall a difficulty in gaining a
reading and so I would need to manipulate the probe
whilst inserted to gain a contact. As I did this I would
be watching it continuously. Overall I think I inserted
the probe about sixteen times.

I noticed towards the end that the probe had some
blood on it. That the probe was causing some trauma

and bleeding to the rectum was unsurprising, bearing in mind the number of insertions. I mentioned the fact of the probe causing bleeding to Angela Nagle [a nurse], so that the cause could be recorded by her. In my opinion, the fact that I noticed blood on the probe indicates that I was paying attention to the task of inserting the probe, taking the temperature and withdrawing it.

This statement, given by a qualified and completely independent witness, is unassailable. Moreover, it fits perfectly with all the other evidence about no attack having taken place at my home.

When Stuart was removed from the pool and taken to hospital he was wearing boxer shorts. These were then removed by the medical staff upon arrival. It was confirmed that the shorts had been tested for blood and none had been detected.

David Corker wrote a long and detailed letter to Essex Police requesting that they reopen their investigation in the light of the new evidence that had been found and indeed evidence that had been always available. We asked Essex Police to reopen its enquiry into the death of Mr Lubbock in order that the issue of how and when the serious injuries inflicted to him be reinvestigated. David Corker's letter of 22 November 2002 to the police was as follows:

This request is made in the context of highly significant new evidence having only very recently become available. This evidence being suggestive that grave criminal offences have been committed whilst Mr Lubbock was in the care of the Princess Alexandra Hospital.

Whilst I readily appreciate that receipt of a lengthy letter from this firm setting out why such a reinvestigation should take place will not be a welcome development for you, I nonetheless would respectfully submit that the matter is properly one of very serious concern both to my client and the public at large and so your personal attention to it is merited.

You will recall that the fact of the injuries having been found by the pathologist Dr Heath on 1 April during the post-mortem caused the Major Investigation Team (MIT) as led by Mr McNeill, to commence a homicide investigation. Since then attention regarding the circumstances of Mr Lubbock's death has continued to concentrate upon the issue of how and where these injuries were inflicted. Bearing in mind the severity of these injuries, the manner in which they were probably inflicted and the continuing mystery surrounding who is responsible, it is unsurprising that this issue remained the focus of both police and public attention and concern.

From the outset of both my client's and my dealings with officers from MIT, commencing on 1 April, it was made clear that there was no doubt as to where these injuries were inflicted. We were informed that the expert and lay evidence established with certainty that Mr Lubbock was attacked whilst at my client's home. Furthermore it is readily apparent that this certainty was also communicated to the media. This, in part, resulting from the arrests of Messrs Kenney and Merritt in June 2001 on suspicion of murder and the decision to continue their police bail in connection with this suspected offence until October 2001. As you will readily appreciate, both the arrest and the prolonged continuance of police bail were predicated on the belief that the injuries must have been inflicted at my client's home.

Bearing in mind that no criminal charges were ever proceeded with against my client, no entitlement to disclosure of police evidence or unused material ever arose. Whilst he and his home remained in the media spotlight, he remained ignorant as to what steps had been undertaken by Essex Police and in particular what matters had been revealed to them by various witnesses. It was not until July of this year that the witness statements which had been obtained, particularly those taken during the period March–June 2001, were disclosed. This disclosure was pursuant to a direction made to this effect by the coroner in relation to the forthcoming inquest.

In broad terms the disclosed statements from the non-expert witnesses can be divided into two groups. First those obtained from persons who were present at the party at my client's home. The 'party' witnesses comprise Messrs Justin Merritt, Kylie Merritt, Claire Jones, Kelly Campbell, Simon Shaw, James Futer, my client and Jonathan Kenney. Second, the statements from the medical team who treated Mr Lubbock during the two-hour period that he was in casualty at the Princess Alexandra Hospital. The hospital witnesses comprise Messrs Nagel, Nairn, Raymon, Nair, Boynton and Hirani. All the hospital statements were taken during the period 8–12 June 2001. Dealing with the hospital witnesses first, there is a striking characteristic common to their statements; no one saw any blood other than that caused by the invasive treatment and no one saw any signs of injury to Mr Lubbock's anus. Most particularly, in his statement dated 8 June 2001, the nurse Stuart Nairn confirmed that he took Mr Lubbock's rectal temperature via a probe on approximately a dozen occasions and saw no significant injury. The only injury he states that he saw was that caused by the repeated insertion and withdrawal of the probe.

As I shall deal further below concerning Mr Nairn's evidence I shall not summarise his account at this point. However in relation to the other hospital witnesses, relevant extracts from their statements which were read to the inquest are as follows:

Dr Nair: '*I do not remember seeing any injuries on the patient. The only blood I saw came from numerous attempts we made to insert "lines" into the patient to assist in his treatment.*'

Nurse Boynton: '*At no time even after Stuart's death was declared, did I see any fresh blood which led me to think that he had any sign of injury. The small amount on the thermometer was the only place I ever saw any blood.*'

Dr Hirani: '*At no time did I ever see any injuries, or blood.*'

Dr Raymon: '*At no time did I ever see any noticeable injury to him. The only bleeding I saw was from medical procedures, i.e. inserting intravenous lines.*'

Nurse Nagle: '*I do not recall any conversation from those persons present about any signs of injury to the patient's anus. Had this been pointed out to me I would have noted this in the medical notes . . . I did not see any injuries other than those caused by procedures.*'

These accounts are strongly corroborated by the evidence of the 'party' witnesses, none of whom in their respective statements and subsequent evidence to the coroner could shed any light as to how Mr Lubbock could have received the injuries. Moreover they each confirmed that they saw no blood, no signs of injury, nothing which would suggest that the assault on

Mr Lubbock took place whilst he was at my client's home.

In relation to the credibility of these witnesses, it is relevant to note that most of them were strangers to each other and so would have no reason to conceal anything from the police. Moreover in relation to at least two of them (Justin and Kylie Merritt), they 'sold their story' to a newspaper and would have had every reason to expose any assault on Mr Lubbock had they known anything about it.

The evidence from some of the party guests, particularly Kylie Merritt also directly confirms that it is extremely unlikely that Mr Lubbock could have sustained the injuries whilst at my client's home. Both in her statement dated 6 June 2001 and in her evidence to the coroner, she was certain that shortly before Mr Lubbock was found unconscious in the pool she saw him swimming and as she put it, 'larking about' there. She also stated that he seemed happy and he had invited her to join him. She concludes her statement, '*I haven't got a clue how these injuries could have been caused. To my knowledge there is no time that it could have happened.*' When her account as summarised above was put to the expert pathologists during the inquest, they were unanimous that it was highly unlikely that Mr Lubbock would have been able to swim and have this demeanour if by then he had sustained the injuries.

Finally in relation to witness statements made available to MIT, I refer to the statement dated 14 August 2001 from the pathologist Ian Calder. He expresses surprise that as the injuries would have caused bleeding this was not noticed by the casualty staff. However most significantly he observes: 'There had been considerable later loss of blood as shown by the blood staining of the sheet as shown by the autopsy photographs.'

In relation to the photographs, Mr Calder is correct, there is blood all around the body and thus prima facie [Latin, meaning 'at first view'] he is entitled to be surprised as to why this could have been missed by the hospital witnesses. Of course, Mr Calder was probably unaware of the evidence of those witnesses summarised above, that there was no blood. The fact of there being unmissable blood at the time of the photographs in conjunction with this evidence from the hospital witnesses further adds credibility to the possibility that Mr Lubbock's body was violated causing the injuries post-casualty but pre-mortuary.

I must, so that you are properly apprised of the position, briefly mention some further important evidence: (a) When Mr Lubbock was removed from the pool and taken to hospital, he was wearing boxer shorts (Exhibit NH/1). These were then removed by the medical staff upon arrival. In reply to an earlier enquiry of mine to your Force Solicitor, it was confirmed that the shorts had been tested for blood and none, at least in the anal area, had been detected. The absence of blood on this garment is of course further evidence that up until the time of its removal, there were no injuries to Mr Lubbock's anus; (b) Despite two extensive searches of my client's home during April and August 2001, nothing was discovered which established, however remotely, that Mr Lubbock was injured there.

It is however unquestionable that those very serious and obvious injuries were inflicted to Mr Lubbock's anal area. The photographs taken at approximately 16.00 immediately prior to the post-mortem by Dr Heath on 1 April clearly demonstrate the nature and extent of them.

Unfortunately the obvious possibility of the injuries having been inflicted at the hospital does not appear to have been investigated at all by MIT. As mentioned above, all the evidence from the medical team and the party witnesses was in the hands of MIT by 12 June 2001 when the statement from the last hospital witness was taken. However despite this substantial volume of evidence it appears that no steps were taken to investigate it.

I emphasise the word 'appears' in this context as of course neither I nor my client are confident that we have so far uncovered the whole picture as to the MIT investigation. Possibly a proper investigation of this matter was conducted during mid-2001 and concerns regarding this are without foundation. You of course will be easily able to ascertain the position by querying this with the relevant MIT officers.

If it is the case that a proper investigation of this matter was conducted by MIT, I ask that you confirm this. I note that in his evidence to the coroner no reference was made to any such investigation by Mr McNeill.

In any event reportage of evidence given at the inquest was consistent with that reported previously; that there was little or no doubt that these injuries were inflicted at my client's home. In fairness to the media this impression was at least in part created or reinforced by comments made by the coroner on this issue in her summing up at the end of the inquest. I quote from the transcript as follows:

'We heard evidence from Kylie Merritt, Justin Merritt, Michael Parker (Barrymore) and Jonathan Kenney. Not one of these witnesses, who were party guests in

248

this house for over three hours has given to this court an explanation about how Stuart Lubbock, a previously fit 31-year-old, should be found floating in the swimming pool at the premises with a significant level of alcohol and drugs in his system, and how serious anal injuries came to be found on his body.'

Bearing in mind the above evidence, which was neither given or read out in statement form to the coroner, it is perhaps surprising that she should have expressed herself in such absolutist terms. Perhaps it was unfortunate that none of the hospital witnesses other than Nagle gave their evidence live before her. For your information, I have already taken this point up with the coroner and in the light of Mr Nairn's new evidence, asked her to reopen the inquest. However she has stated that she is legally unable to do so and in any event would be unwilling.

Taking the above history into account you will understand that subsequent to the inquest my client has wished to do all that he properly could to ascertain how in reality the injuries could have been caused to Mr Lubbock. In particular to further investigate how it could be properly reported that the injuries were inflicted at my client's house whilst the preponderance of evidence as outlined above was clearly against this proposition.

In relation to Mr Nairn, he was clearly a witness whom my client wished to give evidence live at the inquest. Of all the hospital witnesses he was the one who could give conclusive evidence as to the presence or absence of injuries to Mr Lubbock. This was made clear to the coroner's officer and Mr Nairn was scheduled to attend on the final day. Unfortunately this did not transpire. I was informed on the penultimate day that despite extensive efforts to locate him by Essex Police he could not be found. I did not inquire as to what 'extensive' meant in this context but clearly I believed that substantial effort had been undertaken using police resources. I recalled that in relation to Mr Kenney on the previous day, Essex Police had apparently been working in tandem with other forces to locate him which had proved successful. Taking these circumstances into account my client reluctantly accepted my advice that Mr Nairn must have disappeared without trace and so consented to his statement being read out.

Subsequent to the inquest I was contacted by a journalist from ITN who informed me that he had managed to trace Mr Nairn without difficulty via a simple internet search. Mr Nairn was now a lecturer in nursing at the University of Nottingham. I duly contacted Mr Nairn and he was willing to be interviewed by me on 24 September.

Mr Nairn's statement is clearly highly material to the issue of where and how the injuries suffered by Mr Lubbock were inflicted. Mr Nairn, a witness of unquestionable independence, makes plain that when Mr Lubbock was admitted into hospital there were no signs of anal injury to him. He states that during the two-hour period that he treated Mr Lubbock in casualty, he inserted a rectal thermometer into his anus on about sixteen occasions and at no time were there any visible injuries. He states, '*I saw nothing unusual or untoward about it. It was completely normal. If it had been dilated or significantly bruised I am sure that I would have noticed this. Moreover I would have reported it to the doctors.*'

Mr Nairn's statement is unassailable and

---

unambiguous: the injuries were not on Mr Lubbock's body during the time that he was in casualty. They could not have been inflicted whilst he was at my client's home.

Mr Nairn's evidence therefore clearly raises the ugly likelihood that the injuries were deliberately inflicted by someone whilst he was at the hospital. Inflicted some time during the period after he was pronounced dead and before the commencement of the post-mortem, a period of approximately seven hours.

It is clearly a very serious matter that a violation of such extremity could have taken place to Mr Lubbock during this period. Moreover for such an act to have occurred within the confines of a major public hospital clearly must give rise to substantial public concern.

Accordingly I am writing to request that an investigation be conducted concerning this immediately. I request this partly as the other hospital witnesses in contrast to Mr Nairn have, in response to my letters seeking their assistance, declined to provide this. It is however likely those witnesses would be prepared to speak to Essex Police as they have already done this before.

An investigation into this matter would be able to establish the movement of the body between casualty and the mortuary. Secondly who had access to it during this intervening period. Bearing in mind that a Home Office approved forensic pathologist must have been requested that morning to urgently attend the hospital mortuary to conduct an early post-mortem it can reasonably be expected that precautions were taken to restrict access to the body. Accordingly it can be expected that there is a record of whom could have had access to it during this period.

I would be very grateful if you would consider this request and let me know as soon as possible whether an investigation will be conducted into this matter.

I await your reply.

Yours sincerely,

David Corker

I have to say that I was not convinced that the letter would have the desired effect. As no reply came from the police for a long time, my mind had decided that, no matter how compelling the evidence, I was surely dreaming to think that in this continuing nightmare there would ever be a breakthrough. I had taken on the stance of a victim: rounded shoulders and lowered head.

I decided, against my better judgement, to give certain press and radio interviews to at least put my point across. One of the interviews was with Simon Mayo on Radio 5 Live. I was told it would just be a short interview, about the new evidence. Simon asked this, I answered that. He started to put me on trial. I for the first time thought 'I've fucking had enough of this,' but out of respect for the time of day kept the thought to myself.

'Did you?', 'I put it to you' and 'I'll answer you' ensued, as well as seconds of pauses, which feel like an age on radio, and in one of these pauses I could hear the producer telling Simon what to say and ask in his earphones. So now I had two coming at me. I jumped on the situation immediately. I said, 'Don't worry about asking the next question Simon, I've already heard it and here's the answer, NO I DID NOT.' A very embarrassed Simon said, 'I think we had better get these earphones turned down.' It broke his attack.

I even unwittingly made some humour out of the now far

too heavy interview. He said, 'And then, Michael, all your friends deserted you, didn't they?' I said, 'Who said that?' He said, 'Cheryl.' I said, 'Oh, for Christ's sake, not 'er again. It's strange that every bleedin' quote that's made me out to be a monster comes from 'er.' For some reason I went very cockney. 'Anyway, that aside Simon, who did she say deserted me?' Simon looked at the quotes – the producer must have gone quiet! He said, 'Oh, er, Jack Tinker [TV and theatre critic].' I said, 'Of course he deserted me – he died!' Simon tried to stifle a burst of laughter and did not succeed. I continued, 'Anyone else?' 'Er, no, she . . .' 'Who?' 'Cheryl.' 'Oh, just checking.' 'She said that you weren't invited to his funeral.'

I spoke with an 'I've-had-enough-of-this-crap' attitude, 'Simon, no one apart from immediate family went to his funeral, but I did go to his memorial service in Brighton and Cheryl was standing beside me.

Simon read out some emails from listeners, some for, some against, but that's fair. I am realistic enough to know that however much or however long I fight my corner, some people have already decided I'm not for redemption – sad, but it is their problem.

The newsreader handed Simon a piece of paper. He read it, then said, 'Michael, we have just received this from Essex Police.' As he read it, I was imagining the last sentence in my head, '. . . and we are satisfied that everything possible has been done and so we will not be taking any further action.' WRONG.

I was so dumbfounded, it registered on air. Simon asked me what I had to say in light of the police deciding that the case was worthy of further investigation. David Corker's letter had worked, my mouth wouldn't. All I could say was, 'I am delighted.'

Every news programme on television and radio carried the news of the case being reopened.

Here is the letter we received:

Essex Police have recently completed a review of the investigation in accordance with national practice. We are satisfied with the standard of that investigation and the lines of enquiry pursued.

In view, however, of the additional line of enquiry, as set out in your letter of the 22 November 2002, Essex Police will investigate your allegation that the anal injuries identified during the post-mortem had been committed by persons unknown at Princess Alexandra Hospital, Harlow.

I will inform you of the result of the enquiry in due course.

Just to assist even further, David Corker followed this development with more facts that he had uncovered. As he states in the following letter, how much more was there? Or is there? Who knows? Someone does. I know one thing, though, it ain't me. The police also announced that after interviewing all the witnesses that Cheryl had provided them with saying I could swim, they found that all of them only ever saw me standing in the shallow end with someone around.

David's second letter included the following:

MIT officers and specialist forensic personnel commenced a most detailed search of the house, which did not conclude until 19.30 the following day, 1 April. A great deal of property was seized and removed for examination. At some stage, presumably at around 11.30, Mr Macey summoned a Home Office approved

forensic pathologist to conduct a post-mortem
(Dr Michael Heath).

Subsequently, a post-mortem commenced by Dr
Heath during the afternoon and only then, according to
Detective Chief Superintendent McNeill in his evidence
to the inquest, 'the anal injuries outlined in earlier
evidence were discovered for the first time'.

As to the all-important issue of the timing of such
injuries, I quote again from Mr McNeill's evidence:
'... clarification was sought from the pathologist,
Dr Heath, concerning the timescales of the anal injury.
He indicated at 15.25 hours on 1 April that they would
be *no more than four hours old*.'

Subsequent to 1 April all those present at the
party were re-interviewed and in some cases, re-re-
interviewed. Summarising all their accounts Mr
McNeill stated: 'None of the people present that night
made any allegations in respect of any other person at
the party either in terms of sexual activity, assault or
homicide.'

On 10 August 2001, MIT decided to undertake a
second search of the house. The reason, according to
Mr McNeill, being 'based on new hypotheses the
additional experts had introduced'. These hypotheses
were never disclosed. This second search was duly
conducted on 15 and 16 August. Clearly nothing of
significance was discovered as the investigation was
discontinued on 13 November ...

Taking the above into account, I request that the
new investigation addresses the following issues:

All the medical team who treated Mr Lubbock whilst
he was in casualty at the hospital, from 06.28 until
approximately 08.40 on 31 March be re-interviewed
concerning:

The absence of injury and blood other than caused by the medical procedures.

The likelihood, if Mr Lubbock had already sustained the serious injuries and the resultant wounds/blood had clotted, of such wounds not being reopened by the invasive treatment of the following procedures: manual vigorous resuscitation, intubation, ventilation, cardiac arrest treatment and repeated insertion and withdrawal of a metal probe into the anus/rectum. (Such treatment being continuously administered for up to 2½ hours.)

The role played by Stuart Nairn and corroboration of the facts as set out in his statement made in September 2002.

The likelihood of all the members of the team not noticing the extensive injuries.

A reconstruction of what happened to Mr Lubbock's body during the intervening period between pronouncement of death and commencement of post-mortem on 1 April. This to include an examination of all hospital records and identification and interviews of relevant hospital staff etc.

When death was pronounced, it must follow that proper safeguards ought to have been put in place by Essex Police from that moment onwards to ensure that no one had access to and could interfere with the body until its examination by the pathologist, Dr Heath, hours later. Clearly this is both an elemental and fundamental precaution. Any lapse of vigilance, even if only for a short period, would firstly tend to undermine the integrity of any subsequent forensic post-mortem and secondly would also undermine the validity of a presumption concerning the injuries having to have been inflicted at the house.

Mr Barrymore is very concerned to receive an

unequivocal assurance from Essex Police that at all times during the intervening period at the hospital the body was constantly guarded. Unfortunately, whilst the picture is not yet complete, there are grounds for belief that this safeguard was not put in place. I refer to a notebook entry made by PC 4306 Hare covering his time at the hospital on 1 April; it suggests that once the body had been conveyed to the hospital mortuary PC Hare and his colleague (PC Wood?), both then left the scene.

After an extra year's investigation, a spokesman for Essex Police said, 'We are absolutely confident that we have answered everything that needed answering about this part of the investigation.'

David Corker said the police had not given answers to any of the questions he had asked about Mr Lubbock's injuries.

11

The New World

At times I have felt sickness and mental torture. Sounds dramatic doesn't it? It would be laughable if it was only me being a drama queen. Despite what has been written about me, I still have loved ones, and so many others who have given me their support, including so many via my website which I have to thank Joy Padmore for, who has dedicated so much of her time over the last seven years. Between them all they have managed to keep my head held in the position that it should be. Many more events in this yet unfinished story will unfold. The truth is, I don't know what course it will take. The only course I know for sure is that I want to get back to work. Back on stage doing what I know best – making people laugh. Back to what I started doing all those years ago.

God only knows why He made me the way I am, and only He knows why He chose me to be one of His disciples of laughter. He also knows why He gave me times in my life that would test whether or not I could deal without laughter. The ups, the downs, the tears, the frowns and the tragedy that happened at my home.

Prior to moving to New Zealand at the end of 2003, things were hard financially. The taxman had decided to have a close look at me. As far as I was concerned, my accountants had done everything they should have done. The taxman, however, managed to calculate that I owed him a nice fat sum. For legal reasons, I cannot say what happened to my contract with ITV.

I was quickly going nowhere and the income was running down. To top it all, I had no choice but to declare myself bankrupt in the UK. Not surprising, what with the endless lawyer bills, paying everyone's wages and no work coming in. It was one thing after another. It couldn't get any worse. Or could it?

Gray Bartlett, a promoter in New Zealand, promised me he could get me work, but New Zealand is a small country, and budgets are quite different from anything in the UK. But as I had no work in Britain to even turn down, anything became something. It seemed I had two choices, fold up and die or go to New Zealand and start a new life. I didn't run away to New Zealand – it became a life-saving option. A question of survival.

Shaun was a godsend during this period. Coming from a financial background he was quick to help me, working out what we could and couldn't spend. He organised everything and gave me hope that life could go on. We had hardly any money to buy anything, so we rented a house in Auckland, and I soon started to get bits of work to keep us going. I was asked to play Billy Flynn in *Chicago* and that was fantastic. It helped me get back into a work frame of mind.

The people in New Zealand welcomed me with open arms and appeared to see through the tabloid versions of events in Britain. They were non-judgemental and that itself made life so much more bearable. It also helped me to remain sober. Slowly, bit by bit, and with the help of family and close friends, I began to get my life back on track. Jeff Pope who wrote and produced *Bob Martin*, the TV comedy drama, contacted me regularly to see how I was and encouraged me to keep going despite the odds. Diana Howie, a good friend and TV executive, also helped me not to lose sight of the future, advising and assisting me with the small trickle of offers that started to come from the UK. There weren't many but anything rather than nothing lifts you at these times.

Over the next two years in New Zealand I began to find *me*. I had spent so many years making other people happy I had never given any time to *me*. To be honest, the British tabloids did me a huge favour by actually allowing me to start all over and get myself back on track. I suddenly found I could stand up straight; my height came back. I no longer stooped or walked with my head down. For the first time in two years I was able to sit at a café and look at the trees without wondering if there were paparazzi hiding amongst the foliage. I was no longer terrified of my own shadow and my confidence slowly returned.

I was in the middle of the *Chicago* tour when the phone rang in the hotel room at 6 am one morning. Shaun answered it. He paused for just that moment too long, turned to me and said, 'Michael, Cheryl has died.' I wasn't even aware that she was ill.

What was behind the thinking of those close to her at the

time, that not one of them thought, at the very least, to contact me and tell me she only had weeks to live?

When I heard the news my first reaction was to stare straight ahead and rewind my mind through all those years we spent together, all the dreams we had, like all young couples, of how our life was going to be. Even during our worst rows, somewhere among the bad name calling, there always came a point where we would burst out laughing.

I had started to prepare myself for the journey back from New Zealand to England when I was told, via various members of the press and news reports, that Cheryl's last request, according to those around her, was that I should not attend her funeral. I truly was saddened at this information, as it never actually came from Cheryl herself. Cheryl and I always shared everything during our time together 50/50. She deserved everything she had, without her, I was nothing. Yes, she did make me. No, she did not break me.

I am sorry that I took myself away from her. It was necessary for me to do, to survive. From my experience, to invest so much love in one person is guaranteed to bring success. It is also too much for any human being to live with. It is the strangest form of suffocation. That much love paralyses you until you are so still you are of no use to anyone, because all you are doing is breathing. Cheryl took her last breath, the funeral went ahead and although many attended, I did not. I respected her wishes, and just sent flowers. I wrote how much I loved her and quoted her favourite saying about me, which was 'Nobody knows the pain of living with a name'. Yes, Cheryl, I understand what you meant by that, but remember, you created it.

Whatever Cheryl did publicly from the time that I left her, and there was plenty, from accusing me of being physically violent (not true) and saying I could swim (again, not true), I know without question that she loved me from the moment she saw me until the moment she died, and she would rather have mourned my own death than not have me in her life. Sounds arrogant, but true. We never really parted, it was just that we had not seen or spoken for quite some time. Given those years again, would I have married a different girl? Absolutely no way. Only the chosen got to live with the likes of Cheryl. Mx

In September 2005 a few people in Britain started to contact me to sound me out as to whether it might be time to bring me back for certain things. One offer in particular came from Channel 4, to do *Celebrity Big Brother*. When I first heard the suggestion my initial reaction was a resounding no. But they kept coming back to me with improved offers and I could see quite clearly that they were serious about their offer.

I discussed the situation with Shaun and a few close friends, who all appeared to have the same opinion. Don't do it Michael. One night I sat upstairs at the top of our house in Auckland having a cigarette and started to ask myself questions. I thought, whatever happens the press are going to have a go at me – I can't avoid that, it's going to happen regardless of what I'm going back for. But I'm happy where I am. Do I really need all that attention again? If I went back on television with a brand new format, they would delight in cutting me down for that. At least *Big Brother* is an established format. If I can go into the *Big Brother* house with no agenda maybe this could work. The fact that I was to be paid can't be left out of the mix. But there was still the nagging worry that I could be set up.

A few days later Sharon Powers, the executive producer, and, Pete Gair, the talent booker on *Big Brother*, phoned my agent, Karen Kay, to say they would like to come over to New Zealand to talk to me in more detail about the show.

It was then I realised that they were intent on having me on the programme. They were committed. A few days later I signed the deal.

Because of the need to maintain secrecy, the plan was to fly me to Paris, and from there I would travel to London via train so nobody could get sight of me. I did, at this stage, have my moments of doubt, sweating over whether I had made the right decision. I was in now, and that was that. I just had to make the best of it and be myself. I was given so much advice: don't do this, don't do that. In the end I decided not to think about it any more. I went into it saying I would go in the house without any agenda and that's what I did.

When I arrived at Waterloo Station I was put into a van with blacked-out windows, which sped out of the station as if we were on a bank raid. The next morning I was taken from my hotel to another secret location. All the other contestants are there, but all on different floors with their own security staff. The whole operation runs like clockwork. At the hotel I said my last goodbye to Shaun and I was ushered into another car, which was to take me to the house.

As I sat in the back of the car I began to feel nervous for the first time. I knew when I got there it would be besieged with press photographers and I felt numb all over. As we approached the house I could hear the crowd in the background. The car pulled into the studio at a specific point where nobody could see it. I was then sent into a dressing room. By this time the saliva had begun to drain from my mouth. My mouth would not move. This was not another *Barrymore* show, or *Strike it Lucky*. As far as I was concerned, I was about to confront the mob and be stoned. I thought to myself the only thing that works for you is a smile. Stand up to your full height and when it comes at you – duck!

I got back into the car and was driven to my destiny. The car stopped, someone opened the door for me and the crowd went absolutely berserk. Without a shadow of a doubt it was one of the most emotional moments of my life. Not one boo, not one bad reaction, not one bad comment. The noise from the camera motors was ear shattering and the whole commotion froze me to the spot. All I could see were the posters, 'Welcome back Michael', 'We love you Michael'.

All I can say is that it was like a hero's homecoming. I felt like someone who had been held hostage for years; in my case five. I could feel my stomach starting to turn and well-up. I was starting to crack-up emotionally. I couldn't hold back the tears any longer, so in the end I just let go.

The warmth and the human reaction as I walked along that runway was overwhelming. It made me so upset, but out of joy and happiness. People can tell you that they love you, but until you actually see and feel it, it means nothing. At that point, I would have been quite happy to have taken all that good feeling and applause and gone home.

Finally I had to open that door and leave the people outside. I walked down the steps into the house, but it took me forever to get myself together – I think that showed on the screen. I met Chantelle when I walked in, but I don't remember anything I said to her. It was all still a blur and my ears were still ringing with the sound of people calling my name. That whole moment took my breath away and had a profound effect that will stay with me for ever.

In reality it took me over a week in the house before I calmed down. That's why when I was called into the diary room for the first time and asked my reaction I broke down again. I just couldn't hold it back – it was all still too real. I remained numb for about a week. It was so overwhelming and such a huge relief. I remember going to bed the first night and pulling the covers over my head and crying.

The next day fear set in. I had this feeling that at any moment it was all going to go wrong. That perhaps they were going to send in Stuart's father or somebody to set me up. The fact is, I had left myself wide open for any possibility. A sort of paranoia crept over me. It's not that I had anything to hide, but the thought of thirty-eight cameras on you 24/7 is nothing short of terrifying. Very early on I even considered walking out. I missed Shaun terribly. When you are cut off like that from the outside world – no newspapers, no radio and no television – you soon get disorientated.

I cried, I cried, I cried and then I cried – I laughed – I sort of cried. I laughed much more, I cried a little, I laughed till I cried. Then I cried with laughter. I saw the end and wanted it to start all over again. Despite those of my housemates who shouted my name out loud. Shouted my name at me LOUD!

Remember, when you point a finger at any one, three of them are pointing back at you.

For those of you who don't know how *Big Brother* works, nobody has any idea who the other (so-called) celebs are going to be. They just come in one by one. When Pete Burns walked in I sort of knew the face – it is one of those faces you remember! He just walked over to me and said, 'Well, I know who you are.' I suppose the weird thing was that while some of the other contestants didn't know who Rula Lenska or Preston were, the majority of them did know me. What made it easier for me from day one was that there appeared to be a kind of respect thing for me, which made me feel more comfortable.

I didn't feel I immediately had to start performing; I wasn't in the mood anyway. I just wanted the time to get a feel for the place. In some ways I believe that being cut off from all the publicity worked for me – not knowing what was going on outside.

Jodie Marsh was the only one with whom, from the outset, I sensed there was something going on. I knew I wasn't going to get on with her. My feeling was that it wasn't fair to start slagging off Jordan, saying she had saggy tits and looked like a witch. I just couldn't see how that was going to help her on the show. This is a hard enough business as it is without putting each other down. In the early stages I began to believe that Jodie had been put in there on a mission to deal with me and certain events that had happened in my life.

I very soon got into the routine of cooking for everyone. Again, I had not planned to do this. I just instinctively felt that was where I should be – in the kitchen. It was my way of focusing and keeping myself busy. When you consider that we all slept in the same room, had one toilet, one shower – there was no private space – my kitchen became my private space. It became my little stage. It's where I felt safe. In some ways the whole experience became just another rehab for me. The only difference this time was that there were thirty-eight cameras and millions of people watching.

When I knew I was crying on camera my professional side told me, 'Don't do it'. Then I thought, 'Sod it, why not? It's all of me. Why should I hold back? If that's how I feel, then I should show how I feel.' It may have been reality television for most, but it was real life for me. I felt the same way about showing anger on screen. When I lost it with Jodie a few times I thought, 'Why shouldn't I show my feelings?'

Dennis Rodman was one who didn't know me. I think after he had chats with Jodie and the others he found out a little about me. But the thing with Dennis is that I couldn't understand a word he was saying. We ended up having one set-to which got really nasty. He was standing inches from my face, but I stood up to him and looked him in the eye.

George Galloway was one who came with a clear agenda. All he kept saying was that he wanted to appeal to the younger voter. So that clearly failed. However, he also seemed to support me from day one. He kept saying all he wanted was to see me back on television. He said he wanted me to win *Celebrity Big Brother*. He said this out loud to the others. It was at that point I had to leave the room and go outside into the garden. It just hit me. I had not heard that kind of support from anyone in the house. It hit me quite hard. I didn't want to hear people talk like this. I had not expected it. I think I must have built up such a tolerance to people attacking me in the media anything else had become alien to me. I was so defensive when I first entered the house. I expected these people to just come at me. Instead they were talking to me as if they genuinely cared about me. So I sat in the garden and pulled the hood up over my head to try and hide from the cameras, because I could not stop myself from crying. It was just relief.

This scene, I found out later, made headlines in the tabloids, including BARRYMORE CRACKS UP. I suppose it must have made a strange little scene – an odd picture of, in Galloway's words, 'a fifty-five-year-old man out there crying'. (I was fifty-three.) When he and Chantelle came out into the garden it made me worse. I know at the time they meant well. I just needed to be alone with my thoughts. We all need to be like that sometimes. George Galloway kissing me on the head was also an iconic moment. Strange that in the end it was George who eventually turned against me. I just want to take time to explain why I have the need to perform to an audience no matter where it may be – in a theatre, in front of millions on TV, or a few in the confines of my front room – or indeed just to myself.

Most people talk to themselves, I perform to myself, and before you overreact to that statement, performing to yourself is not recommended unless you don't mind people's reaction as you jig furiously down the King's Road, or your local high street of choice, with legs and arms flying in all directions to the tune of *River Dance*, without the music. It is just that recently I have been made aware of people thinking that there is a flaw in my nature. Looking at tapes of *Celebrity Big Brother*, I saw the conversation between George Galloway and Rula Lenska about me always performing. Rula said, 'Michael can be highly entertaining, but after a while can become irritating.'

My initial reaction was, well, Rula, instead of talking about it behind my back why didn't you just say to me, 'Michael, very funny, now can you shut the fuck up?' I would have totally understood and ceased the irritating performance immediately.

Just to give you an idea if you have never watched this particular show or indeed can't deal with any reality at all, this is what happened on Day 19 in the *Big Brother* house.

George: Yeah, well I'm intervening. (Pause for effect.) As you're attacking [Dennis] let me attack you. (Pause for more effect.) You woke me up, and because I wouldn't hand over one of my cigars, you threw a strop, and then at that table you aggressively—
Michael: I think actually you threw the strop George.
George: No, no.
Michael: I asked you if you'd got a cigar. It's a simple question.
[. . .]
George: Michael, you never let anybody speak, so now, this time, you're gonna let me speak. (Here's that pause

again.) Nobody gets one sentence into an anecdote with you before you take it over and turn it into an anecdote about you, so this time you're gonna listen to me.

Michael: (Eyes locked on to George.) Mmm Mmm.

George: I was close to you, and Dennis was close to you and you stabbed both of us because of your mania about hoarding cigarettes. (BIG pre-statement pause.) YOU'RE A REAL CIGARETTE ADDICT! And you ought to address the fact that you've got no loyalty to anybody. When we were sitting in there in that living room, when there was scope for a debate about whether I should have my rights taken away from me, you sat absolutely shtoom and said nothing.

Michael: Mmm Mmm.

George: Despite all the support I had given you, despite all the efforts I had made for you, when it came to a problem that I was facing, you were silent, you know why? Because you care about nobody except yourself. You're the most selfish, self-obsessed person I have ever met in my entire life.

Michael: In your opinion.

George: SO, put that in your pipe and smoke it, if you've still got any cells left in your mind about caring what people think about you.

Michael: In your opinion.

George: (Looking away.) I was expressing my opinion . . . unusually you allowed me to do so.

Michael: Well of course I allowed you to do so.

George: NO, you don't allow anybody to speak.

Michael: Well . . .

George: Every . . . No look, review the footage when you get out of here, everything you speak about, is you.

Michael: I don't need to review . . .

George: ALL you speak about is you, 'cos ALL you care about is you.

Michael: George . . .

George: That's all you care about, number one, Michael Barrymore.

Michael: George, I don't . . .

George: And if, if . . .

Michael: I have to take care of myself, yeah . . .

George: Ahh, yeah . . .

Michael: Course I do . . .

George: Yeah, yeah, number one – that's the only person you care about.

Michael: So I don't care about anybody else?

George: The only person.

Michael: In your opinion I don't.

George: You're the only person you've talked about in here.

Preston: He's talked about everyone nonstop.

George: You haven't even talked about your partner in here.

Preston: He's talked about him nonstop! I can tell you everything he's said about him.

[. . .]

Michael: George, what mission are you on . . . what mission are you on? Listen to yourself, listen to all of ya. (Standing up.) I take no care of anybody else, except me? So I do all the cooking just for me, do I?

George: To be on the camera, to stand in the centre stage.

Michael: Ohhh, excuse me . . .

Maggot: What bollocks!

Preston: George, why don't they move the kitchen over there?

George: You're self-obsessed.

Michael: Oh come on George. George, you're in this frame

of mind, you're in this frame of mind because you've been nominated again, and you take it as a personal slight.

George: Yeah.

Michael: So you thought the most value is to go for me?

George: No. NO.

Michael: I'm an easy target.

George: No, no.

Michael: Is to go for me for the outside world?

George: Poor me.

Michael: You're playing to the outside world.

George: Poor me, poor me, pour me a drink!

Preston: Oh don't fucking bring that into it, that is low.

George: Poor me, poor me, pour me a drink!

Michael: You are out of order . . . you are out of order!

Preston: (Pointing hard at George.) You are a fucking wanker! You are fucking low.

Michael: You are out of order!

Preston: WANKER!

George: Poor me, poor me.

Michael: And you're doing it with a smile.

George: Poor me, poor me.

Michael: You wanna play around with an addict?

George: Poor me, POOR ME!

Michael: Is that what you wanna do?

George: Poor me, poor me.

Michael: That's how caring you are, you care so much about everybody!

[. . .]

Michael: You will be sorry when you go out of here and you review the tapes. You will be the one who's sorry, you're so sensitive yourself. You're the type George, that goes out and buys the papers to see if you're in them. I don't. I don't do that, George, you do.

George: Yeah. Mmm (sarcastically), I'm the self-obsessed one!

Michael: You're gonna be sorry for what you said to the kids, you're gonna be sorry for what you started here.

George: Not a moment.

Michael: You're gonna see how ridiculous . . .

George: Not a moment.

Michael: All I was gonna say when I started is—

George: All you were gonna do was attack Dennis.

Michael: GEORGE, I feel really sorry for you.

George: All you . . .

Michael: You're that sad, no wonder Tony Blair threw you out!

George: Keep on talking, keep on talking.

Michael: No wonder Blair threw you out.

George: Keep on talking.

Michael: You can do that smile, George, it don't work, you need a bigger smile than that for the camera!

George: You're always performing, you never stop performing.

Michael: Absolutely don't, George, absolutely don't never stop performing. I never give anybody any time.

George: IT'S ALL AN ACT!

Michael: That's the trouble – you don't know the difference, you don't know the difference, George, because you're a frustrated performer yourself.

George: You never stop performing.

Michael: You come in here and you try your best and you don't like it, because you might have to go through that door.

George: I don't care about that.

Michael: You're worried about going through that door, George. If you're worried about going through that door . . .

272

George: I'm not.

Michael: Don't go through that door. Sit down, have a
protest, do what you do, shut the whole place down and
let them take you out. George that is your problem.

[. . .]

George: NO! NO!

Michael: You're mean George. You've got a meanness that
started off with one cigar, all you had to say was NO!
Aw George, come on, think about it, just think about it.

George: You think about it.

Michael: George, I'm absolutely clear I'm the best I've
ever been in my life. YOU WANNA HAVE A GO,
GEORGE? GET IN THE QUEUE! GET IN
THE QUEUE, GEORGE, and when you get in it,
go to the end of it, 'cause there's a big long line.

George: You never stop saying that – you're a broken
record.

[. . .]

Michael: I hate the word 'celebrity'. The word's banded
about, used for anybody who wants the name celebrity,
so they are a bit more known than the bloke next door.
He said, they said, she said. This is wrong, that's wrong,
they're right, you're right. Do you honestly think
anybody out there cares? Call me what you like, I don't
mind, I've been called everything there is, believe me,
everything. I have been called everything. But whatever
you say, you can't hurt me any more than I've been
hurt. I've been bashed against every pillar and post.
Giving me a bashing is not gonna gain any brownie
points . . . anywhere . . . except those who wanna favour
you, an' they can go an' jump in the lake. You can do
what you like to me, you can tear me down and rip me
apart. But one thing you can't have is my sobriety.
When you have been to where I have been to, some of

you may know what it's like. Then stand up and have a go at me, until you reach that spot in your life, if ever you reach that spot in your life . . . I beg you, please, to keep your opinions to yourself. And I'll do what I've done all the way through here and keep mine to myself.

[A really long, uncomfortable pause.]

Michael: Coffee anyone!?

I was not immediately aware of some of the things people were saying in the house – in particular the remarks made by Jodie Marsh about the pool incident. In hindsight, it was probably a good thing I didn't hear what she said. I was always waiting for the first person to mention swimming pools – not surprisingly, it was one of my nightmares. Of course, what I didn't know was what the tabloid press had said about me going on the show. It was still so 'anti-Barrymore'. If I had seen that, I would never have gone in there. MICHAEL BARRYMORE IS THE DEATH KNELL FOR CHANNEL 4 said one headline.

You cannot see from inside the house what the crowd reaction is to each housemate that enters. Chantelle kept asking me, 'Were the crowd nice to you – did they love you?' All I could say was, 'Yes, they were fantastic.' I was still in a haze. All I remember saying to her was, 'Oh, I know who you are.' Which goes to prove what a state I was in. How could I know who she was, she was completely unknown!

Chantelle appeared to me to be well cast. Why wouldn't I think she was in a pop band – she looked as if she could be. She was from Essex, a place I knew well. She had an accent that I knew. Although I never really queried the fact she wasn't a celebrity, Chantelle had no experience of the celebrity world and, in my opinion, it was a shame that she got hooked-up early with Jodie Marsh. Jodie didn't help her cause at all. One of Chantelle's finest moments was when Dennis Rodman, who thought he was God's gift to anything in a dress, made a clumsy pass at her and she said "Ere, I'm not goin' ta be at your beck an' call – you can forget that, mate.' I just thought, well done, Chantelle. Whether it was calculated or not, I think she did it really well.

Chantelle and I were the first ones in and the last ones out. I watched her grow in stature and, in the end, I think she deserved to win. If I'm honest, it may have been that this show wrote itself. It provided the perfect conclusion. The show managed to produce a brand new celebrity and, in some ways, made an old one very happy!

The experience of being there had gone way above my wildest expectations. Given my experience as a TV entertainer – doing this show was above them all. It was such a unique experience and nothing comes close. But it did completely drain me.

I remember standing there at the end with Chantelle before they called the winner. All I could think of was getting out and seeing Shaun. Although I had this feeling of foreboding sweep over me again. Wondering how the public were going to react to me. What the press had said.

When I climbed up those steps to come out I felt like a child. When I heard the roar from the crowd, which, by the way, was about three times the size of when I went in, all I could think of was where's Shaun? Suddenly I could hear his voice, then I spotted this rather slick looking new Prada jacket in the crowd. Yes, it was definitely Shaun. Going into the *Big Brother* house was meant to be, and proved, an integral part of my overall journey. I will never forget it.

The moment I came out of the *Big Brother* house, amid the euphoria and the mad excitement, the first person to greet me was my colleague, Chrissy Smith. She told me that a meeting had been arranged between myself and Terry Lubbock with the help of Rebecca Wade, the editor of the *Sun* newspaper. The meeting would be at a London hotel. Naturally I was a bit taken aback – relieved in one way and very nervous in another. Chrissy assured me that everything would be okay and I trusted her, after all I had wanted this meeting for so long. Over the years Chrissy and I had tried to set up a meeting with Terry as I knew that he wanted to meet with me face to face, have eye-to-eye contact and ask me certain personal questions. I embraced the idea but sadly no progress was ever made because it would be insisted that a lawyer and a national newspaper would have to be present. To me this was about Terry wanting closure on what happened to his son that night. I was very aware that it would be a highly charged and emotional time for both of us, one that needed not to be turned in to a media circus. The *Sun* newspaper had agreed to allow us time in private, for however long.

All along it appeared to me that, according to the tabloids, Terry had chosen to blame me for everything. But despite the amount of hearsay printed in the press, some basic facts remained. Stuart Lubbock did go back to my house of his own accord that night, and he chose to continue drinking. He also chose to go into the Jacuzzi and then into the pool.

Obviously I knew Terry from pictures, but had never met him personally. I was nervous, though I don't know particularly what I thought would happen. It did occur to me that he might attack me – it might be just a reaction – but I had nothing to hide and hoped we could work together to try to find some answers. It was what I had always wanted to do.

When I entered Terry's hotel room he was very chirpy and cheerful, and I thought, this is a good start. I greeted

Terry and told him I was so pleased to meet after all this time and he looked me in the eye and said, 'Yeah, and so am I.' We exchanged pleasantries and I held on to his hand and, instead of shaking and letting go, we just sort of held on to each other. It was one of those moments. He had tea and I had my usual Coca-Cola. Chrissy left the room and we were left alone; no journalists, no lawyers, just the two of us for well over an hour.

I told Terry that I was sorry that it had all been dragged out. That I believed a lot of obstacles had prevented us getting together and finding out what actually happened to Stuart that night. Terry's opening bombshell was, 'Let me put your mind at rest straight away. I don't blame you for Stuart's death at all.' I thought to myself, well, you wouldn't believe that from all that's been printed in the press. I smiled and said, 'A lot of things have been said, and it would appear some were said in such a way as to destroy my name and my reputation, based on something I am not responsible for.' Terry's second bombshell was, 'Michael, I know you had nothing to do with it, but you do hold the key to all this. There is no doubt that whatever happened to Stuart, happened at your house.'

'I'm afraid neither of us can be sure of that, Terry,' I said. Terry reached inside his jacket pocket as if looking for something. 'Look,' he said. 'What I want you to do is get a pen and write down on a piece of paper that you believe that whatever happened to Stuart, happened at your house, and sign it. That's all I want you to do.'

It was clear that Terry had come to this meeting with his own agenda. I had come to the meeting with an open mind. I told Terry that if he wanted me to say that, then I would have to state that there was an equal possibility that any injuries to Stuart occurred at the hospital, at some time in the eight hours after the resuscitation team had finished.

Terry stared at me and said, 'Oh no, that's all been gone over, the pathologist's report confirmed that.' I told Terry that we couldn't just pick, piecemeal, bits from here and there to make the story fit what he wanted it to fit – you had to see it from all sides to try and understand what 'could' have happened. Terry was clearly not interested in referring to the documents with all the factual witness statements that we both had brought with us. He went through the motions of putting them down beside him, and that's where they stayed throughout our meeting. I had brought my batch of witness statements because I was under the impression we were going to go over each bit together.

It was then that Terry launched his third bombshell. 'You see, Michael, I hold the key to your future. I want you to get back on television and back where you were, and I can help you do that. I just want you to write down what I said.'

At that point I realised this was not going to go much further. How could I just sign a piece of paper saying the injuries to Stuart happened at my house, when I did not believe they did? I became very frustrated and emotional at this point. I tried to explain to Terry that this was a momentous moment for me, as I am sure it was for him, to have got this far and to be sitting together at last. It had taken nearly five years just to get to this point. I made it quite clear to Terry that I was more than happy to go to the police or do whatever was necessary to find out exactly what had happened to Stuart. But Terry wasn't to be moved – he was on a solo mission. It was as if somebody had instructed him to obtain some form of documentary evidence where I agreed that any injuries to Stuart must have taken place at my house.

Terry had one last bombshell. 'You know this will avoid you having to go through a private prosecution?'

I said, 'What private prosecution?'

He said, 'Well, you know we would have to take a private prosecution to get you to answer things we want answered.'

At that point, I thought it would be wise to ask Chrissy to come back into the room to witness what Terry was asking me to sign. Terry agreed this would be okay and when she arrived I said, 'Terry, would you just explain to Chrissy what you've just been saying to me?' Terry once more repeated his request for me to sign his statement. Chrissy interrupted his flow. 'Terry, can I stop you there?' she said. 'I'm not going to allow Michael to agree to that.' Terry looked hurt. 'Well, why not?' he said. 'All we want to do is go forward and get some progress so that we can fight this together. I hold the key to Michael's career to get him back where he should be.' Chrissy said, 'To be fair, Terry, no one who was there that night would be able to sign this piece of paper.'

I asked Terry why he kept blaming me for everything in the newspapers. 'Because I wouldn't get any publicity out of it if I didn't use your name, would I?' was his response. When Terry made that statement I just stared, not openly at him, just to one side, and thought to myself, this is all so unnecessary and so, so sad.

I tried once more to reason with him. 'I can't give you information that I don't know, Terry. You keep saying you know I had nothing to do with it, yet you're asking me questions that I haven't got answers to.'

By now I was becoming very tired and frustrated. The whole tone of the conversation was starting to shock and worry me. It had all seemed such a good idea, but the meeting had descended into farce and I felt that we had not progressed at all. In the end we both made an attempt to arrive at some sort of compromise.

'Well, we'll have to agree to disagree,' announced Terry.

I thought for a moment and then replied, 'Terry, can we agree that you and I will go to the police and ask for the case to be reviewed and to say that we want certain questions answered? That includes questions that I want answered about what happened in the eight hours that Stuart was left alone.' Terry appeared to agree. He appeared to be anxious to finish the meeting and asked if I was going to join him and the *Sun* reporters for something to eat and drink. I explained I was still tired, having just come out of the *Big Brother* house, so we said our goodbyes, shook hands amicably and agreed to meet up later in the week.

The newspaper took shots of Terry and me shaking hands and interviewed us both separately. They had also carried out their own investigation into the events surrounding Stuart's death and the following morning the photos and the story hit the front page under the headline I DON'T BLAME YOU MICHAEL. It certainly was a momentous day for us both. Finally someone had the courage to print the facts. Sadly, I still couldn't help but feel despondent about certain aspects of my meeting with Terry and I had a feeling that Terry would not let things rest.

Sure enough, a few days later, Terry began talking to other newspapers, claiming he was not happy with our meeting. So it all began again. I was getting frustrated that every time I tried to do something with Terry to try and move things forward the goal posts mysteriously moved.

During that following week communications did indeed break down again. I received a list of eight points that were to be used in a private prosecution that was brought against me – just as I was about to leave for New Zealand. We were back to square one again. My lawyers warned me that if I did go back to New Zealand before the court case it would look as if I was running away. So I asked for the court hearing to be brought forward to the Friday before I was due to leave. I felt so let down. After all, I had agreed to try and sort things out with Terry, while backstage he was planning a private prosecution.

Then came another twist to the story. On the day of the hearing the judge ruled against every single point, the case was thrown out of court and I left for New Zealand as planned.

After all we had been through over the past five years, I felt a certain sadness. In my opinion, nothing Terry and I discussed had anything to do with genuinely finding out what happened to Stuart. And following the court case, and despite the judge stating there were no grounds for prosecution, Terry was pictured standing outside the court with a placard continuing his campaign.

When the mystery of what has actually happened to anyone who dies is answered or solved, the body is then, and only then, released for burial or cremation. This leads me to ask why, if all those concerned repeatedly wanted answers, was Stuart's body released for cremation less than a year after his death? The moral answer speaks for itself; the biological questions can now never be answered.

The bone of contention between Stuart's father and myself is that, although he has said he doesn't blame me for the death of his son, he believes that those injuries happened at my house. I don't believe they did. I didn't see anything happen, the medical team who worked on Stuart for about two hours didn't discover any injuries, so that would clearly indicate that they happened elsewhere.

There is this belief that Stuart was coerced into going back to my home. But Stuart was a 31-year-old man who, of his own accord, chose to get in the taxi. He was a father of two, an adult. Nobody is saying that Stuart was gay.

You can make your own assumptions and conclusions from the toxicologist's and pathologist's reports, but my concern is that nobody seems prepared to push and find out who was in charge of Stuart's body during the eight-hour period that it was unaccounted for. Surely, if injuries of this sort were apparent at 4.40 in the afternoon, they were apparent eight hours earlier?

I believe that these injuries happened to the body during that eight hour period and not at my house.

I understand that Terry needs answers and wants to know what happened to his son, but he must accept that there was no gay orgy at my house.

If a murder took place at my house, then why were all charges dropped? I was never arrested on suspicion of murder – although many people think I was, just by my name being put in front of the many stories about the case.

In the original witness accounts, not one guest mentioned drugs. It was only after Justin Merritt was cleared of suspicion of murder that stories about drugs started to appear in the paper – fictional stories, for which he received money.

Whatever Stuart did that night, he did willingly. He wasn't tricked or forced into it. These are the facts. He went in the pool when nobody else wanted to go in it. It was his choice to drink. Whatever drugs he took, he would have been the only person to know the true amounts.

At our meeting, I reminded Terry that Stuart's boxer shorts were intact, had no blood stains and were only removed by nurses at the hospital. His explanation was that whatever caused the injuries bypassed the boxer shorts, bypassed his outer skin and caused internal injuries. You do not have to have a medical background to work out that that is impossible. When I suggested this, Terry said, well then, the boxer shorts were removed and replaced. I asked Terry if he was seriously asking me to believe that someone removed the shorts in the water, injured him in the water, and then put the shorts back on, in the water? And all done without a speck of blood on anybody, on anything, and with his boxers in exactly the same condition as they were originally? The subject was changed.

Before I left to go back to New Zealand, Terry sent me a letter via my solicitor David Corker following our meeting. It was dated 2 February. In the letter, Terry thanked me for meeting him and confirmed that he did not hold me responsible for his son's death, although he insisted that Stuart's injuries had happened at my house. He suggested that I knew more about the events of that evening than I had told the police, and asked that I reveal this information to them.

My reply, dated 23 February, was as follows

Dear Terry
I was pleased that we finally had the private meeting that the both of us have wanted for so long.

However, I had thought we had reached a basis to go forward, with your acknowledgement of no wrong doing on my part, and an agreement to investigate how Stuart's injuries occurred after he left the house.

It is no use if you continue to ignore the proven facts. Neither the police, nor the three casualty doctors and two nurses, saw or reported any anal injuries. Indeed the nurse who inserted the 3mm thermometer on about 15 occasions saw no injuries.

After Stuart died in casualty, the two police officers signed off his body at 08.10am. There is then an unexplained gap of approximately eight hours before the body was examined by the pathologist. It is this eight hour gap, and the persons responsible for the body, which should form the basis of an inquiry.

283

As you are aware, I requested the police, in a six page detailed letter of 22 November 2002, to investigate this issue. They declined to reopen an investigation.

Terry, if we are to persuade the police to investigate further, we will need some evidence, which neither of us have. However, I note you have received £20,000, presumably from a newspaper, which could be used to fund a private investigation.

If we are to work together it is not constructive to keep saying that I have further information and it is unhelpful if you continue to make unfounded allegations in letters which obviously you have not written yourself. I am concerned that other persons seem to have a different agenda.

Let me put your mind at rest for once and for all. I do not have any further information as to Stuart's death or the injuries he sustained after he died at casualty.

In response to your other questions, I have no idea where Jon is. Furthermore you are wrong to suggest that Chrissy Smith prevented anything being said. What she and I did was to refuse to agree to the point that the injuries could have occurred at the house, and to refuse to sign anything that indicated such.

I am prepared to honour our agreement to work together but you must be constructive and not keep ignoring proven facts. If we can persuade the police to assist, their first enquiry should be into the 'missing eight hours.'

Yours sincerely

Michael Barrymore

I then began to receive a number of emails and letters from Terry and people who were apparently acting for the Lubbock Trust. One dated 23 February 2006 asks if there is any truth in a reported TV deal and goes on to remind me that the anniversary of Stuart's death is approaching.

Terry Lubbock emailed his reply to my solicitor in New Zealand in response to my letter. He said that unless I stop questioning what happened at Princess Alexandra Hospital, he would insist that I was responsible for his son's injuries.

Terry Lubbock told me that he holds the key to my career – that's neither right, nor fair. You cannot say that to someone. I want closure on this as much as he does. Also, what exactly is the reasoning behind emails asking what money I have or haven't been offered? And what is the purpose of ending the same email with a reminder of the forthcoming anniversary of Stuart's death?

I have to ask, what has that got to do with finding out what happened to Stuart? It is totally illegal to threaten someone that if you don't stop saying one thing, I will say that you are responsible for whatever I choose to accuse you of, particularly when they have already said I am not responsible. Part of me believes I was set up.

Now, at the time of writing, this case is being reviewed by a new team of Essex Police officers. I hope they find something and uncover a line of enquiry that leads to the truth. I want it reviewed, I'm relieved that it's being looked at again. I want the truth on this as much as anyone.

Here is a news item that came via the net this morning, 20 June 2006:

A judge yesterday quashed the murder convictions of three men after he deemed that evidence given by a pathologist was 'discredited' and may have misled the jury. The decision came on the day the pathologist, Michael Heath, faced a Home Office disciplinary tribunal into his professional conduct following complaints from his peers.

In his judgement yesterday, Lord Justice Hooper quoted extensively from analysis provided by other pathologists who questioned several of the conclusions central to Dr Heath's evidence. The judge said Dr Heath's claims that the victim may have 'drowned in his blood' because of injuries to his head and lips, and that he had been unconscious after the assault in his flat, had been discredited by his peers.

If the Home Office tribunal into Dr Heath's professional conduct – which opened yesterday – finds he has acted inappropriately, a number of high profile cases could be revisited, legal experts have said. Since his appointment to the Home Office register of forensic pathologists in 1991, Dr Heath has provided post-mortem evidence in a series of cases, including that of Stuart Lubbock, who was found dead in entertainer Michael Barrymore's swimming pool.

Hours earlier, at Dr Heath's disciplinary tribunal at the Old Bailey, Charles Miskin QC, for the Home Office, said, 'It is the belief of the Home Office that Dr Heath has fallen short of the high standards required by the Secretary of State of forensic pathologists.' The tribunal would hear of two cases in which there was 'severe disagreement' between Dr Heath and other 'eminent pathologists', he said. In both cases, Dr Heath refused to back down on his view that two women had been murdered, despite evidence to the contrary, it was alleged.

As soon as I became aware of this report, I asked my solicitors in New Zealand to send a letter to the police to make sure they were up to date with the recent situation.

———

At the time of writing, no ruling has yet been reached at the tribunal. I have already questioned how Dr Heath discovered injuries that, up until his examination, had not been witnessed by any of the eight people at the house, nor by the two paramedics, nor by the two policemen that were with them, nor by any of the doctors and nurses who tried to save him. Twenty-three people who saw nothing to suggest in any way that Stuart was the victim of anything other than drowning, eight unexplained hours, and no answers.

It's not good enough; it's not fair on me and it's not fair on Stuart's dad, indeed anyone related to Stuart. There are questions that need to be answered and I hope they will be, so Terry and his family can get on with their lives and I can get on with mine.

12

Endings and
Beginnings

I had a moment of clarity when I woke up this morning. It's one of those days you wake up and get it – everything that is confusing about life you suddenly understand. We all have them, we just don't realise what they are. The difference between feeling up or down. (If you are following this, you may need to see a doctor.)

At the time of writing, I have a month left till this book has to be delivered to the publisher. So it's time to look back over what I've written so far. Strange that we are encouraged to live in the present and yet I've spent all this time looking back. It's been months since I left the *Big Brother* house. Wow, what a weird time – new highs, different lows, brand-new places found in the head. (Still following me?) Shaun's worried about me. My face is red raw and apparently I've been distant. He can't quite see why, when everything is going so well for me, why I don't look it. (You still with me?) I cannot really give him a decent answer, because he's got to know me so well. I tried thinking what it was like to live with me, got nowhere with that, and marvelled at how he does.

He is fantastic to live with; he's bright, caring, thoughtful and, best of all, he is really funny. He loves me to death, as I do him, but somehow it sounds more convincing coming from him. He has total understanding of who Cheryl was and her part in my life. He's often said he would have liked to have met her. There wasn't much chance of that occurring before, but now, sadly, it can never happen. This morning he handed me some, actually a load of emails that had been sent to my website from fans. Shaun handles all our personal business, he reminds me a lot of Eddie, my father-in-law; I loved him too. Shaun said, 'Read these and see what the people who matter say about you, which I think you forget sometimes.'

Of course, after what you have just read, you'd think it was time for me to be excused from further controversy, wouldn't you? Sadly, some people will try to accuse you of the most preposterous things. Shortly before I left for New Zealand, a young man, who was deaf and dumb, accused me of sexual assault. Of course it was nonsense. He had come to my house to give me flowers, and myself and my friend Jean saw him out together. After the trial in Liverpool, at which I gave evidence by video link from New Zealand, it was shown there was no evidence and the boy was arrested for perverting the course of justice. He was later sentenced to two years suspended.

A few years ago Shaun had seen enough of me staring at the garden walls day in, day out. He said, Michael, if we don't do something drastic you are going to end up six feet under, sober or not. You can't fight the world. For both our sakes we have to start again. Let's pack up everything and emigrate to New Zealand.

I agreed, but didn't really take in the enormity of this decision until the huge removal container filled the driveway. Shaun helped to organise everything. I helped with a few things, but found the experience somewhat numbing. Was I really packing up everything, leaving my birthplace, going to the other side of the world, not for the reasons many do so – to start a new life – but to get my old one back? Had the tabloids done enough to hound me out of my own country? Well, all the bags were packed, the furniture gone. It was amazing that, despite all the time spent following me, not one photograph was taken of the removal, or of Shaun and I leaving. On Christmas Day we were in the air. We had a stopover in Hong Kong and on New Year's Eve were back in the air again, landing in Auckland, New Zealand, on New Year's Day 2004.

At first, I wondered if it was really going to be any different, as a small plane circled the house, snapping pictures to show where we were living. But the first article that appeared had a very different approach. The headline read: POMS WON'T LET UP ON BARRYMORE. It was written by David Hartnell, and the following is an extract.

I'm just staggered at how the British press have tried to crucify this talented entertainer at every turn. Sure, he's been through the mill and, sure, he may have done some outrageous things, which he now regrets. But no human being deserves to go through what he's been through and if the British press have their way they look like they'll hound him till his dying day. Unfortunately I've never met Michael. But I sincerely hope that one day our paths will cross. I'd like to take this opportunity to wish

Michael and Shaun every happiness in their new life here in New Zealand.

David continued to be very supportive. Our paths did cross, they still do, and I have been able to thank him personally.

That article showed me the light we all seek so hard for when our personal tunnel of life closes in on us. I started to relearn what most people take for granted – simple things, such as driving to the shops, alone. Smiling back at those who recognised me in the street. Talking to strangers who knew me and asking them what they were all about. All the things I used to do. All the things I had been made to believe were in the past. Complete strangers telling me to hold my head up high and thanking me for all the joy and happiness I had given their mums and grandmas, dads and grandads, and themselves as well. Asking me if I really understood that they could see through everything that had been said and that I was truly loved. All types, all ages, always there. I had to go back out to find out that I never really had to stay in. I had to travel 12,000 miles to find that shadows don't reflect any different when you're upside down.

I met a man called Bob Jones, who stood at the side of the stage watching me work after I had interviewed him before a huge Kiwi crowd at a business seminar I was compering. Bob and I hit it off straight away, to the delight of the crowd. We went for dinner, where he told me how his life had taken a turn for the worse some years ago and how he had come back fighting and reclaimed himself. Bob had followed my story and relayed to me in no uncertain terms his disgust for certain tabloids and how I was treated. Bob Jones is well known by the Kiwis and, love him or loathe him, you cannot ignore him. He started, mentally, to help me reclaim myself. Just because he believes that's what one human being should do for another. I have tried to thank him many times for what he did for me. If you go to thank him, though, he changes the subject. Last time we talked I said, 'Bob, you are just like I used to be. You have to learn to take thanks with good grace.' He said, 'I don't do grace!' Ah well, I tried.

There is a consistency with the Kiwis that works for me, whatever their background. Gray Bartlett backed me for a tour when no one else wanted to know. Tom Scott, a much-admired Kiwi writer, asked me to take on one of his works called *The Daylight Atheist*, because he thought I was right for the role and based his judgement on that alone. I am grateful to all my Kiwi mates and girlfriends, who have made me proud of being me again. Kiwi Frank, the decorator, who explained exactly which planet I'm on by explaining that the stars in the sky are different over Kiwi land than they are over Pommy land. When I first arrived in NZ, for weeks I pointed heavenward saying, 'Oh look, there's Orion and that's the Anvil. Overhearing me one night Frank said, 'Nah mate, that's Orion and that's the Southern Cross, you won't see Pommy stars from here.' Michael Reed, QC, for proving that there is a lawyer who is true to the saying: 'Do as adversaries do in Law, strive mightily, but eat and drink as friends.' Geoffrey Cone, a barrister with a sense of humour that makes me smile, and leaves others wondering where his nurse is.

I have a lot to be grateful for: I've had good fortune, I have good health, good food and a roof over my head. And I have my sobriety. It's been five years. That's the one thing I am determined not to lose. Sometimes when we moan perhaps we need to remind ourselves of what a friend of mine said when I was moaning about life. He said, 'Have you got a roof over your head today?' I said, 'Yes.' He said,

'Have you eaten today?' I said, 'Yes.' He said, 'So what's your problem?'

I haven't felt this well since I was eight years old. It's taken me forty-six years to get there again. It hasn't been forty-six years of hell; it's been a roller coaster. Some of it was great, some of it was horrible, and it's no good my coming through all of that without somehow improving my lot in life and learning a few lessons. What happened was terrible – Stuart's death, Mum's death, Cheryl dying, the police investigation, the tabloids – and I wouldn't wish it on anyone, but I have gained from it. It helped towards making me sober. When I think back to all the times in the past that I have relapsed with little or no reason, the one time in my life I had the greatest excuse to hit the bottle again, I didn't. I can't allow myself to get too confident, because I'm still an addict, and addiction is always lying in wait to trip me up. I try to live each day as it comes, but I have to take sustenance, rather than substance, from the past to enable me to hold up in the future.

Addiction is a disease. It'll destroy you mentally, leading to a slow and painful death. I will be an addict for the rest of my life. I just hope that I can spend what time I've got left in recovery. I have to remind myself every morning that I'm an addict; I have to be on my guard. Sometimes I get up and can go for three, four hours without remembering what I am – and that's dangerous. On a nice spring day I could go out to meet up with a friend, we could be sitting chatting, I could be feeling confident, and I might just say to the waiter, 'Oh, Jack Daniel's please.' It's a very devious disease, and it's waiting for me to trip up. Every time something happens to test me, the addiction is looking for its chance to get a grip again. But despite all that's happened, I've not had one blip. Not one bubble. I'm not starting that all over again. Just for today.

———

I fly back and forth to England now for work, and I am followed by photographers who report on what I wear, what I buy, who I talk to. If you came round to my house today and we had a nice chat and a cup of coffee, for all I know you could run straight off to the press and claim that we had four pints, then we had an orgy, then the ceiling fell in, then the Martians landed – and they'd probably print it. I've had to put up with some pretty outrageous stuff in the press, but I can't run around denying every single story. Nowadays I just have to believe that most sensible people will realise that the stuff they read about me doesn't always add up, and that just because something is printed doesn't mean it's true. Eventually, I suppose, they'll get tired of reading about me, and the papers will get tired of writing about me, and they'll move on to someone else. Or maybe not.

I try to keep calm, let the photographers get their picture, although I know that it'll appear in the papers with some ridiculous caption saying I'm looking 'tired' or 'tragic', even if I've just nipped out to the shops or come back from an AA meeting. I don't always keep my cool; it's very hard when you know that your every move is being monitored, that they're photographing everyone you meet, waiting for you to make a slip, to show an emotion.

I spent so long running away from things – from my sexuality, from my addiction, from the press – and now I've stopped running.

I don't know what I'm supposed to feel like. My eyes sag slightly, I have a chin I ain't seen before. I love my dog Sprite, who is a bichon frise – strange name, strange dog. I still miss Candy, the West Highland terrier that Cheryl and I had. She was great: she'd rip up every letter that came through the letterbox, she'd bite your nose when you played with her, and she was always there to greet you when you came home, no matter what kind of day you'd had. We went on long walks in the woods together, she never strayed too far without a lead, she slept on the bed and took up all the room, listening to the secrets that I told her. She never agreed or disagreed: she was just happy to be there.

I miss JD, our Jack Russell, named, I'm embarrassed to say, after my favourite tipple from my drinking days. We've just had her put to sleep after seven happy years together. We found her on my nan's farm in County Mayo, when on a trip to Ireland. I showed Shaun all the places I used to play as a kid. It was a hardened Irish farm life, with all the charms and unique qualities that makes my Irish family how they are and, I suppose, a huge part of me.

Shaun loved it. When he was going to the bathroom, Aunt Mary-Anne said, 'What are you doing?' Shaun politely said, 'Just having a bath, is that okay?' She said – actually, no, she shouted – 'Fer what de ye want having a BATH? Didn't ye have one yesterday?' I laughed and Shaun wasn't too sure how serious she was.

The farm dogs loved the visitors, who broke all the rules about letting them into the house or giving them bits of real meat. Uncle Paddy, one of my mum's many brothers, called for the dogs to round up the cattle. As they ran towards him a tiny, far too thin, white and brown Jack Russell followed.

'How long has that little dog been around?' I asked Mary-Anne. She reluctantly got up from the kitchen chair to glance. 'Oh, that little mutt? The tinkers must have left her. She lives under the tyres in the old barn across the way.'

Shaun listened to this conversation with wide eyes. After the evening meal, Shaun asked me where the old barn was. I pointed to a derelict, pre-St Patrick small shed. He went over, looked around the rotting tyre pile and there, tucked away in their warmth, was the Jack Russell. She looked at him and it was love at first sight. For both of them. That night he smuggled her into the bedroom and she tucked herself against Shaun, much preferring his tyre to those outside. He let her out in the morning and a suspicious Mary-Anne said, 'I hope you haven't got that old mutt in this house!'

Mary Ruddy, who lives on the next farm, had helped keep the little mutt alive and said, when we suggested we would take the dog back to England with us, that she thought that would be a wonderful idea. She may have thought, I wonder if I chuck meself under a pile of old tyres they might consider taking me back?

Shaun held JD in his arms as I swayed, leaped and twisted every bend in the road at speed. In that part of Ireland there are no straights! (Professionalism keeps me from the obvious pun.) The little mutt shook, looked terrified at her kidnappers, threw up on every left turning and got her breath back on the rights. Having purchased a dog box and arranged a quick examination by the vet to certify she was still alive, we left her looking through the far too small slits in her new tomb alongside the cases being stowed into the hold of the plane. We landed at Stansted Airport convinced the little mutt would not have survived the flight.

For three months her new home – a London apartment – might just as well have been her pile of tyres, as she never moved unless carried out from under the bed. She never barked, cowered when anyone came near and accepted a collar more out of fear than anything else. The walks around the busy London streets were terrifying for her, and she was always pulling against the lead, away from the noise of traffic, the tractor being the only engine sound she knew.

Food given to her was to be treated with suspicion – and she always took it under the bed to eat for fear it would be taken away. Slowly her confidence grew and the first time she did the smallest of barks she made herself jump, not knowing what it was.

The little mutt from Ireland travelled everywhere with us, on plane after plane, even being allowed to have her own seat to fly to Scotland to spend Christmas at Gleneagles. On that Christmas Day, she sniffed one of her many presents – a designer bed – and jumped straight into the arms of Shaun, not to thank him but to show us she didn't need any labels, she only needed his arm, the best present ever.

I like nice things. I am generous and have always enjoyed giving. I have to learn better how to take things; how to take compliments, and to enjoy it when people say nice things about me. I am very fortunate to have met so many people who have said they love me and thanked me for making their lives better. I have been told that I only have to say sorry once for things I have done wrong, because if you keep saying it you lessen the value of the apology – so I will only say thank you once as well.

So it's been an incredible journey so far and I hope you have enjoyed reading it and are a little more informed. I will miss sitting up until four in the morning putting this book together. I have never put these feelings into words before. Sure, there have been loads of times when I've wished that I could put the biggest distance between the business and myself – but I always keep coming back for more. Now I have a better idea of what I want out of life – not just out of my work, but out of all that life has to offer. This time I'm taking a different path. I'll walk, not run, and see where it leads me.

I was chatting to Shaun this morning and saying, 'It's going to be impossible to thank everyone personally in the book.' To be brutally honest it's a touch like those

Oscar-winning thank you speeches – wonderful for those that get a mention, boring as shit for the rest of us! The other problem with those you feel obliged to mention is that they expect a free copy. It doesn't finish there either, without even opening it, they make a face and say, 'Ooohh, have you signed it for me?' Then, just as they go to open it, 'Ooohh, I hope it's a personal message.' So the following list of thank yous is to those people who have in the past, or can somehow in the future, influence my career. A huge thank you to Donald Trump – Don, when I was at my lowest, every time you said to yet another no hoper, 'You're fired', my day got brighter. To Camilla – darling, what can I say that isn't libellous? And, of course, enormous thanks to Barbara Streisand for the chicken soup!

Anyway, I really wanna thank you. All of you who watched me every week and shared that humour that all of you understood, which left others going, 'I don't see it!' Well, it wasn't that hard really. It's called communication. Seeing what's under the act.

I'd also like to add a huge thank you to my editor, Angela Herlihy, for giving me the opportunity and the courage to speak from the heart.

I have just signed to play the lead role in *Scrooge – The Musical*, written by Leslie Bricusse and produced by Bill Kenwright in a tour of the UK which kicks off soon. So it's time to bring the story of my life so far to a close. Time to learn the words instead of writing them. The words I am about to learn were written by Charles Dickens. The story of a man who sees the Ghost of Christmas Past, the Ghost of Christmas Present and the Ghost of Christmas Future, so that he can become a better person. The words I have written have been about the past and present, so that I can become a better person – around one day, hopefully, to tell you what happened in the future!

Index